The Collaborative Games

*The story behind
the spectacle*

The Collaborative Games

*The story behind
the spectacle*

Tony Webb

First published in 2001 by
Pluto Press Australia Limited
Locked Bag 199, Annandale NSW 2038

In association with the Foundation for Sustainable Economic Development,
The University of Melbourne

Edited and produced by
Bridging the Gap: Publishing & Marketing – btg@cia.com.au

Cover and internal design by Wendy Farley – anthouse@acay.com.au

Index by Neale Towart

Printed in Australia by Star Printery, Sydney

National Library of Australia
Cataloguing-in-Publication Data

Webb, Tony, 1945- .
The collaborative games: the story behind the spectacle.

Includes index.
ISBN 1 86403 163 8.

1. Olympic Games (27th :, 2000 : Sydney, N.S.W.) - Planning.
2. Industrial relations. 3. Industrial relations -
Australia - Case studies. 4. Olympics. I. Foundation for
Sustainable Economic Development. II. Title.

331

Premier of New South Wales

On October 1, 2000 Juan Antonio Samaranch uttered the words we wanted so much to hear but maybe doubted we ever would, "the best ever". He was right. They were. But the success still caught us by surprise ... and it shouldn't have.

In *The Collaborative Games: The story behind the spectacle*, Tony Webb, with the assistance of Max Ogden at the Foundation for Sustainable Economic Development and the research team of Di Pass and David Williams, tell the story behind the "best ever" verdict while memories are fresh and before mythical versions of history are confected.

Sydney 2000 is one story nobody need fake. This was Australia on show as never before – an intelligent, friendly, contemporary society, a society that works. Only the new smart Australia, with its open competitive economy and tolerant multicultural society, could undertake the hardest peacetime event and do it so well.

The Games saw a high degree of social cooperation. Gone were conflict and bloody-mindedness, replaced by negotiated, cooperative partnerships. It was a powerful demonstration of civilised industrial relations and public sector excellence.

The Collaborative Games tells a big story. Of venues built on time and on budget, unprecedented workplace safety standards, fair and strike-free industrial relations, trains and buses running on time, workers well paid and looked after, constant dialogue between the social partners, environmentally friendly practices built into the Games at every point, volunteers trained, motivated and cheerful ... the list goes on.

There was a definite sense of community and national purpose and, at the end, a feeling of purpose achieved. But that sense of purpose had a largely external impetus – the eyes of the world were upon us. The IOC was scrutinising the planning in close detail. Overseas journalists and TV crews were probing our every weakness and exposing them across the globe. Visiting athletes and officials were quick to criticise anything sloppy or second-rate.

The Games were a brief, tantalising moment that took us outside ourselves. The task remains to internalise that sense of purpose and bring it to bear upon the challenges of our time.

Can we replicate that social cooperation on the factory floor? Can governments show vision and leadership on salinity, drugs, medical research or biotechnology? Can we upskill workers with training that really makes a difference? Lift productivity while retaining harmonious industrial relations? Rehabilitate the nation's polluted industrial sites and rivers? Build new energy-efficient suburbs?

Few projects are as specific, concentrated, emotional and internationally important as the Games. To recreate the Olympic magic will take grit and patience – project by project, workplace by workplace, region by region, portfolio by portfolio.

Without something like the Olympic ideal to take us all outside ourselves it seems an almost impossible task. But we have no other choice. Social and economic gains are never guaranteed. They must be constantly renewed. That, in fact, is the salutary concluding message in *The Collaborative Games*.

With Sydney 2000 we set the bar higher for ourselves and vaulted right over it. If ever we are tempted to forget our Olympic experience (and the decade of hard work that made it possible and the 15 years' economic reform that underpinned it) then read this study. It is a map and memento of the biggest and most exciting thing to happen in this nation during peacetime.

This study will become more valuable over the years as a rebuttal to any temptation to retreat from excellence and social cooperation. An even cursory reading will leave one in no doubt as to what we achieved and how we did it. Remembering that will – and ought to – make it hard for us to settle for anything less in the future.

Warm thanks must go to all those associated with the production of *The Collaborative Games*, including the generous corporate and public sector sponsors, the Universities of Melbourne and Western Sydney and the NSW Labor Council. This partnership reflects and honours in microcosm the great partnership that made Sydney 2000 the extraordinary success it was.

I commend *The Collaborative Games: The story behind the spectacle* to your close and attentive reading.

Bob Carr
Premier

Sponsors of
The Collaborative Games

Australian National Training Authority

Bonds

Cleanevent Pty Ltd

Comet Training

Corrs, Chambers, Westgarth

Foundation for Sustainable Economic Development (University of Melbourne)

George Weston Foods

Industrial Relations Victoria

Labor Council of NSW

Multiplex Constructions (NSW) Pty Ltd

NSW Board of Education and Training

Spotless Services Ltd

Sydney Olympic Park Authority

TAFE NSW

Thiess Pty Ltd

Urban Frontiers Program (University of Western Sydney)

Victorian Department – Sport and Recreation

Visy Closed Loop

WorkCover New South Wales

Without their assistance the study and this book would not have been possible.

Acknowledgements

It is tempting to say that no book is ever written by its author alone. This one certainly wasn't. How it was produced is itself a story of quite unique collaboration.

Many people contributed to this study of what went on behind the spectacle of the Olympic Games. Many more will be involved as we take the legacy of this study into future projects. The book is one small milestone in this process of action research.

To all these people, thank you.

Some contributions stand out as particularly significant. First Max Ogden of the Foundation for Sustainable Economic Development and Greg Combet of the ACTU who asked the initial questions. To Steve Bracks, Premier of Victoria, Bob Carr, Premier of NSW, and John Della Bosca, NSW Minister for Industrial Relations, who provided the seed funds that convinced others that we had a viable research project. To Danny Samson and Mile Terziovski at the University of Melbourne Business School and Jane Marceau at the Urban Frontiers Program at the University of Western Sydney who combined to sponsor the whole project, give it an academic base and carry the risk. To the many more who contributed with funds, support in kind, and with their time to enable the project to proceed. A list of the sponsor organisations who funded the research, writing and publication of this book can be found on page viii.

Special thanks go to the individuals who contributed to the steering group discussions that gave the project its focus and a clearer definition of its scope as a feasible program with a definite timetable. Many also read and commented on the drafts of this report. Special mention is owed to Chris Christodoulou and John Robertson of the Labor Council of NSW who contributed significantly to the initial first steps, provided an office for the project and opened many doors to people and money; Kate Barker of Spotless Services for her multiple roles as part researcher, steering group member, and coordinator of hospitality for many project meetings; and Judith Pugh who assisted with research on the Games Ceremonies and the culture of the performance industry. Others who made special contributions to the work include Bill Ford, Brian Tee, Craig Lovett, David Collins, David Higgon, David Wilson, George Kuti, Greg Spierings, Janet Chester, John Stockler, Justin Burney, Neil Watson, Paul Houston, Paul Howes, Ray Harty and Rob Forsyth. There are many others, not least the 100 people who gave generously of their time and their experiences for the interviews. To all, thank you.

We also owe special thanks to the publishing team at Pluto Press: Tony Moore, Kathryn Lamberton and Wendy Farley, who did more than just advise with the task of preparing the words for publication but actually produced it on the kind of 'impossible' schedule that is, itself, another story.

Perhaps the most significant, certainly the most personal acknowledgement is to my colleagues Di Pass and David Williams who did more than just assist with the research but contributed significantly to both the content and, as important, the balance with which we have tried to tell the story. Any errors that remain are mine. Finally to my long-time colleague and mentor Max Ogden without whom it simply would not have happened …

Tony Webb
Project Manager
September 2001

Contents

Timeline of key events leading up to the Games 1993-2000

	Dates	Organising the Olympic Games
1993		Sydney wins Bid to host the 2000 Olympic Games – SOCOG formed
1994		Multiplex wins Stadium contract
1995		Labor government elected in NSW – OCA established to coordinate government Games activities and construction of venues
1996		Construction of venues commences
	May	
	July	Atlanta Games – a 'wake-up' call for Sydney
1997	February	OSCC established to coordinate Olympic Security
	September	
	November	
	December	
1998	February	Showgrounds project completed
	March	
	April	Royal Easter show held at Showgrounds. First test event.
	August	
	October	
	December	
1999	May	All Olympic Venues completed by September 1999 (Test events at all venues by May 2000)
	August	
	December	SOCOG Board calls for audit of Service contracts – identifies problems with costs, delays in finalising contracts, and concerns over recruiting the necessary workforce
2000	January	OCA takes over management of service contracts
	February	
	March	
	May	Main Press Centre fit-out and Olympic 'overlay' at all venues commences Olympic torch relay commences in Greece
	June	Torch arrives in Australia. Media village opens.
	July	Athletes Village opens
	August	Olympic Arts Festival commences
	September	'Live Sites'. 15 September – Opening Ceremony THE OLYMPIC GAMES
	October	1 October – Games Closing Ceremony. 16–29 October – The Paralympic Games
	November	
	December	Cultural custodian deed recognises Aboriginal rights to sections of the Games Ceremonies

Industrial relations 'architecture'	Planning for the Games workforce	
		1993
		1994
		1995
Enterprise bargaining produces project agreements on major construction sites		**1996**
Concerns raised re overseas production of Olympic licensed goods and uniforms	OCA and SOCOG observe Atlanta problems with recruiting and retaining the labour force	
	Specialist volunteer recruitment commences	**1997**
SOCOG and the Labor Council sign Principles of Cooperation agreement, and Code of Practice on Production of Olympic Licenced Goods signed		
Memorandum of Understanding between government and construction unions signed		
Olympic Games Award negotiations commence	'Concept of Operations' plan for the Games workforce endorsed	**1998**
SOCOG and Labor Council sign Volunteer Protocol	General volunteer recruitment program launched	
Games Award submitted to NSW IRC – second round of negotiations with employer peak bodies required	'Gap Analysis' reveals significant shortfall in labour force for Games services	
Negotiations with employer bodies on details of the Olympic Award continue all through 1999		**1999**
TCFUA campaign over labour rights re Olympic goods and uniforms – resolved December		
• Unions 2000 – single union for Games workers • MEAA campaign for payment of key staff involved in the Games Ceremonies – resolved April	Contractors start recruiting	**2000**
Olympic Award finally registered with NSW IRC	• Volunteer training • OLN (Olympic Labour Network) formed	
	Service contracts let	
	Workforce Uniforms and Accreditation Contractor training	
	June-July – workforce rostering	
OH&S, Risk Management audits completed – all sites		
TWU negotiates Olympic Transport Award		
Unions 2000 roster 32 union officials from 5 unions – 24-hour coverage to resolve IR issues	Bus 2000 transport crisis – when the wheels nearly fell off!	
Olympic bonus paid to workforce	The volunteer parade	

Chapter one

The Collaborative Games Study

From beer fountain ...

Monte Carlo, 8.28 pm Thursday 23rd Sept.1993: *"And the winner is Siderney ..."*. As the announcement by Juan Antonio Samaranch and the spectacle of the jubilant Sydney Bid Team is broadcast to the world, one of the union delegates at the party organised by Lend Lease on the lawn outside what is to become the Games Aquatic Centre at Homebush Bay leaps into the air and crushes a beer can in each hand, setting off a cascade of similar 'beer fountains'.

Some months before, Danny Potocki had the task of shepherding International Olympic Committee (IOC) delegates around the construction site. He talked about the company's progress in building the swimming pool – how the workforce had combined to drastically reduce the construction time by building the roof on the ground outside and craning it into position. He talked about the culture of the construction industry that made this and other design and construction innovations possible. He was asked what assurances could be given that Olympic construction would be completed on time. This was, after all, a time when the image of the Australian construction industry needed a makeover in the eyes of the world's media. 'Why wouldn't we? We completed Darling Park on time and under budget' was the simple reply. Now where was the transport that was supposed to take the IOC delegates back to their hotel? No worries. Danny pulls out his mobile phone and arranges a replacement. It arrives minutes later. Back in the hotel and visibly impressed, IOC delegates ask if the company usually gives its union delegates authority to arrange transport like this. 'Why wouldn't we?' is the simple reply. Given the change in the workplace culture and organisation of work practices at Lend Lease that had been started some years before, time and cost over-runs were unthinkable. Both responsibility and the authority to exercise it had long been devolved down the management structure to those on the job.

Between the beer fountain and the river of fire there is a huge story. It is the story about what is, so far at least, the world's largest peacetime event.

How much did this help Sydney's Bid? On its own probably not much. Together with all the other little signals that indicated a community-wide collaboration for staging the Year 2000 Olympic Games in Sydney, it did.

... to the river of fire

And then the Air Force jet lights its afterburner as it flies over the Stadium in Olympic Park symbolically carrying the flame from the cauldron and triggering firework displays all along the river from Homebush Bay to the Harbour Bridge – a 'river of fire'! And the watching world acknowledges and celebrates with Australia the awarding of the accolade of 'the best Games ever'!

Twelve months later, as this book goes to press, there are millions of memories. Some of them are shared, like that moment, several minutes actually, when Cathy Freeman stood under the cascade with the ring of fire that refused to continue its journey up to the cauldron at the top of the Stadium. Or when she won the 400 metres! The swimming events ... That pole vaulter – now what was her name? ... The hilarious F. A. Wombat ... The Opening Ceremony, from Ocean Dreaming to the Parade of Australian Women Olympians, reflecting our culture to the world, and to ourselves. Many more memories will be private ones. The Canadian disabled visitor who found access by train easy enough but then discovered that the people at Central had called ahead to Olympic Park so he would be met and escorted through the crush – and then similarly helped on his return, all the way to Bondi.

NEWSPIX

The cool head of the technician who sat with his laptop and worked out why the cauldron wasn't moving, and got it going again. All those people whose birthday falls on 15 September. Paul McKinnon, head of Olympic Security was one. It was as though Sydney had staged the biggest birthday party of his life. Or the 500 Maoris who came to Sydney to work for the Games – without a job to go to. How they were found work, were housed in a 'Maori village' at the old Arnott's biscuit factory, saved the day when the Opening Ceremony rehearsals were about to be called off, and repaid those who helped them with a traditional *hangi* feast before returning to New Zealand with their stories of coming to Sydney to work for the Games. Some of these and more we will try to tell. Many more will never be told publicly.

When the 'river of fire' reached Sydney Harbour Bridge.

Between the beer fountain and the river of fire there is a huge story. It is the story about what is, so far at least, the world's largest peacetime event. It is a story that can be seen through many people's eyes, each with a different perspective. The list includes spectators, athletes, and games organisers who created the spectacle; sponsors, media organisations and the governments who helped finance it; contractors who provided goods and services; and by no means least, those in the workforce (both paid and volunteers) who built the sporting venues, organised the transport, catering, security and cleaning, sold goods, provided information, made uniforms and Olympic souvenirs (here and overseas), or helped in many ways to make it possible.

How did we do it?

This is a people question. How did we bring together so many people in so many different organisations:

- the government and the Games agencies – SOCOG, OCA, ORTA, OSCC, SOBO ... the list reads like an alphabet soup* but involves thousands of people
- the trade unions, who ensured industrial harmony ruled throughout the Games
- the community organisations across the country who provided so many of the 'wonderful' volunteers
- and the private companies who sponsored the Games and provided contract services that made it possible.

And how did we get all these to collaborate to produce such an unprecedented success – one that even sport-cynics acknowledge as unusual and outstanding?

The Games involved completing a \$3.2 billion construction project on time and within budget and in the process cleaning up what had previously been a toxic waste site at Homebush Bay – with only one day on one site lost to a minor industrial dispute. The training provided during the process significantly improved the skill and the safety culture in the construction industry workforce, and the success of the Games construction projects has attracted continuing investment in the industry and jobs for the future. Staging the Games events in September 2000 involved assembling a workforce of between 150,000 and 200,000 people, a third of them volunteers, to turn up and work for a two-week event

* See glossary on page 218.

and then go away – and have a significant number come back to do it all again two weeks later for the Paralympic Games.

How was this achieved? What dramatic shifts in industrial and human relations cultures made this degree of collaboration between government and private sector employers and the workforce possible? Perhaps more important, what lessons can be learned and perhaps replicated in other events or the many other projects that need to be undertaken if Australia is to position itself in a rapidly changing world economic, social and ecological environment?

Asking the questions – the Collaborative Games Study

It is these questions that we set out to answer. The Collaborative Games Study was conceived as part of a Victorian Government initiative that established a Foundation for Sustainable Economic Development at the University of Melbourne in 2000. A mass of evidence worldwide shows that enterprises with progressive human relations and ecological sustainability policies also achieve sound economic performance long term. What is not so clear is exactly how this synergy of people, environment and economics operates. The foundation was set up to undertake the necessary research and to provide practical advice to industry, government and the trade-union-supported superannuation funds that now provide a significant portion of Australia's investment capital and the retirement income for many of its workers.

Discussions in late 2000 and early 2001 led to collaboration with the Urban Frontiers Program at the University of Western Sydney and the formation of a steering group for this study. The aim was to explore how this 'triple bottom line' of people, environment and economy might apply to the staging of the Sydney 2000 Olympic Games. The group brought together expertise from the two universities and sponsors of the study, including the Victorian and New South Wales governments, companies involved in the construction and service delivery phases of the Games and the Labor Council of NSW. (See Appendix 2 for the list of people who contributed to this steering group process.)

The story of the Games is an open-ended one – and the task of exploring it as long as a piece of string. A number of decisions were made that limited the scope of the study. Perhaps the hardest was to focus on the Olympic Games only and exclude a detailed study of the Paralympics. This was driven by the need to finalise the report for the anniversary of the Games in September 2001 and the limited research funds available. The Paralympic story is a fascinating one in its own right and deserves to be told properly. Some aspects of this study do carry over to the Paralympic Games, but there is much more that was unique and we make no attempt to tell that story here. The other major decision was to limit the study of the 'Green Games' story. Some of this has been, or will be, told by others. Rather than duplicate this work, we have focused on those aspects where environmental and technological innovation required special attention be given to people-management issues for the ecologically desired outcome to be achieved.

There was a hunger for an opportunity to tell the story. For many people there was unfinished business and a desire to pass on the lessons of the experience.

The final decision was not to try to tell the whole story in detail. Rather, we have focused on identifying the basic framework of human relations (industrial, workplace and interpersonal) that was established in the planning and development of the Games, from the winning of the Bid to the Closing Ceremony. We then explore in more detail some of the specific areas of activity as seen through the eyes of a number of the significant actors and directors in the drama of staging the Games.

To those whose company or personal story we have omitted, we apologise. One thing became apparent in the interviews. There was a hunger for an opportunity to tell the story. For many people there was unfinished business and a desire to pass on the lessons of the experience. We hope this book goes some way to meeting this hunger.

What did we expect to find?

Given that the steering group included many people who had been involved, some of them intimately, with the Games, we had some expectations of what we might find from the study. Where exploration of human experience is concerned there is no such thing as 'objectivity'. The best that can be done is to reflect some of the many personal and subjective experiences with as little overlay of opinion or bias from the researchers as possible. It is inevitable that there are preconceived ideas about what will be found and the questions asked will to some extent constrain the answers. In order to make clear its own bias, the steering group discussed what it expected to emerge and what needed more detailed research.

The main points identified were:

- The project management of the Games was unusually collaborative and innovative.

- This collaboration began early, even prior to the Bid, and itself was the result of earlier collaborative experiences in industrial relations and human resource management that began in the mid to late 1980s.

- The world spotlight on Sydney and the Games had a significant impact. Fear of failure was matched by a desire to present 'the best Games ever' despite widespread early cynicism.

- The role of government, many employers and the trade unions in creating an innovative industrial relations climate needed to be explored in detail and lessons, if any, from this passed on.

- Different human resource and industrial relations strategies were adopted by different sectors of the Games operation, for example, construction of the venues, delivery of the Games services and transport. These needed to be compared and lessons identified for the future.

- Innovative industrial relations and human resource management provided the climate to address issues associated with the widespread use of volunteers.

- The collaborative/innovative climate contributed to innovative dispute/conflict resolution.

- The collaborative/innovative approach resulted in:
  - excellent training and on the job learning
  - new work organisation, especially in construction
  - new management methods
  - widespread commitment to the green/environmental objectives
  - low levels of occupational, health and safety problems
  - unusual employee flexibility
  - increased employee involvement and participation in decisions
  - high level of interpersonal trust and co-operation between union officials, Games agencies and private employers; between union officials and shop stewards; and between unions.

■ If this hypothesis were to be confirmed, similar collaborative/innovative strategies might work well on other large Australian projects, including:

- attracting international trade and investment
- improving our industrial relations reputation
- the Commonwealth Games and other major events
- land salination and other environmental problems
- major infrastructure projects.

Asking the people involved

With this in mind, in mid-March 2000 we undertook a pilot survey, interviewing a small sample of the key players involved in three major constituencies:

■ Government and the government-appointed agencies, particularly:

- The Olympic Coordination Authority (OCA) which had responsibility for overseeing the construction of the sporting venues and later coordinating government activity in support of the Games
- The Sydney Organising Committee for the Olympic Games (SOCOG) which, with the Sydney Paralympic Organising Committee (SPOC), had responsibility for planning and delivering the two Games events over a 60-day period from September to November 2000
- The Olympic Roads and Transport Authority (ORTA)
- The Olympic Security and Command Centre (OSCC) which had responsibility for planning and delivery of security for the Games.

■ Private sector companies, including those associated with:

- construction of the venues and the environmental infrastructure of the Games, particularly at Sydney Olympic Park (Homebush Bay)
- delivery of the major contract services for the Games period in September 2000
- support of the Games through secondment of staff or provision of 'value in kind' services as part of Games sponsorship arrangements

- employer associations representing companies in these various sectors.

- Trade union organisations, such as those involved in:
  - the construction industry
  - the service sector, with particular emphasis on those with coverage of cleaning, catering and security
  - public and private sector transport
  - the Labor Council of NSW which coordinated the unions, negotiated the major agreements with the government, OCA and SOCOG, and established a single inter-union agency, Unions 2000, as a one-stop shop for workers involved in the Games.

In order to distort people's stories as little as possible, the survey asked six broad, open-ended questions – essentially 'mouth openers' that guided the interview over the ground we wished to cover. In practice, many people needed little prompting; the stories often told themselves. These questions were:

- How far do we go back to get your story of the Games?
- What were the significant events and timelines?
- Who were the significant players?
- What were the major innovations – things that made a difference?
- What was your strategic thinking at the time?
- What are the major lessons?

These could be asked in almost any order and the interesting details followed up to get a deeper understanding of the person's story.

The pilot survey confirmed not only that there was indeed an important story of government, employer industry and union collaboration, but that the approach of asking a few open-ended questions allowed aspects that we had not considered to emerge. It suggested that there was a clear separation between the construction and service delivery aspects of the Games. It identified the main features of service contracting and workforce planning that together provided the framework for delivery of the Games.

In late April the survey was extended to cover as many as possible of the key people and areas of interest that had been identified in the pilot. In the end we had detailed notes from interviews with

100 people together with a variety of documents provided in the course of these interviews. A list of the people interviewed, in the date order we spoke with them, can be found in Appendix 1. To all of these people who gave so generously of their time and knowledge we are deeply grateful.

These interviews contain far more information than can be compressed between the covers of this book. The Games study team will be organising seminars and forums for different interest groups so that some of this additional knowledge can be shared.

For you, the reader, here is the core of the story. We hope you enjoy it as much as we did uncovering it.

Chapter two

Building the theatre

In the beginning ...

In 1993 there was the Bid.
And the Bid was the word (in several volumes of Bid documents approved by the IOC)
And the word was that the New South Wales government was to build (and pay for) all of the sporting venues needed for the Games – a task given to the Olympic Coordination Authority (OCA)
And that the Sydney Organising Committee for the Olympic Games (SOCOG) would pay only for the temporary fit-out and operation of these venues for the duration of the Olympic (and Paralympic) Games.
Within the Olympic Family the word was that the OCA will 'build the theatre' and SOCOG will 'stage the show'.

For the OCA this involved the coordination of a $3.2 billion construction project, most of it on what, at the time, was a toxic waste site at Homebush Bay close to Sydney's demographic centre in the West. This site became Sydney Olympic Park, home of the Games in September 2000, including an Olympic Village for the international athletes and Games officials. Today it leaves the State with a legacy of world-class sporting venues, a housing estate incorporating many 'ecologically sustainable' features – and a headache. The government needs to attract further investment for development of the site, and events that draw large numbers of people to use it. Success will mean Homebush Bay becomes a viable and vibrant suburb of the city; failure will leave the State government with a white elephant requiring ongoing financial support from the public purse. Whatever the outcome, there is one part of the legacy that will remain in the collective consciousness of Sydney (and Australia) and a large slice of the world population. They were all touched by the events and spectacle of that September.

How was it possible to shift from competitive and adversarial relations that not long ago were rife at all levels within the industry to mutually rewarding cooperation and collaboration?

The story of the Olympic construction project is a marvel in itself. The architectural design of some venues, the Stadium in particular, was on the leading edge of 1990s technology. The 'environmental' features, while falling short of what some Green groups had hoped for were nevertheless significant in scope and scale. And the whole project was built on time, under budget and to high quality standards. Even more outstanding in our view is the human architecture that was designed and built to support the construction process. This is what we will focus on in this chapter. How was it possible to shift from competitive and adversarial relations that not long ago were rife at all levels within the industry to mutually rewarding cooperation and collaboration?

To understand this we will look at the culture of the industry that existed in the early 1990s and the various approaches to driving industry reform. We will then look at the industrial relations framework that emerged in the process of planning the construction projects that became the Olympic Games venues and how this led to a comprehensive training program for all workers involved and significant improvements in the safety culture of the whole industry. Finally we will explore, through case studies, how this human relations architecture operated on the ground. We have called these sections:

- 'The construction industry – competition or collaboration': where we explore the changing culture of the industry
- 'The human relations architecture': where we explore the industrial relations agreements, training and OH&S issues
- 'Building the venues': where we explore as case studies the construction of the Showgrounds Dome, Stadium arches, Athletes Village, Main Press Centre and temporary seating at the Aquatic Centre.

The construction industry – competition or collaboration?

The industry in the early 1990s was in recession. Actually it was at the bottom of a recurring 'boom and bust' cycle that had frustrated strategic planning at the industry level and the economic fortunes of many whose livelihood depended on it. Industrial disputes on the job were reflected in contractual disputes at boardroom level. It is easy to focus on the publicly visible features of industrial conflict such as the 1990 Royal Commission,* the de-registration of the Builders Labourers Federation (BLF) or the Federal and State government initiatives to drive a reform process. In essence there were two contrasting approaches of 'fostering' or 'forcing' change (like the proverbial 'carrot and stick').

These were associated, then as now, with different political persuasions. In the early 90s, Labor in power federally favoured trying to achieve change by negotiation with, and between, industry stakeholders while the Coalition parties in State government favoured legislative approaches to force changes in industrial relations. It is ironic that three years after the Bid Labor was in government at State level and the Federal government was Liberal-National Coalition. The reality was, however, that change was taking place within the industry at a level and in a way that seems, in hindsight, to have been independent of the politics.

We have touched on how the IOC was impressed, perhaps influenced in favour of Sydney, by the work-team approach in evidence at the construction of the Aquatic Centre. The 'whole system approach' and 'learning enterprise' had been translated from philosophy into practice by several of the major construction companies. Lend Lease had proved its value when the Darling Park Project was completed on time and under budget and without industrial dispute. This was an experience shared by a number of the major contractors in the early 90s. It reflected significant effort and commitment to improving the industry culture. For some in the industry, the value of creating a work environment in which skill development, participation, pride and 'ownership of the workplace' no longer needed proving. Critically,

---

* Gyles Royal Commission into Productivity in the Building Industry in NSW, 1990.

Bob Leece, chosen by David Richmond of the OCA to develop the Olympic facilities and supervise the initial contracts, came from the construction industry.

To understand the culture of the industry we need to look deeper into the way that construction projects are put together. There are several types of contracts used to engage a builder. The most common type envisages the client engaging the architects and design consultants. These develop full design documentation that specifies the building to be built. The design documents are then put out to tender. Building contractors compete for the job which is largely awarded on the basis of price. From the client's perspective this competition should be beneficial. The **unintended consequences**, however, often include the establishment of adversarial relations between:

- contractor and client (and sometimes lawyers for each side)
- contractor and design consultants who draw up the plans
- contractor and subcontractor (and people they subcontract to)
- contractor and the client's representatives used to ensure that time, cost and quality standards are met
- and not least between workers and the various contractors and subcontractors as everyone tries to squeeze the 'weakest link' down the line, cost cutting sometimes by cutting corners (including safety).

Alternatives to this 'hardnose' system involve varying types of 'design and build' contracts. The variant known as 'little d' involves the client specifying (called 'novating' in the industry) the architectural design team but the contractor taking responsibility for the documentation of the design and the details of how to build it. In 'Big D' contracts the client specifies the outcome desired (rather than its form) and the contractor takes on the whole job including the commissioning of the design, documentation, and building the project. The **intended consequence** of this approach is collaboration and sharing of expertise:

- between the design consultants and the contractors all the way down to workforce level – often in teams – the 'learning enterprise' referred to earlier
- between contractors and subcontractors – and their 'subbies'[*]

---

* 'subbies' = subcontractors

who need to be brought into the loop – a 'whole system approach' between contractor and client – with conversations that begin 'We think we can do it better this way ...' or 'We ran into a problem but ... what about this? Is this acceptable?' and so on

- also between the client group and the contractor – as a different kind of relationship (and organisational structure) is needed to 'manage the contractor' rather than merely manage the contract

- and, interestingly, sometimes between consultants or between contractors – who now collaborate rather than compete.

Negotiation is the key word here. A collaborative culture is not likely to result from forced change or adversarial industrial relations.

The past decade has seen a significant development in this collaborative culture – driven in some measure by the shift towards design and construct contracting. It was this model that was favoured by the OCA and in very large measure by many of the Olympic venue construction companies. Bob Leece of OCA says:

"With the larger design and construct projects the client worked with the architect and the builder right through the process and produced a far better result. With full design [hardnose contracts] the contractor was focussed solely on the bottom line." [98] *

Hand in hand with design and construct contracting went parallel changes in managing the workforce both in terms of formal industrial relations systems and the interpersonal relations between management, unions and workers. Negotiation is the key word here. A collaborative culture is not likely to result from forced change or adversarial industrial relations. This is not to deny a role for legislation. Sometimes both 'carrot' and 'stick' work together. John Barraclough, of the OCA, says:

"Legislation was needed 'as the big stick' but he [David Richmond] was clever at setting up processes that pre-empted the use of the stick. It meant that it was there if needed – but in fact it never was!" [81]

The OCA was established in mid-1995 after the election of the NSW Labor government and the contracts developed were let in 1996. Most were 'fixed price' and the larger projects were 'design

---

* The small reference numbers in the text indicate the interview from which we source the comment, quote or statement. A full list of these interviews can be found at Appendix 1.

and build'. The list of industrial agreements made around this time (see the brief history opposite) suggests that the collaborative approach was well underway – driven as much by the industry view that this was the way to go as by political ideology.

The human relations architecture

The Olympic Games collaboration between the unions and the NSW government goes back, at least, to 1991. When Sydney was bidding for the Games the Liberal government in NSW under Nick Greiner recognised that success depended on union movement cooperation and that Labor Council involvement in this was critical. To Michael Easson, then Secretary of the Council, the issues were jobs for workers, and the need for contracts that provided certainty for both construction and operation of the Games. He says:

"On the union side we saw this as an opportunity for the union movement – winning the Games would be a fillip for NSW, would be good for jobs and therefore for NSW and good for workers." [11]

Nick Greiner, the NSW Premier, and John Coates of the AOC wanted union movement participation, in part because changing the IR image was critical to the success of the highly contested IOC bid process. They recalled previous support when the Labor Council opposed the boycott of the Games in Moscow (1980, over Afghanistan) and Los Angeles (1984, over Nicaragua). Discussions led to early agreement on both the Bid and the subsequent Games organising. Michael Easson says:

"Initially Greiner wanted a 'no strike' agreement – a blanket agreement. What we settled on was the form of words for an in-principle agreement that there would be no strike provided that the agreements negotiated were adhered to. We copped a lot of flack over this but it wasn't a case of giving away our rights – it was an agreement with two sides to it." [11]

This was tested during the Bid phase. A one-day strike was planned over the Liberal government's IR legislation – inadvertently called at a time when an IOC delegation and President Samaranch were to be in Sydney. Rod McGeoch who was managing the Bid called Easson who recalls:

"We decided to delay the strike by one week. The result was a lot of favourable publicity but also I expended a lot of political capital in getting the delay." [11]

A brief history of emerging collaboration in construction

- 1990 Concrete Constructions (Walter Constructions) awarded Airport Central. Seen as a model project, it spawned a new generation of agreements with building unions based on communication, restructuring, skill enhancement and productivity gain sharing.

- 1990 (Gyles) Royal Commission into Productivity in the Building Industry in NSW – part of a 'forcing' approach to industrial change.

- 1991 CFMEU formed by progressive amalgamation of Construction, Forestry, Mining and Energy Unions.

- 1991 Darling Park Project started – Civil & Civic (Lend Lease) – attitudinal and cultural change – 'learning enterprise', 'whole system approach' based on skill development, participation, pride and ownership of workplace.

- 1991 Construction Industry Development Agency (CIDA) reform strategy launched by Federal (Labor) government – 'model enterprise' focus.

- 1991 In-principle agreement commits employers, including Concrete Constructions, Civil & Civic, Multiplex and Thiess, government and unions to measurable reform in areas of contract definition, work practices, rationalisation of awards and agreements, improved training, and lost time reduction.

- 1992 Major contractors and key unions sign first agreement under new CIDA (Federal) guidelines.

- 1995 Building Industry Taskforce abolished by Carr (Labor) government. Deed Monitoring Committee replaced with Construction Industry Consultative Committee (CICC).

- 1996 Start of contracts for Olympic venues. Pattern bargaining produces a series of site-specific Enterprise Agreements. Award conditions are registered with the NSW IR Commission by consent (binding subcontractors to the Award).

- 1997 (December) Memorandum of Understanding between NSW government, the Labor Council and unions sets benchmark objectives for all Olympic construction projects.

Winning union backing wasn't easy. Some sections of the union movement felt passionately that the enormous amount of money the Games would cost should go to education and health rather than sport.[11] There were also arguments from a militant group about 'collusive leadership' and how this benefited the government but not the unions. All these were aired on the floor of the weekly Labor Council meetings and provided a focus for discussion about supporting the Games. In the end the leadership won.

"I think it paid off in the long term ... we were involved in consultations at all stages of the Games and delivered what could be seen as best practice industrial relations and considerable benefits in terms of training. Unless we'd taken that decision the headlines would have been 'union movement destroys Sydney Bid' whereas the outcome created a lot of goodwill – a perception that the union movement was genuinely willing to be helpful on the Games Bid. When the Games decision was announced and everyone was being congratulated, Greiner called to say he was surprised the Labor Council was not mentioned in this post-Bid publicity as he'd valued the support and seen it as critical." [11]

There were other examples of union cooperation. The Labor Council was called before the Technical Committee of the IOC. Michael Easson took Andrew Ferguson and Stan Sharkey of the Construction, Forestry, Mining and Energy Union (CFMEU).

"This was a case of putting the unions' feet to the fire. The committee quizzed us on how far the union movement was behind the Bid." [11]

And there was a dispute at the Opera House ...

"Workers were thinking of using the concert for the IOC delegates to highlight the issue. We worked through the early hours of the morning with Terry Ludeke [Judge with the Australian Arbitration Commission] to work it out and avoid the strike. In the Opera House event ... the smoke from the stage almost suffocated the IOC delegates – there we were fixing the IR problems overnight to have the performance almost choking them to death in the front rows the next day!" [11]

In retrospect Easson has no regrets:

"The reality was that people got behind the Games. We got good publicity from it and it had good employment practices. There was a willingness to regard the other side as worthy of respect. It's simple rather than complicated. Get people behind you on the idea of sensible industrial relations. A cooperative attitude – not one where you are there to be walked over – but one that contrasts cooperative IR with one where everyone does their own thing." [11]

Working together – sharing the benefits

"With a major project, risk is in retrospect – it looked easy, it went smoothly but success occurs by giving thought to strategy."

Michael Easson[11]

The Olympic sites construction program was one of the largest ever undertaken in Australia. There were over 7,500 workers directly involved on site and approximately 15,000 involved in off-site work. Managing this workforce, particularly in the context of an unstable industrial relations culture, would indeed require some strategic planning.

The Stadium was one of the first contracts to be let. It involved a long construction program, and early completion was seen as essential. Multiplex, who eventually won the contract, met early with the OCA and argued for industrial relations to be managed by individual contract sites rather than have a common 'whole of site agreement' covering the Olympic Park or even the whole Olympic construction program.[19]

Negotiated under enterprise bargaining arrangements set in place by the Federal Labor government, the initial **Project Agreements** were site-specific, based on a pattern developed by the Labor Council in conjunction with the major contractors.* A key element of these agreements was a system of 'productivity payments':**

- Completion to schedule payments – where increases in the hourly rate for all workers on the site are paid for completion of elements of the project to an agreed schedule (or the pay increase forfeited if the schedule is not met).

- Completion to productivity payments – where additional hourly payments are paid on achievement of agreed milestones for project productivity.

In terms of the pay packet this means, for example, a $1.00 per hour increase **when** the milestone is reached, which may be ahead of the date when a further $1.00 per hour will be paid **for** meeting

---

* This 'model' award has since become an industry standard being used subsequent to the Games for projects such as the Eastern Distributor and the M5 Motorway.

** The system of productivity payments was developed and first used by Multiplex on the Bennelong Point project in 1995.

the milestone – a real incentive for **early** completion of each stage of the project.

The agreements also set standards for safety management plans, security, and dispute resolution procedures. Maintaining strict security with swipe-card access to all projects was seen as necessary for site management. It also allowed unions to know when any contractor or worker came on the site. It allowed union delegates to discuss union membership with workers, to communicate the cooperative ethos that was the norm for the project, and to pick up any issues before they became problems and work with the company to find solutions. Having the unions know who was on site was not always welcomed. For some subcontractors where there was a history of unresolved industrial dispute it operated, as one HR manager said, like

"a cleaning agent in the industry – fixing up problems that had been hanging around for a long time".[24]

The Project Agreements became the basis for 'Consent' Awards under NSW Industrial Relations legislation.* Unlike Federal legislation, the NSW Industrial Relations Commission (IRC) allows parties to register agreements between the company and the union that are then binding on anyone who may be involved in the project. This 'Common Rule' system is particularly useful in large projects involving subcontractors who will not be chosen until much later.

Late in 1997 a Memorandum of Understanding for the Olympic Construction Program was signed between the NSW government, the Labor Council of NSW and the main unions in the construction industry.** Covering all 18 Olympic sites then planned or under construction it provided a framework for the many

---

* For readers unfamiliar with Australian IR legislation an 'Award' is a registered agreement covering aspects of wages and conditions which acts as a 'contract' between unions and employers. It is unique in that it is part of a national arbitration system established over 100 years ago with support of all sides of politics that established a legal framework for negotiation of disputes.

** The Labor Council of NSW; Construction, Forestry, Mining and Energy Union (CFMEU); Communications, Electrical, Electronic, Energy, Information, Postal, Plumbing and Allied Services Union (CEPU); Electrical Trades Union (ETU); Australian Workers Union (AWU); and Transport Workers Union (TWU).

(company/site-specific) project agreements. It committed the unions to ensuring 'delivery of all 2000 Olympic and related projects in time and within budget in an industrial environment based on cooperation and stability'. It also set out the common understanding on issues such as dispute resolution; occupational health and safety (OH&S); project productivity allowances; and especially on training. Of particular significance, it led to the negotiation of a common $1.85 per hour bonus for all workers in the Olympic Construction Program. Technically this could not be framed as a 'site allowance' (it was couched in terms of a productivity agreement designed to ensure that construction was completed on time) but in effect it operated as such in all but name across the whole program. For John Robertson of the Labor Council who coordinated the negotiations on the memorandum, there were two objectives: to re-establish the idea of overarching project awards and agreements; and to develop employment and training opportunities. To the employers the memorandum had elements of an 'all of site' agreement but did not fundamentally change the agreements already in place. Matt Stagg, a Director of Multiplex, says that, despite their initial opposition, the all-sites agreement

(The Memorandum) committed the unions to ensuring 'delivery of all 2000 Olympic and related projects in time and within budget in an industrial environment based on cooperation and stability.'

"sort of happened anyway – but there wasn't a central organisation industrially ... It was a model of government and everybody working together. Collaboration. The government didn't want it seen as a disaster and they pulled out all stops. Good luck to them." [19]

So, the key elements of the industrial relations framework that emerged were:

■ An overarching understanding at the highest level that
  • a culture of collaboration was needed for the whole Olympic construction project
  • it was worth paying a common Olympic site bonus to all workers involved in the construction program on Olympic sites to ensure on-time and within-budget completion
  • this 'site allowance' would be capped for the duration of the Games program (and though not explicit would also apply to all other sites in the Sydney area for the same period).

■ Enterprise Agreements made with individual companies and registered as Consent Awards – based on a pattern that

- set milestones for achieving specific stages of projects
- tied productivity payments to achievement of these milestones
- provided incentives to reach these milestones early
- locked all subcontractors into the common rules.

■ A basic award framework that was untouched by the above. This included pre-existing trade-specific awards, over award payments, and additional company-specific allowances that set rates of pay and conditions for different trades or sections of the industry.

The agreement was respected throughout the three to four year construction period despite changing economic circumstances, opportunities and pressures to negotiate improvements. It is worth noting that the unions settled for an Olympic bonus of $1.85 per hour. In 1996–7 the industry was just coming out of recession. It is widely acknowledged that a rate of $2.50 an hour or higher could have been negotiated, especially later as the economy improved. The $1.85 bonus was never renegotiated and all other construction sites across the Sydney region operated within this cap. The unions were determined that higher rates elsewhere would not be allowed to draw workers away from Olympic construction work.[11 22 23]

The NSW CFMEU leadership has come under fire from militant elements, mainly in other States, for its collaboration during the Games. The arguments are that the union should have exploited its bargaining position for maximum gain, that union officials were too cooperative with management and that organising opportunities to recruit members were lost during this period.[22 23 47] The current union leadership agrees that a better deal might have been struck. Against this it argues that all sites had enterprise agreements, recognised delegates and a high level of union membership. Backing the Games was a strategic decision designed to change the culture within the industry and its image in the eyes of the people of Australia and the investment community, here and overseas.[23 46 47] In the long term (and there are signs that it is working) the result should be greater investment in construction and in jobs for construction workers. In the process, the union leadership also argues that a unionised building program completed on time and within budget will enhance public support for trade unionism. And for the workers in the industry there have been direct and measurable benefits in training and safety. There is also the intangible change in the quality of life for people who go to work where their contribution to a common task is respected, acknowledged and rewarded, and where they are given responsibility and involved in a learning culture – where they are empowered to take decisions. Whether these are seen as part of a process of collusion and self-exploitation or part of a culture that is valued is a matter for the membership within the union.

The CFMEU is the dominant union within the construction industry with about 80 percent of the membership. Collaborative relations between the union and construction companies were fostered in several ways. First, the major contractors each employed one of the more 'industrially mature' CFMEU site delegates. These were senior delegates (members of the union's elected management committee) who had the respect of both company representatives and workers on site. They provided the company with a direct link to the workforce, ensuring that all workers (including subcontractors) understood the nature of the project and the culture being developed. Their role was to act as a channel for workers' concerns and deal with issues as or before they arose. They had special responsibilities in the area of safety and training. The bottom line was that they ensured that the commitment to deliver on time and in budget was achieved – safely! [7 9 23 24 30 31 46 47]

For the workers in the industry there have been direct and measurable benefits in training and safety.

The construction companies also developed collaborative relations between themselves and with the network of subcontractors over bidding for design and construction on the various sites. Overall, the performance indicators of safety, skill formation, lack of disruption, mediation of disputes, on time and under budget delivery mark the construction phase as a huge success.

Skills for the Games – and the future

A key element of the Memorandum of Understanding was the need for training. It specified that:

The parties are committed to the establishment of project specific on-site and off-site training approaches to increase training opportunities and provide training in areas in the industry where there is expected to be a shortage of skilled and competent workers. This training will also include on site practical training in areas of work that cannot be taught in a classroom situation.

Construction industry training during the Olympic construction period involved collaboration between government and private

It leaves NSW with a larger pool of qualified, skilled workers.

sector training providers; the construction industry; and the unions and Labor Council. The NSW Department of Education and Training (DET) coordinated a $10 million construction training strategy.* A preliminary analysis identified the areas where there were or were likely to be skill shortages during the construction phase. Nationally accredited training in these skills was then delivered through a network of State and private Registered Training Organisations (RTOs) and through on-site skill centres. Overall, training was provided for 12,250 workers; 30 percent were new to the industry.

On-site induction and safety training was provided for all 7,500 workers on the main Sydney Olympic sites. Accredited skills courses leading to recognised qualifications were provided both on and off site. Fifty to seventy percent of people involved in the skills courses undertook these on their own time. Employers used down time (bad weather) for training to minimise slowdown of the construction work. They also created opportunities for the workers already on site to acquire additional skills that the company would need in the next stages of the project. The training program ensured that the number of skilled workers were available as needed for the different phases of the construction project. It leaves NSW with a larger pool of qualified, skilled workers. Many are now multi-skilled workers who have experience in working in an environment where 'working fast is not at the expense of working safe'.[23][47] They also experienced work on a site where collaborative working relationships were the norm throughout the three years it took to complete the Olympic venues – longer for those involved in the Games 'overlay' work, which we will discuss below. It also leaves the industry with skills and experience in organising 'just in time' training. Margaret Ryan, former Director of Strategic Planning and Resource Management for DTEC (now DET), said:

"It is a testament to what could happen with a very targeted industry driven approach." [87]

TAFE NSW provided 40 percent of the training. It provided a 'one-stop shop' at Homebush Bay for two years and worked closely with the contractors and other RTOs. Some of the more innovative

---

* This $10 million was made available from interest on the Building and Construction Industry Long Term Payments Scheme.

RTOs piloted special programs for people who do not usually receive this kind of structured training experience including housing sector workers (for the small subcontractors in the Olympic Village); workers from Aboriginal and non-English-speaking communities; a pre-vocational program for school leavers; and an IT and business management skills program for small business owners.* These were collaborative efforts, some breaking new ground in the definition of the 'skills' needed in construction. For example, Comet Training, a joint venture between the Master Builders Association and the construction unions, developed a program that trained 15 Aboriginal people. One of them was certified as a scaffolder and is now a leading hand. Another of Comet's programs was a ten-week pre-vocational training course that trained twelve students from St Thomas Catholic School in Lewisham. All went into employment.[13A] Another example is the Building People Program subsequently established by Lend Lease that involves managers and front-line supervisors as mentors for new trainees.[46]

Comet Training originally tendered to manage the training for the Showgrounds project. This developed into the skill centre for many other parts of the program. In 1997 Comet's facility at Lidcombe became the skill centre for the whole Olympic program. Content and practice of the skill centre training was a collaboration between DET, the unions and the industry. Comet also had a collaborative relationship with Multiplex, which had its own skill centre for the Stadium site.[7 13] Ray Harty of Comet says the experience highlighted the need to go beyond technical training as part of the national vocational training program:

"... the trades are not the only area of skills shortages – the non-trade needs have come of age." [13]

Training to be a rigger is one thing. Training a rigger (or a site manager) to be part of the collaborative 'design and build' team effort that can deliver integrated projects on time, under budget and in safety is another. Andrew Ferguson gives this a slightly different slant, one that has support from management in several companies: [7 13 24]

---

* For detailed analysis of the Olympic Training Strategy see Building and Construction: An industry training strategy for the 2000 Olympic and Paralympic Games, Nexus Management Consulting Pty Ltd, May 2000 (unpublished).

"WorkCover requirements for site specific induction and OH&S is the law. There was more compliance ... and ... government involvement in the project but the main difference was the attitude." [23]

Site-specific training and OH&S are not new, particularly to the large contractors.[7] What is unique here is that this was a collaborative project between government, industry and the unions across **all** of the contract sites. It provided a skills development program based on detailed analysis of the skills that would be needed for different stages of the whole Olympic construction program. It was strategic coordinated forward planning of the training needed to deliver the necessary skills matrix at the right time. It combined:

- comprehensive induction, with a focus on safety

- 'just in time' approaches to assembling the skilled labour and the work practices on the job, where these skills were applied.

The effect has been to produce a change in the construction industry culture.

Occupational health and safety – everyone's business

Training doesn't just improve skills; it saves lives! The OCA noted that

"The training provided ... has resulted in a general level of skill improvement which will result in productivity and safety improvements."

There was one fatal accident in the whole of the Olympic project. This occurred on the Olympic Village site. A pallet of bricks on scaffolding at first-storey height had been stripped from one side only leaving an unstable wall of loose bricks on the outside.

Tragically, these fell on Tom Pascoe who was working below. [23 46] According to the site delegate, who is still affected emotionally, it 'could have been avoided by better training'.[46]

The only significant work stoppage on an Olympic site was over a safety issue. The Olympic Games required a massive 'overlay' of temporary seating in a number of the venues. During the construction of the 12,000 seat temporary stand for the Aquatic Centre (which we explore in more detail later in this chapter) workers were concerned for the safety of the structure and those working beneath it. Several weeks work was delayed while both design and structure were rectified. This perhaps serves to indicate that collaboration is not simply about avoiding conflict but having the trust and respect to know that when conflict arises there may be a good reason behind it. In the area of safety, it is 'everyone's business' to address the underlying concerns.

Building the venues

Each of the 18 sporting venues built for the Games is a story in itself. The early work on Olympic Park Station not only showed that the contractors could deliver on time, it also allowed the organisers to flag that the Games would be 'car free'. Its architecture is recognised both for its aesthetics and its 'ecological' use of passive ventilation systems. Similar features stand out for many of the others. To tell the whole story is beyond the scope of this book. What we can do is give a few examples where collaborative relationships came together around some particularly challenging projects. To do this we have chosen as case studies:

- the construction of the Dome on the Exhibition Halls at the New Sydney Showgrounds

- the construction of the 'arches' that support the roof of Stadium Australia

- the incorporation of ecological sustainability into the construction of the Athletes Village

- the construction of the temporary 'overlay' that converted some of the facilities for Games use. Here we use two examples
  - the fit-out of the Main Press Centre
  - the temporary seating at the Aquatic Centre

On the ground; in the air – the Showgrounds Dome

The challenge was to construct a dome, 50 metres high and 100 metres across, at the Exhibition Halls of the New Sydney Showgrounds in Olympic Park. The project contract had very tight deadlines and presented significant challenges in terms of building the structure 'at height'. Work high above the ground involves significant safety issues.

The Showgrounds project was managed by John Holland and the dome project was contracted to Thiess. When it went to tender in

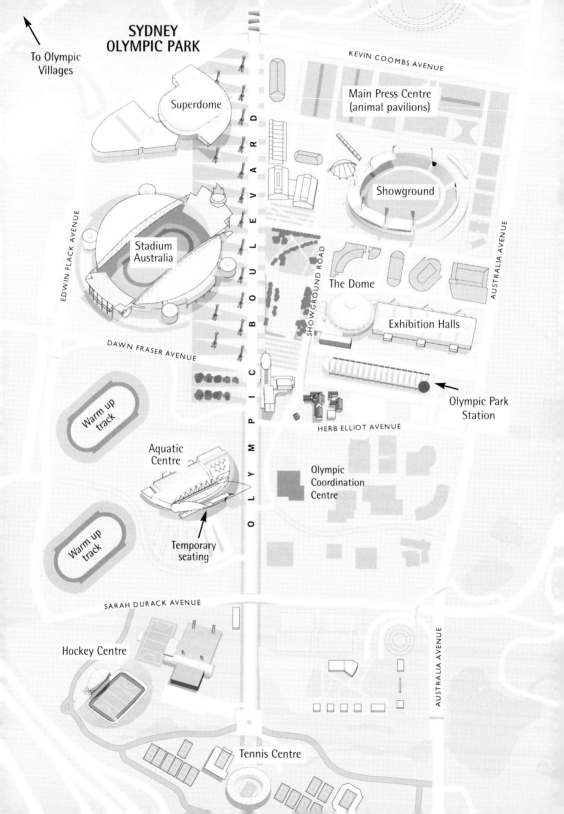

SYDNEY OLYMPIC PARK

To Olympic Villages

KEVIN COOMBS AVENUE

Superdome

Main Press Centre (animal pavilions)

Showground

Stadium Australia

EDWIN FLACK AVENUE

BOULEVARD

DAWN FRASER AVENUE

SHOWGROUND ROAD

The Dome

Exhibition Halls

AUSTRALIA AVENUE

Olympic Park Station

HERB ELLIOT AVENUE

Warm up track

Aquatic Centre

OLYMPIC

Olympic Coordination Centre

Warm up track

Temporary seating

SARAH DURACK AVENUE

Hockey Centre

AUSTRALIA AVENUE

Tennis Centre

1996 the project deadline was for early 1998 – to be completed in time for the old showground to move from Moore Park. Project Director Ian Buchan is credited with the idea of building the Dome on the ground and then jacking it up. Thiess won the contract in October 1996 on the basis of this methodology and completed it in time in February 1998. There is general agreement, in retrospect, that it couldn't have been built any other way. The achievement is one acknowledged by Michael Knight who says that

"The Showground was built on an impossible timetable, several engineers didn't believe it could be done. The workforce felt they were engaged in something special and building the Showground . . . was building a part of history. At the opening all the workers who had worked on it were invited and had a sense of being part of it." [68]

By building the top of the Dome at ground level first and then progressively jacking it up as each lower section was added, the safety risks of working 'at height' were drastically reduced. Subsequent work was done out of cherry pickers and other safe work platforms with nobody climbing on scaffolding. Thiess described it as 'simply working on the ground in the air'. All the electricals and lighting were installed progressively as each stage of the Dome was erected, reducing both time and cost and leaving ground space free of scaffold for other work. It was learning on the job. Scott Gartrell, the HR manager, says:

"We'd never done it before. It was only theory so we had to work out how this thing was going to happen. We had a big design team working on it very closely with the crew. That was also unique. Design usually precedes construction so that was pretty important. Steel work was subcontracted ... [as far away as Melbourne] ... so pre-planning was vital. All subcontractors were included and played a part in the planning and the design process and they were kept in the loop. We had regular meetings. Everyone was caught up in the spirit." [24]

Scott Gartrell said he needed 'a sound industrial relations platform to run the job'. Hollands and the Labor Council had negotiated the Showgrounds Project Agreement and had this certified by consent as a State Award. As contractor, Thiess was bound to this Award. Gartrell says:

"It was a very successful formula. Not because of what was in the document. The document was essentially a very simple thing. It was successful because it actually had commitment – it's one of those old-fashioned things – it was seen by both sides as a good deal – so it stuck. An interesting thing about

COURTESY OF THE SYDNEY OLYMPIC PARK AUTHORITY (BOB PETERS)

The Showgrounds Dome under construction.

it – it was taken almost verbatim to the Eastern Distributor and used for the construction period there and I picked it up for the M5 when I came to Baulderstone's and used it almost verbatim. It has provided us again with a very good framework. So I have to say it's now a standard. A simple agreement that fits the Federal and State Law – is acceptable to clients as well as the industry as being something that delivered a lot of value." [24]

Not that everything always ran smoothly:

"There was great cooperation – a good relationship with the unions – everyone was getting on very well when I got a call one day from a project manager that this new union organiser had parked his car across the gate and was blocking a concrete pour. Now I hadn't seen the blockage of a concrete pour for ten years! Not only was it unusual in the industry generally – it just hadn't happened. So I rang him up and I said, 'What's going on …?' He said, 'I came here this morning and your manager agreed to this … they haven't … I've come back … and that's it! I won't give you a second chance.' So I said, 'Well that's not how we do things here, this is a different philosophy. If you've got a problem ring me and we'll resolve it.' That conversation was conducted with both of us screaming at each other. But at the end of the day he acknowledged that the site was different and that they were not going to take preventive action and from that point on

we didn't have one single occasion where that sort of response was taken to an issue. That's different because it resumed straight after the Games on some building sites though not on big civil construction sites." [24]

We'll let Scott tell the rest in his own words:

"... most subcontractors are little businesses – many of them had no idea of how to put an EBA * in place. What we constantly find is that we the managing contractor spend a lot of our time advising subcontractors on how to view IR – and employ their people – and all modes of labour issues. So because we weren't fighting at the outset of these projects the cooperative spirit grew up very quickly. When you've got that general good will it carries through so that when you do have a problem there is a better attitude towards resolving it. That has stayed with us. You agree on the approach at the outset – you nominate all the issues that are going to arise in the project, agree a response to them and get on with the job. We tried to really focus on who worked there – which is not what's done generally. We are getting better at it as an industry but we really tried to understand the employees, the subcontractors, making sure what their skills were, and where there were skill gaps.*

"The unions' attitude was very simple. They said that their role was to ensure that their members were paid properly and work in safe conditions. Although I must say the deal ($1.85 per hour site bonus) probably wasn't as high as could have been achieved on a one-off basis. I think that the unions showed great restraint." [24]

Training would be essential to completion of the project on time and within budget. The Showgrounds became the model for skill-centre training. Ray Harty of Comet Training describes the proactive approach:

"We determined ... what the skill matrix was likely to be at any given point in the construction phase. So we knew for example, at excavation stage, just getting out of the ground, that the sorts of skills we would have on site would be concreters, steel fixers and form workers etc – and further in, once we gained some height we knew we would need riggers, doggers, people who knew how to work elevator platforms etc – so having mapped the project and the various stages of the construction phase we then set a training calendar that operated three months in advance. We would then offer courses during any month that matched the skill matrix. As each month dropped off it became a very useful diagnostic tool for us, because it enabled

---

* Enterprise Bargaining Agreement

*us to analyse what courses were supported and what not supported, which
meant that when we added the new month we were able to make adjust-
ments to the training program for that month that reflected where the
construction phase had moved to, reasons why particular courses hadn't
been supported, and where demand lay. As a strategy this actually worked.
At the end everyone was surprised with the result we got because in that one
calendar year we actually trained 1,244 people.*" [13]

One focus of training in high demand was risk management. This
was a particular OH&S focus for leading hands, foremen and
supervisors about the whole jobs safety approach.

In terms of the analysis we have developed, this was a 'little d'
contract – the contractor completing the design documentation,
and constructing the project. It had significant technological
innovation supported by a collaborative IR and HR culture
involving the whole contractor and subcontractor workforce with
a significant focus on training and safety.

Golden arches across the world – the roof of Stadium Australia

It would be almost exactly three years after Sydney won the Bid
that the first sod was turned on the most important of the new
venues – the Stadium. This was the project that everyone had
dreamed of. Two full years in its planning and design stage, it was
built over and over on paper, and it would be another two and a
half years before it reached practical completion.

Construction of the 110,000 seat Stadium was an extraordinary
task in terms of the management of people, time and tools. Early
construction would allow testing of the essential systems (crowd
control, catering, security and transport) that would be needed
during the Games. There was an imperative for on-time delivery,
with severe cost penalties for failure. It also had the 'eyes of the
world' ever present. One of the many challenging features was the
construction of the steel arches; the 300 metre long, 14 metre
deep steel trusses spanning the entire length of the Stadium and
supporting its roof (6,000 tons of steel). At one stage 35 cranes
were being operated simultaneously on site. The world's largest
land-based mobile crawler crane was needed to lift the four end
sections into place. Each of these end sections was attached to a
concrete thrust block with a single (1.8 ton) pin requiring precise
coordination of machine and manpower.

The Stadium under construction.

The Stadium contract, won by Multiplex in mid-1994, was to 'design and construct'. As Director Matt Stagg says:

"The Stadium was very much Big D design. The design part of that from our perspective was at least as big a task as putting the thing together. This involved team work – architects, engineers, contractors, subcontractors and workers, working together, with mutual respect at every level." [19]

A lot of thought went into selecting and building relationships with the subcontractors who Multiplex thought could do some of the unique jobs involved. Similarly care was taken with selection of supervisors and a union delegate who would have the respect of both management and workers. Employee Relations Manager Dave Higgon:

"I have to say – the Labor Council and CFMEU did everything possible to make the project a success. One key element was having a capable site delegate – one who not only had the respect of the company, but also the respect of the workforce and unions, and who was also able to work with management to anticipate problems before they emerged. Multiplex's industrial relations strategy recognised that successful management of IR is very much an outcome of good relationships, good safety, concern for the

welfare of individuals and constant attention towards developing a good working environment. The site delegate and other delegates worked closely with Multiplex in achieving these outcomes." [7]

Eric Rolls, Project Manager with responsibility for construction, observed:

"I had never been involved with a project before the Stadium where the benefits of people working together cooperatively was so clearly demonstrated. I think the workforce, subbies and management all learnt valuable lessons. The exercise for all of us is to keep the momentum going." [7A]

Multiplex employed Mario Barrios, a senior CFMEU delegate, to assist with workplace relations and day-to-day implementation of safety management. He describes the task:

"We had a thorough site induction process – specifically regarding OH&S – and told all people working on the site, 'If you have a problem with safety then come see us'. There was immediate investigation of any safety issue or accident, followed by a rectification procedure. We kept everyone informed about the process. Each and every accident, no matter how minor, each incident – the same procedure. We pinned up a notice straightaway – the incident report – what happened; the outcome; the cause; follow-up procedure; action to prevent recurrence. It was important to anticipate – to know what could happen and to then try to avert it. Don't let it happen! Deal with issues. Keep people informed. These were the key elements." [47]

As union delegate he had freedom to organise among all workers on site. The company had a card security system in place so it and the union knew at any time who was on site and ensured all workers went through site induction training.

For most of the construction period (two and a half years) Multiplex had a workforce of 1,000 on site at any one time. Prior to commencement of the project, Multiplex anticipated skill shortages. A training program was developed in consultation with Construction Training Australia (CTA), the national industry training advisory body. This ensured that, as well as meeting the needs of the project and individual employees, the training was also consistent with National Industry Competency Standards. An on-site Centre for Entry Level Training (CELTA) was established between Multiplex and the Building Workers Assistance Centre (BWAC) to provide a single entry point for apprenticeships and traineeships. The CELTA assisted the employment of approxi-mately 150 people, a significant proportion being young people and indigenous Australians. An on-site skill centre supported by DET was established to meet the project's training needs. Other stakeholders such as the Building Careers Advisory Centre, TAFE, secondary schools career advisers, community groups and training providers were invited to use the resources and the high profile of the Stadium project to promote the common industry agenda for training and skill-formation. The legacy of the Stadium training experience is the ongoing communication between the parties involved and the recognition of both its domestic and international potential. In the words of Ray Hutt, CEO of Construction Training Australia:

Many of the workforce skilling issues identified during the Olympics building program are of importance domestically and in relation to industry export potential. Multiplex and Construction Training Australia are currently participating in a feasibility study with our UK counterpart, the Construction Training Board, towards establishing international building industry competency benchmarks.[7A]

On-site, joint monitoring meetings were held monthly between contractor, subcontractors and union representatives to discuss issues of relevance, past present and future. Meetings with union representatives confirm that there has been a culture shift. Some elements of this can be seen in the comments that follow.

"There is always a problem with the subbies but it is easier now – people are talking more about safety. There's been a culture shift. Ironically it's harder with the membership. A lot of the young guys don't realise how hard we had to work for all this. It means there has to be a change in union tactics. We have to work harder to explain how we got it – the wages, allowances and the training – then they come around. I picked up three tickets on this job." [(Joe)47]

"We could always have got a better deal on top of what we got – but to do so would be to commit suicide. First the public would see us as greedy and we wouldn't be able to maintain the conditions that we have now – we'd lose them after. Same with membership – people saying we should have 2,000 members and the like but get them the old way and the whole industry might suffer and jobs wouldn't be there and if there's no jobs where do we get the members. It's jobs that aren't as well organised where people have to look for excuses to pull a stop. On the Stadium no-one was looking for problems – issues yes, and if anyone found them they were brought to attention and got fixed. In the 80s it was the workers who pulled the 'business union' delegates on – still do – but this is different – it's not doing deals. People are starting to realise that if there is an incident we have a meeting **when we have the answer** *– we keep people informed. Like the*

Crane incident ... people demanded a meeting but we said no – you'll ask questions and we won't have answers. We got it investigated and kept people informed by notices and then ten days later we had a meeting to report on it. It was a human error – the person was suspended but wasn't stigmatised. Before we'd have had a meeting when something occurred and people would have gone home, often not knowing why, and come back next day to the same mess." [(Mario)47]

Before the Olympics waste minimisation and separation was seen as appropriate at home but impossible to do on a construction site.

"There's lots of little things about the Showgrounds as well as the big stuff. Like the nails left sticking out on the lift shaft. Usually we'd knock them off with a hammer. The formworkers came up with the idea of using a metal tube to break them off – much safer – lots of little things like that when you give people ownership. A lot of work is lost in this business due to hot or wet weather. We'd get the weather report and find alternative work for the hot hours – start people on outside jobs early and then put people under cover doing these jobs when it got hot – little things like getting the steel under cover before it got too hot to handle outside. All this isn't new it's that we were involved in the planning." [(Tony)47]

"The other thing we had was we could get things to happen outside the job where it affected work for the Olympics – like the [public transport] buses were not starting early enough or the problem with the mosquitoes – we could go to the Minister – we got the bus schedules, and pellets were dropped by helicopter for the mozzies." [(Mario/Tony)47]

"Whereas this kind of collaboration was common on large sites during the Olympics it is now being found on much smaller projects down to the $1–5 million contract level. The stewards talk particularly of the multi-skilling that was made possible." [(Joe)47]

"And there was good money – a real incentive to work – after all you work to live not live to work." [(Mario)47]

Before the Olympics waste minimisation and separation was seen as appropriate at home but impossible to do on a construction site. Today all Multiplex sites have separation and recycling as part of their environmental management procedures. Jo Drummond, who worked with Multiplex developing the company's Environmental Management System, describes how she recently observed

"... a young plumber's apprentice walk up to a set of waste bins carrying a big cardboard box. He took out some pieces of plasterboard and put them in the plasterboard bin and some bits of steel into the steel bin. He then tore up the box and threw the pieces into the cardboard bin. He was left with a short piece of PVC piping which is currently not recyclable." [53]

On the management side there was a preparedness to look at anything that someone thought might establish better relations on the site. As the goal for the Stadium was to be the best in the world, the Stadium construction would also be a model of 'world-best practice'. As Dave Higgon says:

"This isn't rocket science – if you treat people properly you have a much better chance of getting a good outcome. It shows what you can achieve when people work together." [7]

Green as grass – and fit for the world's best

"The very next day, after Sydney won the Games, they came in droves. Fellas in utes, dog in back – a whole busload took a detour into Homebush – all of them with the same question. 'Got a job for us mate? We've come to help.' We had to turn them away, disappointed. And still they came."

Danny Potocki [46]

Homebush Bay was still a cattle yard when Lend Lease first arrived. The swimming pool (to become the Aquatic Centre for the Games) was accessed via a dirt track and there were acres of concrete slabs everywhere. The occasional truck still sneaked in under cover of dark to dump an illicit load of waste. Lend Lease was there before anyone else. They had taken on board the idea of restructuring workplace relations. If anyone could persuade the IOC that Australian construction could pull it off, Lend Lease could – and they did.

The Lend Lease site delegate Danny Potocki had been at Homebush Bay since 1992. Of the party thrown on the night the Bid was announced he said:

"There had been a huge amount of hype around it all. There were 2,500 people there. Everyone wanted to be there. There was an amazing atmosphere. We had accumulated RDOs so that productivity wouldn't be affected by a whole weekend celebration. We were very confident that we'd win it! Then after the announcement – it was just the most incredible experience. Really macho men were hugging and dancing with each other – the euphoria truly something that I will always remember. There were a number of us that did the beer-can thing! There was no class distinction – managing directors hugging labourers and politicians hugging delegates – everyone was equal. It went on and on (felt like for days). Then it was back to work and get on with it!"* [46]

---

* rostered days off

Being the first contractor on site at Homebush Bay gave Lend Lease access to many other opportunities. The company was short-listed for the Stadium contract but ended up (in a consortium with Mirvac) with the job of constructing the Olympic Villages. This would be a tough one as part of it involved building many (relatively) small houses – very different from a single large 'construction' project. Within the industry the 'house-building' culture is very different from that in commercial construction. The contractors would have to deal with a large number of small subcontractors and still meet the unions' expectation for organising rights and an enterprise agreement that covered subcontracts. Industrial relations strategy was going to be critical to the success of the project. The challenge for the Mirvac/Lend Lease Village Consortium was to bring the domestic sector of the building industry into what was, traditionally, a union-oriented industrial framework. In this the company had two levers. One was health and safety. The other was the environmental sustainability criteria that had been built into the 'green games' rhetoric when Sydney bid for the Olympics in 1993.

The contractor used the strategy of establishing a skill centre, site induction and OH&S training to deliver the message that 'working safe isn't necessarily working slow'.

In the Village Project Agreement, signed October 1997, the unions acknowledged that house building was different from commercial building and also from home-unit building. The agreement focused on the need to create opportunities for long-term benefits through acquiring new skills and learning innovative and safe ways of working. It also acknowledged that the best way to effect change in the workplace was through consensus and working in partnership towards common goals and objectives. Perhaps more simply put as 'collaboration'. As this was a Consent Award all subcontractors were bound to it. The awards provided the level playing field. Les Tobler, CFMEU organiser for all the Games sites, describes it bluntly:

"There was no screwing the arse off the subbies and the subbies weren't screwing the workers." [75]

To drive the safety program the contractor used the strategy of establishing a skill centre, site induction and OH&S training to deliver the message that 'working safe isn't necessarily working slow'. By extending the kind of working relationships it had with its own workforce to the many small contractors, Lend Lease built a commitment from the employers to safety and safe working practices. It took time but it worked. Eric Hensley, Lend Lease

COURTESY OF THE SYDNEY OLYMPIC PARK AUTHORITY (BOB PETERS)

Employee Relations Manager, says:

"The culture of the cottage industry isn't used to the implementation of good OH&S procedures. But we had them captive for over 18 months and they did a number of houses over this period so their processes of safe working procedures got developed and honed. Our feedback is that a lot of these builders are practising the same processes that they acquired on the Olympic village. It's not uncommon now to see full scaffolding and particularly edge catch-scaffolding for roof tilers. In the past this was very rare." [30]

From Homebush Bay to 'Newington Green' – the Athletes Village under construction.

As with other Olympic contractors, Lend Lease employed an experienced union delegate, Danny Potocki, as part of the core workforce for the project, with the job of identifying safety problems and fixing them at source. This gave the unions a presence for organising on the site but equally important was the task of building respectful working relations with the subcontracting employers. Potocki said that the union saw it as an opportunity to make an impression on the industry on behalf of the membership.[46] The impact of the training and the OH&S – the one fatality excepted – is impressive.

Within the union movement there are criticisms of this approach, and of the CFMEU in particular. For some, the unions exist primarily to press the case for improved wages and conditions and to maximise the involvement of the rank and file in this struggle. Danny Potocki points to some of the gains from the alternative (collaborative) relationships that evolved during the Games:

"For the first time you had labourers being able to pick up a hammer and carpenters able to wheel a wheelbarrow! Although this was something the Olympics gave us, in this instance we were the leaders in workplace reform … we were given the reins to lead ourselves. Management are to be commended for that. That was a huge risk! They really let the workforce run things. It was just amazing how it all came together. Everyone was excited, learning new things, the subcontractors also had a training allowance, to encourage them on board, so we were actively promoting it and using ourselves as the benchmark." [31]

Between 1992 and 1996 there was no dispute. Indeed the young people coming on to the site believed that everything they got was merely given by the employer. All the agreements – the cross-skilling, the safe site, the clean site, good canteens, sheds, transport, site allowances etc – everything was taken for granted. They didn't know that all of it had been fought for and elaborately negotiated for over a whole decade. [46]

A link to the world – the Main Press Centre fit-out

It was decided to put the Press Centre at the hub of the Games. About 6 million people would visit the Sydney venues to watch the Games events. Some 3.5 billion worldwide would watch on TV and many more would listen to radio and read press reports, collect magazine photos of athletes, heroes and so on. Of the $3 billion sponsorship budget to stage the Games over $1 billion came from TV rights alone. Having the facilities to mount this exercise was an essential part of preparation for the Games.

The Main Press Centre refurbishment and fit-out by Thiess was a logistics marvel. It was completed inside three months between the Easter Show and the Olympics Test Events (May to July 2000). One look at the statistics on the MPC and any project manager in the construction industry would predict that either it could not be completed in time, its costs would blow out, or there would be serious quality problems; or perhaps all three.

The challenge was to convert the NSW Royal Agricultural Society's Horse and Cattle Pavilions (to all intents and purposes a very large tin shed) into a 40,000 square metre high-tech facility* as a working base for nearly 6,000 local and international journalists covering the Olympic Games. It was then to be modified again, inside a seven-day window between the Olympic and the Paralympic Games, to include television crews and some Paralympic sports – and then returned to its original animal house status at the end of the Games. In addition to office accommodation, the fit-out included:

- the largest film processing lab outside the USA
- an 800 seat media auditorium
- eight retail outlets including a bank, travel agent, newsagency and hairdresser
- Etna's Kitchen, a 120 seat, fine dining restaurant
- additional 2,500 per sitting catering facilities
- five press conference rooms
- more than 500 TV sets and 2,000 phone lines.

As well as the risk for the contractor there was an even greater risk to the Games. As Venue Manager Reg Gratton put it:

"The success of the Games is judged by the world's media."

The strategy to deal with this risk was to get both the workforce and the press 'on side'. Ian Buchan described how

"everyone was caught up in the spirit of it. Pre-planning and prefabrication were the keys to its success. All subcontractors played a part and were included in the pre-planning process. The needs of the press were part of the design process and they were kept in the loop. Regular meetings were held – all parties in attendance. There was full participation. 'Ownership of the workplace' was the name of the game." [52]

Thiess had already delivered a large component of the Showgrounds some one year earlier and were still on site managing the IR for the 'overlay' works in various venues for the OCA. With the IR architecture still in place and the main venues now complete, there was a large pool of skilled labour available. This labour pool

---

* Think of this as about the size of eight football fields!

From animal house to Main Press Centre.

COURTESY OF THE SYDNEY OLYMPIC PARK AUTHORITY (BOB PETERS)

ROGER SCOTT/SOCOG

MATT TURNER/SOCOG

had furthermore been properly trained and site inducted at a variety of Homebush venues. The on-site skill centre alone had trained some 1,250 people by this time. The 'zero tolerance attitude' to breaches of safety standards, that had been part of Thiess' induction workplace safety training, stood them in good stead as there were no accidents or stoppages. These foundations contributed to a unique set of circumstances that achieved productivity levels four times the industry average by 300 people working around the clock in shifts. Leighton Contractors (having completed the Aquatic Centre 'overlay' – detail below) installed suspended flooring at the rate of 90 square metres per man-day! Partition walls were installed at a rate of 80 linear metres per man-day! Carpet was installed at a rate of 100 square metres per man-day!

At the end all flooring systems, wall partitions and many other materials were recycled. The people of East Timor gained partitioning for housing as part of the suppliers' disposal plan.

More bums on seats – the Aquatic Centre temporary seating

IOC President Juan Antonio Samaranch described the Aquatic Centre as *"the best swimming pool I have seen in my life"*.

For the Games it was essential to maximise the number of spectators (and ticket sales) for the more popular events – none more so than in the swimming and aquatic sports. The seating capacity of the Aquatic Centre was increased from 4,000 to 16,000. Behind this 'overlay' there is a story in the construction of the temporary 12,000 seat stand, not an easy task and made more difficult as the Aquatic Centre had to remain open to the public throughout the construction period. The seating extension had a dramatic appearance with the size of some steel beams arguably matched only by that of Sydney's Harbour Bridge.

We have selected this as a case study for this book because it went wrong. We are not interested in the detail of what or why it went wrong or because of who might be to blame (the courts will decide that). What stands out is how the main stakeholders dealt with the issues and got on with the job. In construction management 'there are no problems, only opportunities'. The problem was perceived structural design faults in the seating stand of sufficient concern to workers and the union for these to involve the union's Monitoring Committee. The 'opportunity' was to develop a cooperative approach to finding the solution. Without the Games-

An additional 12,000 seat temporary stand for the Aquatic Centre (see arrow).

wide 'best practice' approach to OH&S and workplace safety procedures the hold-up might never have occurred. Equally, the reason why there were no crowd injuries, let alone fatalities, at the Sydney Games is, in part, because of the stringent workplace safety procedures adopted during the construction of the venues.

Leighton won the $19.4 million contract by competitive open tender. But from the outset there was close collaboration between client and contractor. Lee Price, Leighton's construction manager, said:

"During the bid for the contract the OCA were very conscious of who and how. The lowest price was not necessarily the most important consideration. Industrial relations and the environmental issues had a high profile.

"I have never been on a job where the government and the private sector have knitted quite like that. There was a genuine effort to make it work. Everyone put their egos aside. Both Leece and Barraclough [OCA] have a background in construction. They knew what made it tick – take away the conflict, then it's just 'what's fair and reasonable?' The problem was

perceived design faults. It created a major industrial problem. We had the Olympic trials looming up [11th May]. Work was stopped on 28th February. It was April before we got back [five to six weeks]. Even then it wasn't all go. Barraclough stepped in to take control and give direction from the design perspective." [93]

The involvement of the client in the execution of a project is unusual but these were unusual circumstances. John Barraclough had been responsible for the 'overlay' program since July 1997. Faced with the 'opportunity' he brought contractor and workforce representatives together to get a clear and common understanding of the perceived problem, organise the engineering checks and agree on the design rectifications. This design review took two to three weeks. Communicating it all took another week. Rectification works for another two to three weeks brought the project back on track.

Lee Price says:

"We worked round the clock. We had a 24-hour maintenance operation. Anything went wrong – we went out to rectify it." [93]

The project was also a model for the 'green games' approach to construction and recycling. More than 90 percent of the steel dismantled from the Aquatic Centre was bought by Wollongong Sports Ground Trust for the grandstand at WIN Stadium. The roof-sheeting and ceilings, as well as the precast planking from the concourse, were reused on other construction projects. Of the effort, John Barraclough of the OCA said:

"It gave people the opportunity to achieve – to take on responsibility and accountability. Everyone collaborated. Everyone wanted the Games to succeed, or rather no-one wanted it to fail." [81]

As we said earlier there are many more stories – and many more examples of collaboration in 'building the theatre' but it's time to turn attention to the spectacle of 'staging the show' – the Sydney 2000 Olympic Games!

Chapter three

Staging the show

'Caesar conquered Gaul. Did he have no cook in his army?'

Bertold Brecht

The Sydney 2000 Olympic Games was arguably the world's largest single peacetime event. It was seen by 4 billion people around the world and about 6 million people in the Olympic venues over the 16 days. Alongside the Games, Sydney organised a series of other events, such as the Arts Festival and 'live sites' that attracted and entertained one and a half million more.

We all saw the athletes and the media commentators. We watched star performers and noticed some of the several thousand people involved in the Opening and Closing Ceremonies. We saw fireworks, the Stadium, the cauldron, Olympic Park, various sports venues and happy smiling spectators. We might have noticed some of the dignitaries and sporting officials from around the world and heard the head of the IOC declare 'best Games ever'.

If we were there, we might also have noticed some of the other people, like the wonderful spectator services volunteers and the people on the train platforms and the buses. We might have seen the young backpacker wearing the uniform of one of the cleaning companies – faced with the mess of a small child who had ice-cream all over his T-shirt, she not only cleaned up the mess but made sure the child had a new ice-cream within minutes and a clean T-shirt in half an hour. Had we been in the right place at the right time we might have noticed senior executives from the NSW Premier's Department doing shifts at the information booth in Martin Place, or State Rail managers helping direct crowds on the platform at Central Station. Overnight at Sydney Olympic Park we might have seen the truck driver picking up bins of waste carefully sorted into compost, recycling and trash or spotted the logistics crew putting matting down on a slippery walkway. In the middle of the day we might have noticed one of the union organisers standing in the crowd with a mobile phone to her ear dealing with yet another case of a Games worker who hadn't been paid that week and not asking which union the worker was in, or if he was in a union at all.

There are more stories here than can ever be told. Behind the spectacle and the enjoyment, a large number of people worked to make it possible. The full number will never be counted. It all depends where you draw the line. The Games events alone required a workforce of at least 125,000 people. At least 60,000 of these were volunteers, many with specialist skills. Often they were working alongside people who were being paid to supervise, or deliver the core services of cooking, serving, cleaning and waste disposal, or marshalling or providing information, security and transport. Without them all the events just could not have happened. Include the many others who were not counted in the Games workforce but without whom the city and the Games would not have functioned and we estimate a total workforce in excess of 200,000.

Not all of this ran smoothly. As we will see there were a number of areas where there were significant problems, but none of these caused major disruption to the Games. It is as if, when the wheels fell off the Games truck, people held it up and very rapidly got some new wheels under it. It is this collaboration that we are exploring. How was this possible? What were the features in the human relations architecture of the Games that made significant contributions – and perhaps more important in the long term, can any of these be replicated in other projects?

In this chapter we outline the framework of industrial and human relations that were established during the planning and lead-up to the Games. In the next chapter we will explore how this operated in practice in each of the major areas of service delivery. We also explore how, in some of these, environmental innovation and human relations worked together to the point where Sydney 2000 can legitimately be described as the 'Green Games'. We try to tell it as it was, through the eyes of those directly involved, 'warts and all'. Drawing attention to problems as well as the success stories will help to illustrate that 'the best Games ever' was achieved with something more than the spirit of goodwill generated by a unique sporting event. This spirit was nurtured and built on a framework of human, industrial, workforce, workplace and interpersonal relations without which this goodwill could so easily have turned into recrimination – something all too evident in the legacy now carried by a number of previous Olympic Host Cities such as Toronto, Barcelona, Seoul, Atlanta and Berlin.

Staging the show – easier said than done

Within the media-driven language of the Games organisers the division of responsibility was that the Olympic Coordination Authority (OCA) would 'build the theatre' and the Sydney Organising Committee for the Olympic Games (SOCOG) would 'stage the show'. As we will see this line became blurred at times, particularly late in the planning and preparation. Also within the planning structure were the Olympic Roads and Transport Authority (ORTA) with responsibility for coordinating transport, and the Olympic Security and Command Centre (OSCC) with responsibility for security. Add in a few others like the Sydney Paralympic Organising Committee (SPOC), the Olympic Media Organisation (OMO) and the Sydney Olympic Broadcast Organisation (SOBO). Despite the common perception much more than SOCOG was involved in staging the Games.

SOCOG was in fact a very small organisation. At its peak it employed a mere 3,500 people. Most of these were initially recruited to manage some 90 program areas. As the Games deadlines approached most of these people were 'rolled over' into the venue management teams at the various Games sites. OCA and ORTA were even smaller. So the skill of the people in the coordinating agencies was in mobilising, motivating and supporting 120,000–200,000 other workers:

- people employed in Games sponsor companies or those providing contract services

- people seconded or on leave from other work

- people providing goods, equipment or 'value in kind' (VIK)

- people recruited just for the Games

- people working as volunteers providing specialist medical and technical services or helping guide people around Olympic Park.

And let us not forget the many more whose work contributed to the Games in producing equipment, uniforms, Games licensed goods and literally millions of other ways both within Australia and worldwide.

It is worth noting the political collaboration across parties and ideologies which delivered such an outstanding result. SOCOG was created to run the Games under the political philosophy of a NSW Coalition government (when Labor held power in the Federal Parliament). As such it was set up to be at arm's length from government and mobilise private-sector resources for the event. From 1996 it was ultimately accountable to a State Labor government (while the Coalition held power federally). The SOCOG board under the presidency of the NSW Minister for the Olympics also included members of the Opposition party including the former Coalition Premier, Nick Greiner.

As the lead agency in staging the Games SOCOG has come in for a fair degree of criticism, some of it justified, some perhaps not. Apart from establishing the structure little was done in the three years 1993–6. Some of this delay is understandable in light of the subsequent media exposure of the political paralysis on the SOCOG Board. The conflicts with the AOC explain (though hardly justify) an apparent inability to make decisions in the early days and the high turnover of senior staff. The AOC view is that there was too much involvement of the board in what should have been management decisions[71] while at the same time key issues do not seem to have been raised at board level.[33 37] It is not the concern of this study to reinvestigate these issues.

Similarly it is not our role to analyse in detail whether the division of responsibilities between the various agencies was the best way to organise the Games. The separation between SOCOG and OCA created a number of problems, as did the decision to have transport planning in ORTA, and the Ceremonies planning seemingly independent of SOCOG or anyone else's control in the early stages.[17 33] Suffice it to say that there was tension, some say enormous tension between OCA and SOCOG. 'You build the theatre and we'll organise the show' was good rhetoric but it was inevitable that once the venues were built OCA would be seeking a wider role. Also the government was the major sponsor of the Games and when SOCOG (a) didn't raise enough money from sponsorships[17] (b) caused a public outcry over importing marching bands from the USA[33] and (c) created a major public embarrassment for the government over the allocation of tickets[33 68] there was an excuse if not a reason to step in. This happened in early 2000. There were substantial changes in the Games organisation from then on with the establishment of the Sydney 2000 group and the merger of OCA, SOCOG and ORTA over a period of time, with David Richmond of the OCA emerging as the director of Sydney 2000.[68] A number of the SOCOG program areas, particularly those associated with the management of contracts for services such as cleaning, waste management, catering, security, environment and spectator services, were 'outsourced' – effectively managed by the OCA.[81] Some people in SOCOG resent this. Some see it as an issue of loyalty to the SOCOG CEO Sandy Hollway. Some also recognise that, apart from managing the service contracts, OCA played a crucial role in pulling together all the government agencies (police, transport, waterways, health services etc) in a way that SOCOG couldn't have done. Whether it was necessary to take over areas of contracting that were clearly in crisis in the immediate pre-Games period is an academic question. In the end the two key players, David Richmond in OCA and Jim Sloman in SOCOG, ensured that people with knowledge and expertise worked together to get things back on track. As Jim Sloman puts it succinctly:

"It's a question of relationships and respect – and it doesn't mean you have to like the people to get on with the job." [17]

Should there have been a single agency to administer all aspects of the Games? With hindsight the answer would probably be yes and the money would be on the OCA rather than SOCOG to be it. But hindsight always has 20–20 vision whereas at the time things are rarely so clear. Michael Knight who, as Minister, had perhaps the best overview says now:

"With hindsight we can see that the structure we inherited and worked with wasn't the optimum. John Coates (of the AOC) would say now that we wouldn't have a separate SOCOG – we would have a separate Sports Commission and marketing arm – and have the rest under OCA but he

> *The government was the major sponsor of the Games and when SOCOG didn't raise enough money from sponsorships, caused a public outcry over importing marching bands from the USA and created a major public embarrassment for the government over the allocation of tickets there was an excuse if not a reason to step in.*

also says that if this had been put forward seven years before he'd have died in the ditch to prevent it happening." [68]

The challenge ahead – lessons from Atlanta

The change of political control in 1995 was closely followed by the wake-up call that came from Atlanta. It is worth noting that this was the first time in the history of the modern Olympics that successive Games had been held in countries speaking the same language. The opportunities for transfer of knowledge were thus unique. The true legacy of Atlanta is probably less stark than the way it was perceived in Australia at the time but the effect was to focus attention on the massive task and the likely pitfalls that Australia would face in assembling the Games workforce. Myth or reality, the story that people brought back from Atlanta seemed to indicate:

> *It is worth noting that this was the first time in the history of the modern Olympics that successive Games had been held in countries speaking the same language.*

- A blow-out in labour costs – in some cases rising to four times the hourly rate before the Games – with serious budget implications.

- A major problem with recruiting and retaining a reliable labour force for the various Games services in the lead-up to the Games. Often people would be interviewed, recruited and sometimes trained and accredited and would then take up offers, going through similar processes with other Games contracting employers. To be sure of having 1,000 workers at Games time many employers found they needed to recruit up to 4,000.

- Poaching of the volunteer workforce to fill shortages in the paid workforce leading to gaps elsewhere in the planning and delivery of services.

- A problem of retaining staff (and volunteers) over the duration of the Games period. A number of workers turned up on day one, received their uniform and were never seen again.

Recruitment and training of volunteers was a function managed within SOCOG itself and as such under its control. We will explore this in some detail below and show how it was managed to achieve such an amazing outcome. Though this was a separate area of recruitment, one of the key decisions of SOCOG was to always refer to (and consequently encourage everyone to think in terms of) 'the paid and volunteer workforce' – an integrated workforce – rather than the division that would have been represented by language such as 'paid workers' and 'volunteers'.

The biggest problem SOCOG anticipated involved the private sector contractors for the service areas of catering, cleaning, and security.[17] If Atlanta had problems in this area then Sydney could expect them, and more. Atlanta was a major city in a country of 260 million people. Sydney was a city in a large island nation remote from the rest of the world with a total population of around 18 million. A population the size of the whole of Australia could be found within a six-hour drive of Atlanta. We will explore how SOCOG and its contractors, with help from Olympic sponsors and the trade unions, rose to this challenge in each of these service areas in the next chapter. What we now turn to is the framework of industrial agreements under which these workers were to be employed and the strategies crafted by SOCOG, the NSW government and the trade unions to address the problems anticipated by the Atlanta experience.

The industrial relations infrastructure

*"Construction was business as usual – we knew how to build large venues etc. The delivery of Games services was business as **unusual**. We were doing something different – that hadn't been done before – that's what made it interesting."*

Jim Sloman [17]

Collaboration between the major government, industry employer and trade union stakeholders in the Games had begun with the Bid and carried through into the construction phase. This was a good news story but in reality it was nothing new. SOCOG's Deputy Director, Jim Sloman, was a former Lend Lease project manager and already part of a culture of collaboration. It was already the norm in construction to work closely with trade unions, build a culture of respect between workers and managers, devolve responsibility to work teams, and reward performance. The challenge was to translate this approach to the very different workforce needed for a public entertainment event lasting a mere 16 days – and then repeat it two weeks later.*

---

* With the shoulder periods leading up to and following both the Olympic and Paralympic Games there were 60 days that defined the Games period, but for many workers their involvement would be little more than the two-week Olympic Games period.

An integrated workforce – business as un-usual

What industrial relations infrastructure would be needed for the massive 'temporary and casual' workforce for this event? How could three categories of workers be integrated into a seamless operation?

- The core SOCOG and venue management staff who needed to plan and supervise the recruiting, training, rostering, accreditation and uniforms, payment and recognition of this workforce.

- The large temporary workforce recruited to work in:
  - catering, cleaning, security, spectator services and merchandising
  - logistics – the procurement and delivery of the supplies needed by these services
  - waste management – the disposal of the wastes generated by the whole event on a daily basis
  - accommodation, feeding and transport of this workforce many of whom would come from outside the Sydney area.

- A volunteer workforce who, while working unpaid, would be providing both essential specialist services (e.g. medical/first aid) and general services (e.g. meeting, greeting and directing spectators) – all of whom would need training, accreditation and material support to work for the Games period.

According to Ian Clubb, the manager of workforce operations at SOCOG, in the early days people thought the greatest risk was technology. After Atlanta Sandy Hollway and Jim Sloman are quoted as saying that it was the Games workforce that 'kept them awake at night'. The team of Jim Sloman, John Quayle (Operations Manager), Ian Clubb and Rob Forsyth who handled much of the detail had many sleepless nights ahead.

The first and perhaps most strategic decision was to consistently refer to and regard the workforce as an integrated one – all workers, paid or volunteer, were part of the 'one team – one tent' approach and consistent or at least parallel approaches were used for each as far as possible. How this workforce was assembled, trained and managed is the subject of the next section. In Chapter 4 we will look in more detail at how it operated with varying degrees of success in each of the main service areas. What we will look at here is the industrial relations architecture that provided a framework on which this mammoth management exercise could be built.

Competition or collaboration?

We have seen that Atlanta faced several major problems:

- problems with recruiting and retaining the number of workers needed in each sector of service delivery prior to the Games

- a blow-out in labour costs

- significant 'no-shows' – people not turning up to work during the Games.

All the signs of an unhappy, discontented workforce. At the very least, Sydney needed to be able to achieve a high degree of control of these workforce issues, including wage rates and flexible working arrangements, if it was to avoid a repeat of these problems.

It is hardly surprising that the decision was to seek agreement on IR collaboration by negotiation with unions and relevant private sector companies. What is surprising was the phenomenal success achieved by this approach.

In this it faced a choice. Atlanta was a deregulated labour market in what in the USA is known as a 'right to work' State. The US Labor movement prefers to call these 'the right to work for less States' – where trade union rights to recruit members are severely limited and wage rates and workers' conditions are generally much lower than in those States without such restrictive legislation. Sydney could try to achieve where Atlanta had failed by following the labour market deregulation agenda advocated by the Federal government. This would involve reducing involvement of unions in collective bargaining, basing wages and conditions on 'individual contracts' and reducing industrial award agreements to core conditions. The theory would have it that this 'competition' in the labour market would keep costs down. Alternatively it could use the existing State industrial relations framework to negotiate a tripartite agreement between the State (as the major banker for SOCOG), the trade unions, and the companies who would be providing the major Games services.

In 1996–7 NSW had a State **Labor** government. It had a union movement that had demonstrated its commitment to support the Games. It also had a number of senior managers in SOCOG who had come from industries where this kind of collaboration was the norm. It is hardly surprising that the decision was to seek agreement on IR collaboration by negotiation with unions and relevant private sector companies. What is surprising, as we will see, was the phenomenal success achieved by this approach. It is interesting to speculate whether this success could have been achieved if the other route had been chosen.

The principles of collaboration

Little had been done to build on the early cooperation between the winning of the Bid in 1993 and 1996. One employers federation had reviewed the 1956 Olympic experience in Melbourne and met with SOCOG shortly after the Bid to discuss what might arise.[27] Two of the key service sector unions, the Australian Liquor Hospitality and Miscellaneous Workers Union (ALHMU) and the Australian Workers Union (AWU), had given some thought to the impact of the Games on membership and the latter had discussed these with the Labor Party in opposition.[1][21] Following the ALP conference in 1997 Michael Costa of the NSW Labor Council met with the NSW government Minister for the Olympics, Michael Knight. An inter-union committee brought together the major unions representing workers in the service industries.[*] A series of key documents outlining the framework for collaboration were then negotiated between the unions, SOCOG and the NSW government. These included:

- **The Principles of Cooperation** between SOCOG/SPOC and the Labor Council of NSW, signed 21 November 1997 (see Appendix 3). This established a Coordination Committee to negotiate detailed agreements designed to deliver certainty and flexibility for the 60-day period of the Games such as:
  - common wages and conditions for all employees
  - training and accreditation for union representatives servicing the Games

---

[*] The unions initially involved were the Australian Liquor Hospitality and Miscellaneous Workers Union (ALHMU), Australian Workers Union (AWU) and Media, Entertainment and Arts Alliance (MEAA). At later stages the inter-union collaboration also involved Shop Distributive and Allied Workers Union (SDA), Transport Workers Union (TWU), Rail, Tram and Bus Industry Union (Public Transport Union) (PTU), Textile, Clothing and Footwear Union of Australia (TCFUA) and the Australian Council of Trade Unions (ACTU).

- opportunities for union membership and recruiting
- preferential employment for existing Olympic site/venue employees, and
- a protocol for the use of volunteers.

■ **The Volunteer Protocol** – an agreement between SOCOG/ SPOC and the Labor Council on the use of volunteers for the Games, ensuring:

- agreement on appropriate roles for volunteers and ongoing consultation on these as required
- appropriate skills and training for volunteers
- appropriate benefits for volunteers including: catering, uniforms, transport, accommodation and acknowledgement of their work
- health and safety, insurance and income protection.

■ **The Code of Labour Practice for the Production of Licensed Goods** – an agreement between SOCOG/SPOC, the ACTU and the Labor Council signed November 1997 to ensure that all licensees, contractors and subcontractors adhere to basic international labour rights standards, including:

- freely chosen employment
- international rights on protection against discrimination
- non-use of child labour
- freedom of association and the right to collective bargaining
- legal minimum standards on wages, hours of work, working conditions, employment and training.

The Code set out implementation and monitoring procedures, and sanctions for non-compliance. In Chapter 4 we will explore some of the problems that were not anticipated in the operation of the Code.

The Olympic Games Award

The Principles of Cooperation was an agreement between SOCOG and the Labor Council. The next stage was to translate this into an industrial instrument that would specify the wages and conditions for workers at the Olympic Games to be held nearly three years away.

Originally the thinking had been that all service staff might be directly employed by SOCOG. Then that there would be a single labour hire company providing staff at SOCOG managed venues. Eventually a system of contracting of services to specialist companies in key service areas was adopted. The view of John Quayle, Operations Manager for the Games, was that, with the scale of the event, it was impractical to have 30 awards. SOCOG needed budget certainty to be able to plan and a common award delivered this financial certainty. Thus HR strategy was seen as essential to budgeting certainty. Managing the large number of employees at Games venues was always going to be a problem. HR management was seen as critical to the smooth running of the Games, including an agreed dispute resolution/settling machinery.[1]

The employer representatives from a number of major companies were brought into the negotiations with SOCOG and the unions, starting with major catering contractors, then cleaning, security and venue services. The objective was to achieve a consensus on a Sydney Olympic and Paralympic 2000 Games Award that would cover all workers recruited for work during the Games period. The strategy was to negotiate first with the 'industry' of the Games on the whole award and then negotiate details with the four sectors separately to make the changes necessary to accommodate their specific issues – mainly on rates of pay.

The third tier of negotiations involved the employer industry groups, notably the Employers Federation (now Employers First), Australian Business Ltd, NSW Chamber of Commerce, Restaurant and Caterers Association and Australian Industry Group.

The major elements of the agreement include:

- Defining an 'industry' for the Games that embraced all of the services to be provided to SOCOG by private industry contractors so that common conditions could be specified for workers across all these services – reducing the scope for resentments over differences and pressure for 'leapfrogging' claims later.

- Defining clearly the Games period for which the award would apply. This avoided the creation of precedents based on the unique Games situation. Existing award conditions would apply up to the Games period and be reverted to after.

- Defining wage rates to apply in each of the major service jobs that would represent a fair and appropriate rate at the time of the Games in September 2000 taking into account the unique nature of the event and the flexibility in working patterns required. This provided budget certainty for SOCOG, and for the contracting companies as the contract price would be based on these wage rates. This avoided two of the main problems of Atlanta – 'leapfrogging' of wage rates as contractors competed for scarce labour and the loss of recruited workers to other sectors as the wage rates for different jobs changed.

- Defining an Olympic Bonus of $1.50 per hour to be paid at the end of the Games to all workers who completed 95 percent of the shifts they were rostered for. This overcame the problem of people dropping out of the workforce part way through the Games leaving significant gaps in the workforce.

- Establishing dispute resolution mechanisms for dealing with problems as they arose – avoiding disruption in the lead-up to and during the Games.

- Guaranteeing union rights of access to the workforce at each stage in the process, particularly during the recruitment, training and accreditation processes and during the Games itself. This ensured that the collaboration between SOCOG, contracting employers and the unions was a visible feature of the Games. It ensured unions would be proactive in identifying problems on site and it established effective communications for dealing with these when they arose.

- Guaranteeing that the special conditions of the award would not set a precedent for future awards.

Perhaps more important, though unrecognised at the time, the award and the processes through which it was negotiated and implemented, resulted in an unprecedented level of trust and some abiding personal relationships between key union organisers, company representatives and the SOCOG IR and program managers. Words on a paper agreement can help define rights and dispute mechanisms but openness, interpersonal trust and the ability to work together on solutions to shared problems counts for far more, particularly when working under pressure.

How was the Award negotiated?

In many ways the Award is a unique document. The details are a matter of public record, as is the transcript of the decision handed down by Justice Wright who said that the evidence indicated:

- *... the major, unique and important nature of the Olympics event, the employment in relation to which is to be regulated by this award*

- *... the importance of cooperation in ensuring that the award operates in the public interest to enable the effective carrying out of the major events associated with the two Olympic Games*

- *... that detailed consideration has been given to the labour force aspect of the Olympic Games held in 1996 in Atlanta and that a real attempt has been made to learn from and to cure some of the difficulties that were experienced with the labour force in those Games.**

What is far more interesting is the process by which it was negotiated and the strategic thinking of the stakeholders in the outcome.

For the unions there was a natural desire to have a unionised workforce with decent wages and conditions. They wanted to avoid some of the worst excesses of subcontracting like cash in hand payments, and protect the jobs of people already employed at the Olympic venues when these were transferred to SOCOG for the period of the Games. There was also the long-standing commitment to support the Games and a sense that Sydney would be under the spotlight of world attention and could not afford to have labour disputes during the Games. Somewhere along the way the attitude shifted. As Chris Christodoulou of the Labor Council says:

"My initial questions were what can we get out of it for the union movement and the workers who would be employed. Could we have a unionised Olympics with the best ever wages and conditions. Along the track two other questions became important. We can't afford to stuff up and then as we got into it, seeing that we had a positive role to play in making it the best ever Olympics." [1]

But we jump ahead. Organising the workforce would first require organising the union movement – overcoming a long history of inter-union rivalry over membership and demarcation disputes over recruitment of new members.

Fortunately Chris Christodoulou, then at the ALHMU, had developed a working relationship with key organisers in two of the other unions, Michael Taylor of the AWU and Michel Hryce of the

---

* Industrial Relations Commission of NSW Matter No. IRC 6387 or 1998 Sydney Olympic and Paralympic Games 2000 (State) Award, Friday, 29 January 1999.

MEAA, as a result of an earlier demarcation dispute. Despite the inter-union history, suspicion, and political differences there was a basis of personal trust that eventually built cooperation between the unions for the Games. The Labor Council provided leadership in this cooperation. Michael Costa replaced Peter Sams as the Labor Council Secretary, and Chris Christodoulou was hired to coordinate the unions' Games initiative. Later the SDA, TWU, PTU and TCFUA were brought into the process. The inter-union collaboration led to the formation of Unions 2000[*] as a single shop-front point of entry for recruiting temporary workers as union members during the Games. This was a single 'Games union' run by the Labor Council and serviced by the five unions with a flat fee (15 cents per hour or $6 a week) for membership.

The unions also assisted with recruiting of workers in a number of areas. Some 4,500 'expressions of interest' for work at the Games were gathered and passed on to employers. Around 2,500 of these were employed to work for the Games. During the Games itself, 32 union organisers were rostered to provide 24-hour coverage of all Games sites. Their primary role was to identify and respond to workers' problems so that morale was maintained and none of the problems led to breakdown of services. As we will see in Chapter 4, this union collaboration was matched in a number of areas by unique partnership arrangements between employers, particularly in the areas of logistics, packaging, catering, cleaning and waste disposal.

Industrial relations in Australia have a long adversarial history with peak bodies on both sides staking ambit claims that are then negotiated to a compromise middle ground. What was needed here was some lateral thinking for a unique event.

The decision to include the major employers, many who would subsequently win contracts for Games services, and exclude the employer peak bodies from the initial round of negotiations was a strategic one. Industrial relations in Australia have a long adversarial history with peak bodies on both sides staking ambit claims that are then negotiated to a compromise middle ground. What was needed here was some lateral thinking for a unique event. Unlike the unions, there is no single peak body that can claim to represent all employers in NSW. Several overarching bodies either compete for or cross-represent the same member companies. Others represent employers only in partic-

---

[*] Unions 2000 involved the Labor Council and four unions, ALHMU, AWU, MEAA and SDA.

ular sectors, e.g. the Restaurant and Caterers Association. SOCOG, the Labor government and the unions were concerned that competing peak employer bodies would challenge any innovations out of fear that these might become precedents, and a focus on traditional adversarial issues would stalemate the process. To some extent this concern was justified as we shall see.

Inviting companies that might be expected to tender for the service contracts was also part of an emerging 'partnership culture'. SOCOG had already developed close working relations with companies who were Games sponsors, using these as preferred suppliers. This was later extended to other contractors. Tendering for contracts was an open process but the development of the framework and criteria for the contracts involved discussions with the companies in the industry that SOCOG saw as potential partners. Given that the major task of service contractors would be to supply and manage labour for catering, cleaning, security etc, the Olympic Games Award was a critical part of this framework. While some individual employers might have concerns over pay rates above the norm SOCOG would be picking up the bill so their companies had nothing to lose. It also meant that the major cost (i.e. labour) of the contracts was fixed – both for SOCOG and the employers. Competing for contracts would thus not be on the basis of cutting labour costs, but on the companies' skill and efficiency in managing the large temporary 'event' workforce. SOCOG also sent very clear signals that working closely with the unions was its preferred approach to industrial relations for the Games. For employers who might think otherwise there was an implicit suggestion – cooperate if you want to be considered for a contract! The main elements of the award were thus negotiated between the key players who would, in the main at least, be those working together to recruit and manage the workforce for the major contracts. The potential contractors, SOCOG program and IR managers, and the unions would all have hands-on roles in implementing the agreement affecting the people who would work for the Games.

To develop the award rates, negotiators collected a number of previous agreements which were 'all over the place on both pay and conditions'[16] and worked to develop something out of these that would:

- represent a good solid wage rate across that sector of the industry

- make allowance for likely wage increases between 1998 and 2000

- add 5 to 7 percent for the 'trauma' of the Olympics

- incorporate the bonus of $1.50 per hour contingent on the worker staying with the one employer and completing the rostered shifts. [1 16 21 42]

The bonus was seen as essential. Looked at in terms of the budget it was seen as a small price to pay to prevent the two to four-fold blow-out in wage rates experienced in Atlanta. Looked at through the eyes of a worker, an extra $150 at the end of the Games would be worth considering after one week of hard work and (even if frustrated) enough to make it worth going back for the rest, thus eliminating the high drop-out rates experienced in Atlanta. The consistent view of all the interviews we conducted in this study was that the award, and particularly the $1.50 bonus, made a significant contribution to the success of the Games.

The employer peak bodies were not happy, even though most of the major companies involved were members of these peak bodies and were able to keep them informed of the early negotiations and take advice if it was wanted. The framework agreement on the award was in place and presented to the NSW Industrial Relations Commission in January 1998.[1 16] At the hearing Justice Wright expressed concern that the deal had been done between SOCOG and a number of the larger companies and asked for the employers' peak bodies to be included in a further round of discussions. He also asked for a 'no precedent' agreement to be built into the award.[1 16] While this was agreed to, the view within the SOCOG IR team[16 17] was that the award **was** establishing a precedent in terms of a range of issues relevant to organising this and future major events. These included:

- Unique cooperation between the award parties around a venues-based award rather than the traditional divisions between trade union coverage, and enterprise/employer based awards.

- Unique flexibility where any employee could work in another venue in either the same or another trade. They could even switch between jobs on the same day, working in another sector for up to two hours a day without change in rates of pay or conditions. A cleaner could assist with catering and vice versa provided they had the appropriate training or qualifications.[16 17]

Rob Forsyth who handled most of the IR negotiations for SOCOG and who was one of the venue managers during the Games observed:

"The effect of these arrangements was to create a camaraderie between various groups of workers." [16]

It also allowed for cross-union coverage with officials from different unions dealing with any workplace issue regardless of the job the worker was doing or the traditional union coverage of the trade involved.

The final round of negotiations was a long drawn-out process. In the view of some of the employer peak bodies and the unions, it 'fine-tuned' the award particularly in areas where the smaller companies wanted details such as rostering, leave accumulation and payment of the bonus.[1 27 28] Tim McDonald of Employers First says:

"Our role was to reflect the agreement in an appropriate form for industrial regulation in light of the existing legislation." [27]

An alternative view from the unions was that the employer peak bodies played a role

"as a cooperative partner by clarifying what the draft meant. They became the official 'nit-pickers'." [1]

Apart from limiting the scope for building a different kind of award that could have been a precedent for a different kind of industrial relations, there were other unfortunate consequences. Most of the SOCOG program managers dropped out of the process and had little further exposure to the union/company collaboration. Some employers dropped out leaving the negotiations to the relevant peak bodies. This broke down the collective participation of the key players and some of the momentum that had been generated. More damaging, it set back the timetable for the industrial relations framework by over 12 months. The award was an essential part of the contract process, providing budget certainty for SOCOG and a fixed price for the contractors' labour costs. Many contracts could not be let until after February 2000! In practice SOCOG and the contractors held their breath and proceeded on the assumption the award would be ratified, but the uncertainty didn't help the already complex planning process.

The amendments that were made hardly seem to warrant the time and effort since the 'no precedent' point had been established. Some details were not picked up in the review anyway and outstanding queries or disagreements were ultimately resolved by reference to the original Principles of Cooperation agreement.[116] One benefit of the process was however the extremely good interpersonal relationship that developed between the union organisers and SOCOG and between Chris Christodoulou and Rob Forsyth in particular. This would prove to be invaluable later when aspects of the Games planning started to unravel.

The amended award was finally registered in February 2000. There were some minor variations to this up to September 2000. Mirror image awards were created by several of the major contracting companies. These were a cut and paste of the general agreement with minor variations on matters like the dates of operation including the run-up and shoulder periods of the Games. In fact mirror awards were the preferred option for any variation given the protracted negotiations among the many parties that were required to vary the primary award. Justice Wright also made a federally binding Enterprise Agreement to ensure that the conditions would apply to Games workers employed by contractors not covered by the State legislation.* Industrial tribunal variations to existing agreements of contractors and amendments to State awards were made by reference to the Games Award to allow for Olympic Games payments. Elements of the Games Award were also incorporated into the award for public sector workers involved in the Games.[67] We will touch on some of the collaboration involved in the volunteering and secondment of government workers to Games activities later. There was also an Enterprise Agreement negotiated (a handshake deal, never formally signed) between SOCOG and the MEAA covering the Opening and Closing Ceremonies. Complicated as this network of industrial instruments may sound, all of it is based on the IR framework negotiated for the Olympic Games Award. There was no Federal government presence in any of this. It was predominantly a NSW issue and one with clear political implications given the national debate over workplace and industrial relations reform.[33 42]

One major service area not initially covered by the award was transport. Transport planning and management issues were coordinated by the Olympic Roads and Transport Authority (ORTA), outside of SOCOG. The State Transport Authority negotiated with the Public Transport Union (RBTIU); while the

---

* For example the Games workforce involved in the football preliminaries played in Brisbane, Melbourne, Canberra and Adelaide.

private bus consortium, Bus 2000, dealt with the Transport Workers Union (TWU). Elements of the Olympic Award were later incorporated into their agreements but with markedly different outcomes. Public transport workers received the flat-rate $2.50 per hour Games bonus (awarded to all public sector workers for the Games period) and an additional $3.00 per hour in recognition of the unique pressures on the transport system.[66] The Games Award was varied to include private sector transport workers who received an extra $1.50 an hour for delivery to the Games sites in compensation for additional access and security requirements.[18] Drivers working for private bus contractors received additional special payments in settlement of problems that led to a near disaster on the eve of the Games.[18 26 33 36] We will explore the details of this, and its origins in the failure to establish a collaborative relationship between Bus 2000 and the TWU, in Chapter 4.

The significance of the agreements and the relationships developed in the process of negotiating this Games Award should not be underestimated. Apart from delivering the basics of industrial harmony, budget certainty and flexibility in work practices, it laid the foundations of trust and respect that were to prove invaluable later on.

The significance of the agreements and the relationships developed in the process of negotiating this Games Award should not be underestimated. Apart from delivering the basics of industrial harmony, budget certainty and flexibility in work practices, it laid the foundations of trust and respect that were to prove invaluable later on. We will return to this point many times as we explore the details of the Games operation. For now a couple of points to illustrate this:

■ SOCOG needed to say to the unions 'this cannot be done – we just can't afford it' on several occasions. It helped to have established trust so that this was accepted as the reality and not the starting point for bargaining.

■ The union organisers needed to say to SOCOG on several occasions 'this is an issue we **have** to deal with'. It helped that the trust was there and SOCOG and other stakeholders could recognise immediately that this was for real and not a 'try-on'.

There were many times during the Games when this trust would be called on.

Collaborative industrial relations?

If there was one person who was in the middle of this somewhat tortuous process in the years leading up to the event, and in the thick of the consequences at Games time, it would be Rob Forsyth. This is what he has to say about building a culture of collaboration.

"Firstly it is about building **trust** *– practical trust – you need to see both sides of the fence and have people from both sides engaged in the process. The outcome can be people who trust each other – despite fundamental differences of views – to negotiate and work through to an outcome that both sides agree is fair. Each knew they wouldn't be 'dudded' by the other – so could speak their mind and respect the other's opinion without having to agree with it. This issue of* **fairness** *– overseas people commented on Advance Australia 'Fair' – they had a different take – a different slant on our national anthem. It's closely tied to* **respect** *– there was the example of the union delegate who tended to get on his high horse in a confrontational style – but he was respected and valued nevertheless.* **Empowerment** *– it's also about empowering people at all levels – it's easy if not empowered to keep referring matters to the masters before making decisions. In general the culture was one where people didn't – they were empowered to make decisions and there to fix problems.* **Openness** *was also critical – ability to share problems and not necessarily have the answers – to search together for a solution and to back each other in finding it (and selling it after the event) – for example occasions in the Industrial Relations Commission when SOCOG was assisted by the Labor Council in explaining the point to the Commissioner – a cooperative or collaborative approach rather than the usual adversarial one.* **Self-Esteem** *– positive self-images not bound up with ego not God/right on my side and/or the knight in shining armour stuff. In this culture the* **outcome** *was what was important – not 'win-win' but something that was* **rational, fair, logical and timely.** *People felt they were right and at the end of the day were vindicated. The culture we built was one of 'don't prevaricate' – 'get on with it' – and 'we're not doing this for practice' – a lot of it was about understanding the Australian culture."* [16]

These elements do not always come together in industrial relations. Something pushed the Games stakeholders beyond adversarial power-based relationships towards a culture of collaboration. In the process, we discovered genuine personal and cultural pride in achieving a 'best ever' outcome. A key element in this appears to be the global spotlight of attention. We may be prompted to change when (and perhaps only when) as Chris Christodoulou said, 'we can't afford to stuff up'. It is then we realise we have to move beyond old ways of relating and create a new culture.

Planning the workforce

"one team; one tent"

Jim Sloman, Sandy Hollway, et al.

Running parallel to the negotiation of the industrial relations framework was an equally intense program assembling the workforce for the Games. This involved management and coordination by SOCOG of

- an analysis of the available labour force

- the plans for the recruitment, training and retention strategies

- the logistics of accreditation, uniforms, accommodation, transport, catering and recognition of the close to 150,000 workers directly involved in servicing the Games.

This was perhaps the most significant achievement of the Sydney Games. As we have seen this is where previous Games, and particularly Atlanta, fell down.

In the language of the Organising Committee there were three groups of workers:

- 'Paid' – those directly employed by SOCOG – a total of 3,500

- 'Volunteer' – specialist and general volunteers who worked unpaid for the Games but received training and supporting services from SOCOG for their job at Games time – a total of 60,000

- 'Contractor' – those seconded by Games sponsors or working for companies providing services on contract to SOCOG – a total of somewhere between 60,000 and 80,000.

The lines between these were often blurred. Working within a SOCOG team at any time might be paid SOCOG staff, specialist volunteers and people with particular expertise from sponsors or contractors. In Chapter 4 we discuss the case of the contractor who organised Games merchandising for the torch relay and the Games but worked **within** SOCOG throughout the lead-up to the Games. This case study also illustrates the 'preferred partnership' culture in which SOCOG was always seeking people and organisations it could work closely **with** rather than merely hire to provide services.

Key elements of the strategic framework for assembling this

integrated workforce involved the following:

- SOCOG undertaking to organise both the Olympic and Paralympic Games. SPOC had difficulties raising sponsorship money. It made no sense to duplicate planning for events separated by two weeks. SOCOG organised all the statutory/legal requirements of both Organising Committees for OH&S, public and workforce liabilities, human resources and industrial relations infrastructure.

- A decision to structure SOCOG around a range of functional areas such as human resources, workforce planning, volunteers, accreditation, etc – and then in the lead-up to the Games to 'roll over' the key SOCOG staff into venue management teams to run each of the specific Games sites.

- The strategic decision by SOCOG to contract private companies to provide the bulk of the Games services. These companies employed their own workforce to deliver the services.

- The industrial relations strategy detailed above which delivered a measure of certainty to the workforce budget for both SOCOG and many of the contractors as the terms of the Olympic Award applied to all casual workers employed for the Games period.

- Research into workforce availability – particularly the 'Gap Analysis' which identified the likely shortfalls in the labour market for each of the major service areas, particularly catering, cleaning and security.

- Developing partnerships with the contractors that assisted in their recruitment strategies by:
  - sharing intelligence on labour market analyses
  - setting early recruitment milestones and timelines
  - developing detailed requirements for numbers, rostering and payroll.

- Adopting a consistent three-phase approach to training of **all** workers for the Games:
  - an orientation to the Games, its ethos and values, and what was expected of a worker with a job for the Games – paid or volunteering

- site orientation – introducing the workers to the particular Games venue or work-site they would be working in, the associated services for meals etc, the venue management and the people they would be working with
- job-specific training to equip the worker with the skills needed to do the particular job.

■ Coordinating operational functions for the workforce at the Games: accreditation, uniforms, accommodation, transport, catering etc.

■ Managing the event – organising the logistics of supply of equipment, materials, packaging, cleaning and catering supplies and the ecological recycling or disposal of these as part of the 'Green Games' undertakings.

And of course much more, all of this overlapping and intersecting so that the whole came together to meet strategic needs at critical times. To those who worked within the process we apologise sincerely for oversimplifying such a complex operation. Some of the detail will be illustrated in the case studies that follow in Chapter 4 – along with the pitfalls, mistakes, miscalculations and their consequences.

SOCOG staff

SOCOG was a lean organisation, made leaner throughout most of its life by budget constraints. SOCOG had already developed close working relations with companies who were Games sponsors, using these as preferred suppliers. This was later extended to other contractors. Tendering for contracts was an open process but the development of the framework and criteria for the contracts involved discussions with the companies in the industry that SOCOG saw as potential partners. Given that the major task of service contractors would be to supply and manage labour for catering, cleaning, security etc, the Olympic Games Award was a critical part of this framework. Shortage of funds led to a series of hiring freezes in SOCOG recruitment. Known as 'scooping', the money saved by delaying recruitment was transferred to contingency budgets and used to deal with problems that arose later. The consequences of this were that existing staff were carrying large workloads, some planning decisions were delayed and in particular some contract details were not finalised until very late in the process. Some of these consequences we will explore in Chapter 4.

What was required was therefore a highly skilled and motivated staff – one that would acquire a unique set of skills, knowledge and experience during the planning process and whose skills it was vital to retain once the planning was done and the operation phase of the Games commenced. The solution to these pressures was the strategic decision to 'roll over' the SOCOG staff from their functional roles into venue management. SOCOG realised that many of the staff would be subjected to a great deal of stress and in 1998 it introduced an 'employee assistance program' for staff and their families.[60]

SOCOG's human resources functions were largely outsourced to Adecco, one of the Games sponsors. In 1997 Adecco was commissioned by SOCOG to produce a detailed study, 'The Concept of Operations for Games Workforce'.[*] This identified workforce needs and strategies for obtaining the necessary human resources for the Games. It was developed through extensive consultations and workshops across the many internal and external functional areas, sponsors, unions, government bodies (including immigration and tourism), ORTA and the OSCC.

Adecco also handled advertising and recruitment of paid (permanent and temporary) staff through the Olympic Recruitment Centre from June 1996. Over 50,000 applications for SOCOG paid positions were screened for the various SOCOG positions. Despite the 'temporary' nature of the jobs within SOCOG, delays caused by hiring freezes, heavy workloads and lower pay than comparable work elsewhere, many people left secure positions and successful careers to work for the Games.

Maintaining the morale of the staff through an extended period (five-plus years for some) was achieved by a variety of people-management strategies including an internal communication strategy with

- an all-staff newsletter (later internal e-mail)

- monthly all-staff meetings profiling Sandy Hollway as the CEO and providing information-sharing and networking opportunities

---

[*] 'The Concept of Operations for Games Workforce' (SOCOG, 1998) was prepared by Di Pass, a member of the research team for this Collaborative Games Study.

- lunch-time seminars, primarily providing additional information on the 28 sports included in the Games.[86]

These communication platforms were particularly important in the later stages of the Games planning, when SOCOG came under attack over the marching bands decision and the ticketing fiasco. Ian Clubb, describing the working conditions for many of the staff, states:

"We had to adopt a siege mentality to survive! There were so many things to distract the workforce at the time when the clock was ticking fast." [60]

As we will see, some delays early on had compounded into significant problems. Whatever the arguments about competency in dealing with these, it was a matter of working to fix the problems not apportioning blame.

SOCOG relied extensively on expertise and secondment of staff from sponsors and other companies. The Olympic Management Development Program involved over 100 staff (30–40 from industry and 65 from the Greek Masters Program) being seconded to SOCOG. The employer paid salaries and SOCOG provided mentorship and 'guaranteed a learning environment'. These people, selected for ability to 'think outside the square' and work in problem-solving teams, were used in tackling a variety of problems as they arose. One example was the problem of getting detailed information from poolside to the media room in the Aquatic Centre during a test event. The solution to overcome the delays was to hang a bucket over the balcony. Information hauled up this way met the journalists requirements. Cathy Tomkins who organised the program said:

"Often we were not looking for Rolls Royce solutions – this one was timely, practical and it worked." [34]

Volunteers

The initial challenge was to have a workforce in which there was a clear delineation between volunteer and paid work but without demarcation issues between the volunteer and paid workers. The Principles of Cooperation between SOCOG and the Labor Council acknowledged that volunteers would be needed to complement the Games workforce and agreed to establish a protocol for the use of volunteers. The Volunteer Protocol, negotiated in 1998 and formally signed in August 1999, defined the areas where volunteers would be used. It ensured that, generally, volunteers would not be used for jobs filled by the paid or contractor workforce. It also provided for ongoing consultation over differences in interpretation. With the evolution of the collaborative relations between SOCOG, contractors and the unions, considerable flexibility emerged in the interpretation of this in practice. One area where use of volunteers caused industrial relations problems early on was the Ceremonies. The MEAA and SOCOG negotiated successfully over who among the 20,000 performers involved would be paid. Similarly, the ALHMU negotiated over where volunteers were to be used to plug gaps in the (low-level) security service. We discuss these in more detail in Chapter 4.

The Volunteer Protocol, negotiated in 1998 and formally signed in August 1999, defined the areas where volunteers would be used. It ensured that, generally, volunteers would not be used for jobs filled by the paid or contractor workforce. It also provided for ongoing consultation over differences in interpretation.

Initially the target was for around 50,000 volunteers. In the event some 62,000 had jobs at the Games. Back in 1996, many in SOCOG did not recognise that volunteers were needed; some wished they weren't. Few understood volunteers or volunteering – their role, the types of people who volunteer, their motivation and volunteer management issues. There were a lot of assumptions about volunteers, most of them wrong, like, 'You can't rely on volunteers' or 'My work is too important for volunteers'. It took a huge amount of work by the Volunteer Program for people to see that many were not amateurs but capable people often with professional backgrounds, and the Games required that professional expertise. About half the Sydney Games volunteers were recruited as specialists with qualifications and skills to do specialist jobs as doctors, nurses, physiotherapists, etc. The other half were generalists working mainly to assist the public and spectators.

A Volunteers Advisory Committee brought in expertise from the State Emergency Services, Rural Fire Services, YMCA, YWCA, Rotary, Lions, Surf Lifesaving, Australian Institute of Sport, State and national peak bodies such as Volunteering Australia and leaders of Aboriginal and ethnic communities. This met every three to four months to discuss processes for recruiting, training, retention and management, and the acknowledgement and appreciation program.

The Atlanta experience where spectators were sometimes given wrong information highlighted the need for training. However, as important was the need to ensure that SOCOG and the other Games partners understood about volunteers. A lot of the training was **about** volunteers – not just **of** volunteers. Many SOCOG staff attended a three-hour 'event leadership' training program. An element of this was cultivating in volunteers the sense that they had a meaningful job. SOCOG produced 4,000 distinct job descriptions giving individual volunteers information about their roles at the Games.

The volunteer management strategy was one of 'centralised administration and decentralised operation'.[35] SOCOG centrally coordinated recruitment but devolved a large portion of the training and communication functions to local management in the various sectors. For example 4,000 medical specialists were recruited but the SOCOG people who communicated with them were the managers of the specific area where these volunteers would work. In September 1997 there was a low profile launch targeting organisations to source the specialist volunteers in four areas: media and communications, technology, languages, and medical. Many of the thousands needed would come through universities so these were involved in identifying suitable volunteers. In October 1998 when the recruitment program for general volunteers was launched, the universities distributed and collected expressions of interest for return to SOCOG.[35]

Back in 1995 the University of Western Sydney and the University of Technology Sydney collaborated with SOCOG by developing degree and graduate level management courses on 'Interviewing for Major Events'. The courses developed awareness of differences between volunteers and paid staff and practical skills in volunteer recruitment. About 150 people from these programs were used to interview all the general volunteers and some of the specialist volunteers recruited for the Games. The courses also developed HR skills needed in the management of the Games venues.[34]

Of the 75,000 volunteer applicants, 62,000 worked at the Games contributing around 6 million hours of free time. Around 85–90 percent of these were locked in with an offer of a job and had returned acceptance forms by May 2000. The last 15–20 percent were difficult to finalise. Contrary to the common assumption that volunteers are generally older and mostly retired people with time on their hands the applications were received from across the age range.

In the six weeks before the Games two areas, spectator services and transport, needed 1,000 extra volunteers. SOCOG organised recruitment, last-minute training and accreditation under pressure. The attrition rate for volunteers over the Games period was under 6 percent, way below previous Games.

The test events, starting with the sailing in September 1998 and the rest from August 1999, proved how dependent the Games would be on **people** and that the key issues would be feeding, rostering, training etc. People became the dominant issue in planning from then on and the volunteers were included in this. David Brettell who coordinated much of the volunteer program says:

"A major element of the workload was people management – that in HR terms we had to identify needs and get it right. This meant getting down to a level of detail like: how long would it take to get a bus from A to B – so we didn't give a volunteer from Penrith a job for the sailing at Rushcutters Bay etc. How were we going to get the volunteers fed, rostered, moved from job to job [rotation] or from place A to B so the level of interest was maintained." [35]

Age range of volunteers applying to work for the Games	
Under 24 years	24%
25–34 years	18%
35–44 years	18%
45–54 years	18%
Over 55 years	22%

Recruitment, training, scheduling and keeping up the enthusiasm for work for a short-term event months away is all about communications. SOCOG seriously underestimated the amount of time needed to prepare each volunteer. The program areas that did best were those who participated in the 'pioneer volunteer program'. This recruited 500 volunteers early and trained these to assist with the management of other volunteers. One of the lessons learned here was that volunteers love being managed by other volunteers.[34] The team of 500 pioneer volunteers provided a total of 200,000 hours of service to SOCOG from 1996 and were regularly used to lift the profile of volunteers within the organisation.[35]

It is worth noting that, unlike some contractors who insisted people wanting to work for them had access to E-mail,* most of SOCOG's communications (planned and unplanned) with volunteers were by phone call and letter.

---

* The 'E-mail revolution' occurred in the middle of the Games planning period but SOCOG was slow to make the transition. The companies provided advice and assistance for their staff to get connected via sharing of facilities, use of library services and free E-mail systems.

COURTESY OF BONDS

The volunteers parade, Sydney, November 2000. Public recognition of their contribution to the Games.

The initial reason for using volunteers was undoubtedly financial but volunteers are not free. Recruitment, training, accreditation, acknowledgement, uniforms, feeding and transport for volunteers all cost money. SOCOG spent around $50 million to run the volunteer program. In the process it gained 60,000+ workers and, perhaps more important, it established community ownership of the Games. People all over the country had a sense of participation in the delivery, not just attending the Games. The volunteers took ownership, decided the Games were theirs, became advocates for the Games.[35]

SOCOG spent around $50 million to run the volunteer program. In the process it gained 60,000+ workers and, perhaps more important, it established community ownership of the Games.

In all contacts with volunteers the aim was to make the experience one where he or she felt it was meaningful and enjoyable. A lot of the responsibility for this fell on the local (venue/site) management and the volunteer supervisors, some who were often volunteers themselves. Getting the messages right involved understanding that people volunteer for what are in the long run 'selfish' reasons. They want a good time or something 'good for me' out of it and so the task is to create a stimulating environment where they have a good experience. David Brettell says:

"They can be motivated, driven internally, if we respect, value and appreciate them and they enjoy it. This involved feeling part of the team and being kept in touch. We might have stimulating videos etc in the training but the aim was that they walk out knowing what the expectations are; that they can meet them; they will be managed well; and trained well." [35]

The recognition program was an important part of this. David Brettell again:

*"We used items of recognition to **thank** – not as an **incentive**. All through we stressed that being a volunteer would be tough. We tested applicants' sincerity. We knew many more would apply than would be needed and the logistics of having to process and then reject people were horrendous. So we consciously went out of our way to tell them how hard it would be and only at the end said how good it would be – we drew the analogy between being a volunteer and being an athlete – said it would be hard work for no gain; lots of training; reduced social life; **but** despite all of that we could guarantee the greatest experience of their life. We always knew we'd give some things in recognition – but wanted these to be a reward for performance not as an inducement to volunteer. People didn't expect it. When it came it was appreciated and people felt thanked and recognised."*

Would he do anything differently?

"None of the successes in the volunteer program suggest it couldn't be done differently or better. I'd free up the managers of particular events/venues to recruit people – identify people they knew who wanted to volunteer and get them to enrol them. I'd also have more targeted recruiting through organisations and groups for the general pool as well as for the specialists and I'd have targeted organisations with strong volunteer programs already." [35]

At the end of the day we can only agree with J. A. Samaranch when he added to the accolade of 'the best Games ever' the phrase *'and your wonderful volunteers'.*

A tiny piece of the volunteers' story

Margaret Hird, a former teacher, and husband Ken, a retired Qantas engineer, were inspired to become volunteers after watching the Atlanta Games. With previous supervisory and volunteering experience, they were assigned as team leaders at the beach volley ball stadium at Bondi Beach. Margaret, who would do it all again tomorrow, recalls the experience:

"So many people from so many walks of life! The camaraderie was unbelievable! Everyone came together, really wanting to make it work, wanting to show what Australia can do. We volunteered not for the uniform, not because we might see some of the events but to be part of it, and to help get the job done for Sydney."

There are over 60,000 others. Hopefully one day another book will be written devoted to their stories.

Contractors – competition or collaboration?

Given that the 'Gap Analysis' had revealed serious shortfalls in the pool of available staff for Games services in the Sydney region SOCOG set about challenging the contractors' thinking on recruitment. Much of this was about raising what Ian Clubb dubbed the 'Oh shit! factor'. It involved asking the hard questions such as:

- Where is your information on workforce numbers and skills coming from?

- Your casuals, how will you hold onto them when they are also being recruited by others? Most people in the casual labour pool will be working full time during the Games – either with you or your competitor (not both)!

- As the Games will be in school holidays, how many of your people won't be available?

- How will you get people to work if travel time during the Games is longer?

According to Cathy Tomkins, SOCOG's strategy was to scare the contractors into thinking about staffing problems – to demonstrate that, while they knew their business, SOCOG had the big picture of the Games situation.

"We never had any doubt that we'd get the people for the Games but this would have been no achievement if we did it at the expense of all the other enterprises in Sydney at the time. We didn't want to leave other services short. We wanted visitors to have a good experience of Sydney as a whole not just the Games. We were making people think – realise that this was not like any other event. For example on catering, our view was there were not enough people overall or with the right skills, so we developed a cooperative spirit among competitors for the catering contracts. The award discussions helped this." [34]

SOCOG requested recruitment plans be submitted, helped contractors to get these in shape, and developed training and retention programs. It was 'more asking questions than having the answers'.[34]

The Olympic Labour Network (OLN)

This was originally conceived as a one-stop shop for contractors seeking 'top-up' casual labour for the Games workforce. The OLN

brought together eight labour hire companies under the leadership of Adecco, a Games sponsor, who had been actively involved
in the Games from the time of the Bid.[*] In the 'Concept of
Operations' mentioned above, the OLN concept was proposed as
a way of maximising the available workforce. It was endorsed by
SOCOG, TAFE, the Australian Human Resources Institute
(AHRI), Recruitment and Consulting Services Australia (RCSA)
and the NSW Labor Council. Its target was to be able to supply up
to 12,000 staff. Due largely to the success in pushing the contractors to undertake their own recruitment and retention programs
the OLN was only called on to supply 5,000 at Games time.

The collaboration between labour hire companies was unique.
There is usually intense rivalry and competition in the recruitment
industry. The OLN organised fortnightly meetings of all eight
agencies for discussion and presentations on a wide range of
Olympic issues: the Olympic Award, Unions 2000, OH&S and
workers compensation, Olympic history and knowledge, advertising,
candidate capture, communication guidelines, Olympic training,
uniforms, transport, catering, accreditation, etc.

An OLN website and an Olympic Job Opportunities section of the
Federal government's Australian Job Search on-line service were
also used to advertise and recruit for jobs at the Games. Although
there was a clear preference for hiring Australian citizens, arrangements were put in place with Australian Immigration to allow
holiday work permit holders to work beyond the customary three-
month limits as a one-off exception for year 2000.

The OLN faced a number of problems. Many contractors for services
such as catering, cleaning and security traditionally recruit their
own casual staff. Some argue that the charge of $4 per hour per
person recruited through the OLN was too high and concentrated
on recruiting their own. Consequently it was often used as the
labour source of last resort. Rostering and scheduling of staff was
problematic. Some catering contractors turned OLN recruited
staff away when they found there was a lack of demand for casuals
on particular shifts. Along with other areas of the Games there

---

* The OLN companies: Adecco, Drake, Julia Ross, LLEM, Pinnacle
Hospitality, Catalyst, Integrated Workforce and Workforce International
– dubbed affectionately by the union movement as 'Snow White and the
seven dwarfs'.

were problems with payroll caused by the number of casual workers involved in varied shifts and the absence of an electronic time recording system. This was consistent across the whole of the Games workforce, as we will see in Chapter 4. There is an ongoing debate about whether a magnetic or barcoded system linked to the accreditation pass, albeit costly, should have been used for the Games. Undoubtedly it will be considered for the future but in Sydney the technology went backwards to the days before clock cards, relying on paper timesheets signed by managers at the venues. As employees of the OLN, but managed by the contractors, the problems for these staff were, if anything, greater than the norm.

Among the lessons of this exercise is the undoubted value in having a labour reserve – though whether it would be organised this way in future is contested.[1 15 17 21 25 29 34 42] Despite the problems, the value of the OLN both as an 'insurance policy' and in terms of what it delivered is evident. The OLN proved useful to some of the international contractors who did not have their own Australian recruitment infrastructure, and to some of the smaller contractors. Overall it provided 5,000 casuals delivering more than 500,000 hours of labour to 30 companies across 400 different locations. Job roles included hospitality, catering, retail, labourers, event staff, vehicle access controllers, rail departure hosts, team leaders for spectator services roles, payroll clerks, secretaries, drivers, runners, porters, concierges, messengers, newspaper sellers, roving film sellers, airport coordinators, chauffeurs, cleaners, transport assistants, car detailers, fleet dispatch, load zone officers, hosts, customer service officers, luggage handlers, logistics personnel, stores supervisors, stadium chefs, stores attendants, bump-in/bump-out stores assistants, cash counters, cash collectors, data entry, kitchen hands, kitchen runners, demi chefs, sous chefs, head chefs, forklift drivers, front of house hospitality staff [15] – and a few more we have undoubtedly missed!

Training

The 'Gap Analysis' had revealed a shortfall in skills among the potential workforce. Competency for the job at Games time was a requirement for both contractor and volunteer staff. SOCOG and the contractors provided training during their preparations for the Games. Perhaps more important than job competency was the orientation training. There was a need to ensure that all those working for the Games understood the unique nature of the event, and the primary task of serving the wider public for whom the Games needed to be a memorably enjoyable experience. It was also important that all workers could respond to requests for information from the public and hence needed to know their way around the Games venues. The training program for all workers had therefore two core training elements – general Games orientation and site-specific training – as well as specific job-skill development.

There was a need to ensure that all those working for the Games understood the unique nature of the event, and the primary task of serving the wider public for whom the Games needed to be a memorably enjoyable experience.

TAFE NSW was the Games training sponsor and primary supplier of this phased training program. Others provided specialist skills. Overall TAFE provided training for around 110,000 workers for SOCOG across the Games operation. It trained 2,000 of the 3,500 paid employees and provided 11 customised employee-training programs. It developed and assisted with delivery of the three-phase training program for all Games workers. Eleven TAFE staff were seconded full time to SOCOG, 15 were located at one external site and 100 trainers were used as consultants as needed. SOCOG had two paid staff to liaise with TAFE and co-managed the program. Beyond its contracted obligations TAFE also trained about 20,000 bus drivers for ORTA and 16,000 staff in Games affected industries through a 'Customer Relations 2000' program.

The paid, volunteer and contractor training programs had been developed separately but were brought together early in 1999.[70] SOCOG conducted five major presentations for training HR managers representing the contractors and sponsors, to ensure that all policies were understood and reinforced by the contracting organisations. More than 44,000 people attended 52 orientation sessions in the capital cities; 82,000 people participated in venue training at 42 venues. Workforce training kits covering the key phases of the training program were provided free to 500+ contractor/sponsor organisations along with programs for company trainers on how to train the workforce. Three thousand SOCOG and contractor people involved in venue management received event leadership training. The objective was to motivate the workforce to do their best, to feel valued, to reinforce personal worth and enthusiasm. This was seen as more important than competency, though there was a lot of attention given to knowing where to get information if you didn't have it. Orientation training kits were developed with an emphasis on self-paced training. Major elements included:

- history and importance of the Olympic Games
- customer service standards – treatment of visitors to the Games
- understanding what to expect during a major event
- expectations for the workforce, e.g. code of conduct.

Recognition was given to the fact that anyone in a uniform would need to be an Olympic ambassador and able to deal with a wide variety of requests.

Venue training was conducted in teams that brought together people who would work together during the Games. It was built around the concept of a treasure hunt in which members of teams were actively involved in learning about the venue with the Olympic 'overlay' in place. Fun was a key element and the emphasis was that every job was important. The training involved collaboration between many groups including the venue managers and OCA who provided detailed maps etc. All workers received a pocket guide with a sleeve for job-specific training notes. Venue managers and the contractors' staffing managers delivered most venue training, with support from SOCOG risk and operations managers.

Event leadership training for venue and staffing managers highlighted the importance of decision-making in an event environment – where thinking on your feet and having the communications network in place so you know who to call if necessary to confirm a decision is crucial. Union input was valuable in this regard as the Games were operating under a unique award structure. A wide range of event scenarios from Nagano, Atlanta and other Olympic Games were explored, including drug use, sexual harassment and inappropriate behaviour in view of spectators.

TAFE NSW prepared job-specific training for about three-quarters of the 60,000 volunteers. Contractors provided job-specific training for their workforce. TAFE NSW developed eight job-specific training videos and modules for 3,000 job descriptions across 42 functional areas of the Games workforce. In many cases this aspect of training was short term and highly specific to the Games task and not articulated within the nationally accredited competency-based training system. For some areas of work such as security, licensed qualifications were required though even here special arrangements for recognition of equivalent interstate or overseas standards and Games-specific training and licensing were made. All policies and the core training materials were developed with input from the unions – usually prepared by the TAFE/SOCOG team, then reviewed by the Labor Council. SOCOG training manager Claire Houston says:

"We experienced some contention and disagreements but always knew that we would come to a place of agreement in the end." [70]

For example, the Labor Council wanted to make a presentation at all venue training sessions. SOCOG argued that only a third of the venue team members were subject to the award and that discussion of these matters could highlight the difference between the paid and unpaid workforce. As a compromise, the union representative was introduced at the training and a union desk was set up so that information could be provided.

TAFE made a significant contribution in another area. Teams of staff and students from cooking, catering and hospitality courses were recruited to work in catering areas for the Games. The Adelaide-based Regency TAFE hotel school provided one of the catering companies with more than 500 people to work in the hospitality suites and corporate boxes at the Games.[*] This gave the students real on-the-job practical (and a once in a lifetime) experience, and was worth $2.4 million in wages to them.[94]

Overall, this short-term training successfully prepared the workforce for a common task – delivering 'the best Games ever'.

Risk management and occupational health and safety

SOCOG's risk management planning involved liaison with the OCA over the construction of the Olympic venues, insurance for the Games events and its workforce, and contingency planning for a wide range of emergencies known affectionately as the 'what ifs'. This involved developing detailed responses for incidents such as power loss, accidents and medical emergencies, bombs, fires and threats, building failures, and those caused by human relations

---

[*] These people travelled over 2,000 kilometres from Adelaide to Sydney to work for the Games.

problems. Like most other aspects of the Games the problem was unique and the solution required innovation. Evacuation procedures for example needed to cater for the vastly increased density of people both inside and outside the main venues.

Risk planning brought together very different cultures and tested both the emergency services and SOCOG. The pre-Games test events provided a basis for learning but were no real test of the Games period, which would involve much higher people densities. Scenario exercises involving police venue commanders and venue management led to closer cooperation and new approaches. Workshops involving venue staff and police, fire and ambulance officers rostered to specific venues built up practical expertise and laid the foundations for a three-day exercise in which all the command centres and procedures were tested. According to SOCOG's Peter Himmelhoch it was

"not just what you did but who do you talk to and how do you get people talking and how people talked to each other – this was the key – the human aspect – getting people working as a team." [45]

Occupational health and safety was another example of collaboration. Five firms of consultants were involved in identifying OH&S issues for each venue with the venue management teams and developing safety management plans. During the Games 50 specialist volunteers were used as safety officers in the venues and SOCOG had a roving crew on OH&S from midnight to dawn when some of the issues could be seen more easily – and fixed before they became a problem. SOCOG involved NSW WorkCover in all key decisions. WorkCover observed and commented on compliance issues at two of the test events and inspected all the venues early. In August 2000 it conducted a comprehensive safety inspection with the Olympic 'overlay' in place. SOCOG was cleared to run the events without further inspection during the Games. According to WorkCover there were only 63 accident notifications which, given the scale of the event, was exceptional.[32] This is not to say that there were no problems. One person was injured in an incident involving a fire-safety shutter, and another when the cover was removed from a computer. Otherwise the Games were relatively accident free. Catering had problems with slippery flooring. Cleaners using petrol-driven blowers were assisted to find safe storage for the fuel. There were minor injuries at several sites and a needle-stick incident in the Athletes Village. The scale of needle use by some athletes, even if only for vitamin injections, horrified cleaners. Athletes were told that if needles were not disposed of in the special bins provided then their rooms would not be cleaned.

How was this 'exceptional' outcome achieved? Peter Himmelhoch said:

"Running the Games was the easy part – the hard bit was before. It is important to involve people early – make them aware of OH&S and other risk issues in a manner they can absorb realistically – relevant examples of realistic risks – then help them solve these without dictating. As soon as you dictate you lose them, then it becomes your problem not theirs. Involve people. No-one is stupid – if it's logical people will abide by it and people perform better when they are involved. It's commonsense really – easier said than done and it takes time, but if you involve people then you get the outcomes that they own and they adhere to. Where we did these things it went well." [45]

"Running the Games was the easy part – the hard bit was before. It is important to involve people early – make them aware of OH&S and other risk issues in a manner they can absorb realistically ... then help them solve these without dictating. As soon as you dictate you lose them, then it becomes your problem not theirs."

Accreditation

"Accreditation underpins the efficiency of Games operations by ensuring that everyone with a job to do in a complex, congested environment, can receive access to all applicable areas, quickly and efficiently, without being obstructed by those who aren't meant to be there." [84]

Geoff Parmenter, SOCOG Accreditation

Once again SOCOG benefited from the Atlanta experience where accreditation was hampered by the late completion of construction and poor planning. Thirty thousand applications for accreditation passes were received in the three weeks prior to the 1996 Games. In Sydney the only significant problem area was in transport for reasons we explore in Chapter 4.

All workers, athletes, officials, media and a variety of other groups required accreditation but 80 percent of the task was meeting the needs of the workforce. Personal details needed to be gathered and linked to Games-time role, probity checks run and then an official pass laminated and issued along with uniform and information through the Uniform Distribution and Accreditation Centre (UDAC). Details on paid staff and the Games volunteers were under SOCOG control. For the contractor workforce the task was more difficult. Accreditation is 'the last domino' in the stack of workforce planning functions – the one which, if it falls over,

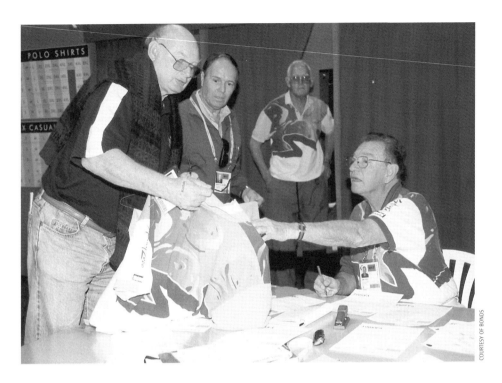

COURTESY OF BONDS

*Games
accreditation:
passes and
uniforms were
provided for
all workers.*

can bring the rest falling flat on their face. The delays that can be traced back to late awarding of contracts flowed through to late development of operational plans and recruitment, and late notification to SOCOG of the numbers for accreditation. The biggest problems were with spectator services and, to a much greater extent, the private bus transport sector. All contractors were given milestones and timelines for recruitment and notification of worker details. However delays in planning of numbers meant these were late. To cap it all, accreditation staff encountered a further late problem. Forty percent of the passes had been produced. The laminating process had been tested in the USA but at local level the process caused ink-runs. Money, people and time were needed to fix these problems.

Overall, however, despite the delays, most people got passes in time. One of the factors in this was the strategic use of 'two-part passes' used extensively for accreditation of the Games workforce. This enabled SOCOG to provide contractors with a fixed number of 'first-part passes' which designated the location, time and access details, while providing an almost unlimited number of 'second-part passes', which designated the individual who could legitimately be assigned to the first-part pass. This assisted Games contractors, giving greater flexibility in rostering individuals around the clock for each approved and accredited job role.

Union recruitment – members and Games workers

Part of the original Principles of Cooperation had been a guarantee of right of access by unions to Games workers. Following the award negotiations Unions 2000 was launched by the Labor Council, with the backing of SOCOG and the Minister, as a single organising vehicle for the Games. Rather than recruit workers union by union (with the risk of demarcation rivalry) the unions agreed to work together to recruit (and subsequently service) members through Unions 2000. The slogan 'Unions 2000: with you at work' was about marketing the trade union movement as a major Games supporter – reflecting the positive support for the Games and support for people getting work during the Games.

The unions negotiated agreements with each of the contractors under the terms of the award for access to workers to discuss union membership during the companies' induction processes. In some cases special forms were produced with company backing and handed to workers as part of the induction to complete and return if they chose. SOCOG gave the unions access to the UDAC and a roster of union officials provided extensive coverage, allowing both a presence and an opportunity to talk to workers about membership. Labor Council organiser Chris Christodoulou says:

"Most of the recruitment was done by union officials talking one-on-one with people. Logistically this was organised around rosters [for union officials] on duty at the UDAC – for 92 days building up to 7 am to 7 pm seven days a week at the end, in which all the unions cooperated. People were approached on the way in and on the way out. We recruited into Unions 2000 – with a generic form – people were signed up ... got a copy of the generic agreement and were serviced by the team of union officials coordinated through the Labor Council. Some employers posted out forms as well."[1]

In all, over 12,000 people joined Unions 2000 in addition to the already unionised workforce in areas such as transport, police and the public sector.

As noted previously the unions organised 'recruitment drives' for Games workers though union journals, leaflets and posters linking Unions 2000 with work at the Games, and around 2,500–3,000 of the 4,500 people who registered as seeking work were employed at Games time. A number of contractors preferred to use the unions as the advertising was targeted to people with skills in some of the key areas, e.g. catering and retail services. The unions learned from this that people have a more positive response to unions if they are trying to find work, that if asked, people will join a union, and that employers will take labour from a union referral.[1 21 29 54]

Industrial relations at the Games – how it worked on the ground

"It got to the point where we almost forgot sport was involved we were so caught up in dealing with the problems on the site." [1]

Paul Howes, Unions 2000

What the unions also learned was that for all the planning some of the arrangements for the Games workforce would be found wanting during the Games operation. Two weeks before the Games the unions were given accreditation for an official at each venue, allowing direct contact with the workforce, and 32 union officials from five unions were rostered to provide coverage throughout the Games. In addition members could access union support through a general call-centre number linked to a Unions 2000 office on site in the OCA building at Olympic Park. The plan was that unions would be in touch with the workforce and on call to identify and deal with any workplace or industrial relations problems that arose during the Games. In order to ensure efficient handling of disputes all officials involved went though a three-day training program organised by the Labor Council and SOCOG. On site the rostered union officials had status on a par with venue staffing managers. The industrial structure envisaged by SOCOG was that each venue management would supervise the Games venue staff and volunteers allocated to that site. Contractor companies in the venue would have their own management and supervise their workers but report to the venue manager.

Fortunately a range of disputes in the 12 months leading up to the Games had helped in the building of trust between the unions, SOCOG and the companies. There had been:

- changes to the awards

- issues over paid and volunteer workers for the Ceremonies

- the question of bonuses for bus drivers

- a major dispute over young people, some as young as 14, employed as vendors who were being defined as 'contractors' with full responsibility for self-employment

- the problem of New Zealand security workers recruited without licences or job guarantees

- underpayment of wages at Bondi Beach Stadium

- and a number of others.

All had been resolved satisfactorily and a large reservoir of trust and respect had been established. But nothing like the problems encountered during the Games had been anticipated.

Even before the Games some problems were apparent. The opening of the Games villages in June 2000 exposed a lack of understanding among staff of the systems, particularly payroll for workers. The unions assisted with presentations to supervisors and helped with the interpretation of the award. Within a few days of the Games Opening Ceremony, caterers struck problems. People were simply not purchasing food on the scale anticipated and the contractors proposed to lay off 1,000 staff. Using the award provisions for flexible working the unions negotiated redeployment of some to other Games work. SOCOG staff used E-mail networks to contact a number of industry groups, letting them know that there were people willing, keen and available, and asking if they needed any staff. These industry groups sent the message on to their members and within minutes SOCOG had E-mails from all over town saying they had openings for this or that number, skill etc. and a hot line of positions found many people work. For the remainder, the unions and caterers negotiated an across the board reduction of hours rather than lay-offs so that no-one was without a job.

But above all the problem was with the payroll. Day in day out there were problems with people not being paid, in some cases for weeks. It was not that these were unusual, complicated or difficult to resolve. It was the sheer unremitting volume and the knowledge that the problem was a generic one – that the systems were simply

Unions 2000 – a one-stop shop for union members working at the games.

inadequate and could not be reorganised during the course of the Games. We will see this story repeated again in Chapter 4 in some cases from the employers' side where it was just as distressing.

In all the unions negotiated 12 major disputes, eight with 'real strike-potential', during the Games period that required intervention from SOCOG at a senior level, and dealt with over 2,500 individual problems mainly over pay. The official procedure for dealing with issues through the venue manager was largely bypassed. Most problems were resolved directly with the companies involved. Many employers had people in place who were committed to resolving issues as they arose and networks of personal relations between the unions and these companies had been established. Some problems the unions stepped back from – judging that employers were acting with goodwill and working to deal with the issues, as we will see in the next chapter.

One example might illustrate the nature of the collaboration. As part of the major problem we discussed earlier where caterers were laying off staff early in the Games, 20 workers in four bars in the Stadium threatened to walk out because three of their workmates had been laid off by the catering contractor Sodexho. Chris Christodoulou says:

"It took three meetings, at 10 pm, 12 midnight and 5 am, along with help from John Quayle, from SOCOG – along with a few drinks in the bar under the Novotel with the key workers in the dispute to fix it." [1A]

Paul Howes describes another:

"There were just two food halls for some of our people to take their meal breaks. We had employers saying the meal break starts when they leave work and they would have to get back in 20 minutes. As you know everything was jam packed on the site so it could take that long just to get between the buildings. SOCOG overruled the companies, saying that it starts when they get to the food hall but, during the Games, there were long lines in the halls – it could take ten minutes to get served – so it was changed again – based on the principle that workers deserved a real break – they had to be fed properly – we gave flexibility on meal times and short breaks – and the companies gave back within a human relations principled framework. Nobody abused the system and morale stayed high." [1]

In all the unions negotiated 12 major disputes, eight with 'real strike-potential', during the Games period that required intervention from SOCOG at a senior level, and dealt with over 2,500 individual problems mainly over pay.

Overall the Games were a success, 'the best Games ever'. In the face of this the problems, large and small, pale into insignificance – unless that is, we wish to learn from both our successes and our failures in order to better understand:

- What are the underlying components of the human relations framework that made this success possible?

- Which aspects were not in place in those 'near-disaster' areas and did their absence contribute to the problems?

- Why did these areas nevertheless succeed in spite of the problems?

- Whether any of these lessons might be useful in planning other major events or projects requiring collaboration between large groups of people in the future?

Some of these lessons of the Games will be explored in the case studies that follow in Chapter 4.

Chapter four

On the job –
how it worked in practice

The previous chapter outlined the strategic framework for assembling the Games workforce of SOCOG staff, volunteers and contractors. In this chapter we will look at how it worked in practice for the people involved in different aspects of delivering the essential services of the Games:

■ The Ceremonies, and other performing arts events – illustrating how the trust built in establishing the industrial relations framework overcame a significant dispute over paid and volunteer workers.

■ Security – illustrating some of the recruitment problems in this sector, the organisational partnerships, and the goodwill that ultimately provided the service.

■ The 'closed loop' industrial partnership strategy that integrated packaging and service equipment supply with catering, cleaning and waste disposal; and how the contractors in each of these areas recruited, trained and supported their workers in delivering one of the outstanding success stories of the 'Green Games'.

■ Production of the Sydney 2000 licensed goods and Games uniforms – illustrating how the ethos and values of the Olympic movement can and should be extended to all those who work for the Games – not just those in the home country where it is staged.

- Transport, perhaps the area where we came closest to a disaster just before the Games commenced – illustrating the different human relations outcomes that flowed from the markedly different collaborative and competitive industrial relations philosophies of the State and private transport sectors.

- Worker participation programs – how so many companies, large and small, involved their workforce in supporting the Games and some of the changes in workplace culture that have flowed from this.

Some but not all of these are 'success stories'. The 'best Games ever' leaves considerable room for improvement, but that is how it should be. We hope the lessons learned here will be applied in Athens in 2004, Beijing in 2008 and beyond, and that Sydney's achievement is only a benchmark in the process of translating Olympic values into practical relationships among those who work for as well as those who perform at the Games in the future.

The biggest show on earth

The Opening Ceremony on 15 September 2000 was watched by an estimated 3.5 billion people on TV around the world and an almost full house of 110,000 in Stadium Australia at Sydney Olympic Park.

How many people switched on their TV that night because 'we are going to end up paying for it anyway' and several hours later were transformed?

In the lead-up to the Games public attitudes towards the Games had been on a roller-coaster ride. The initial euphoria of the Bid had given way to either lack of interest or outright cynicism as the Organising Committee went through changes of leadership, financial crises, public relations disasters (marching bands, ticketing, IOC family nepotism at the start of the torch relay, and the rail and bus transport crises). Some of this was antici-pated and planned for. Some was countered by fostering community ownership through the volunteer program. Some was expected to and did turn around with the arrival of the Olympic torch in Australia and the relay. But for some, this author included, a certain cynicism about a mega sporting event

remained – right up to the moment of the Opening Ceremony. How many people switched on their TV that night because 'we are going to end up paying for it anyway' and several hours later were transformed? Around 16,000 people,[8] most neither stars nor celebrities, staged a spectacle that (with cultural respect, humour, a tinge of self-mockery and legitimate pride) reflected a history of Australia, its people and culture back to the population and outwards to a watching world. And for a nation that coined the phrase 'cultural cringe' it was an image that went beyond 'beer, beaches, prawns on barbies and sport'.

At the other end of the Games, the Closing Ceremony staged a different spectacle, more in the form of a celebration of the stars, including both the glitter and glamour, the icons of success, the partying of 10,000+ athletes, the very visible and pointed 'SORRY'[*] that reminded us that values are still contested in the

The Opening Ceremony reflected a history of Australia, its people and culture.

---

* The band Midnight Oil appeared wearing clothes prominently displaying the word 'SORRY' – a reminder that the Australian Government has yet to offer a formal apology to the Aboriginal population for the actions of white settlers over the past 200 years.

political world by entertainers as well as politicians. Then there were the speeches, the accolades, the handover to Athens, the 'best Games ever' and the 'river of fire' – going out with a bang that could be seen by astronauts in space.

These events were the bookends for the Games story for many. Staging both was a major logistical exercise and one that created its own human relations challenges. In addition, throughout the Games a number of Olympic 'live sites' provided various forms of entertainment at other locations including the Sydney Opera House forecourt, Darling Harbour and Martin Place in the city centre. At many events there were smaller side-shows provided by stilt-walkers, 'fire-eaters', jugglers and other performers. As well as providing entertainment, these assisted in crowd control by slowing down mass movement from venues to transport points and releasing groups of people in manageable numbers as the performances ended. These performers were also strategically used as part of the security arrangements, entertaining the queues of people necessarily delayed by bag searches at venue entrances.

The Ceremonies were unusual in that they were regarded by the rest of the Games organisers as being part of a different culture. Some of this is valid. The performing arts do manifest a particular kind of creativity and have traditional work practices that are not found in many other workplaces. This culture gap might explain, but hardly justifies, the unique place in the organisational structure of SOCOG that left these largely outside the necessary controls on budget and content. The Games paid a high price for this, as we will see.

Rick Birch had come to the Games Bid team with an enviable reputation, one that survived the almost universal cringe in Australia that was felt over the 'kangaroos on bikes' stunt at Atlanta.[8] He had a contract under which he reported directly to the SOCOG Board and to a sub-committee chaired by Games President Michael Knight. This by-passed much of the rest of the SOCOG structures.[8 33 83] A significant portion of the $50 million Ceremonies budget was spent early in 'creative planning', 'team building' and transporting the people for these to resort locations.[4 8 71] This may be part of the performance culture but didn't go down too well with the rest of the organisation where the staffing and budget freezes were used to save funds for later.

What will concern us here is not the outcome so much as the

process. Not what was staged but how? What characterised the relations between the people who were involved in staging this show?

Let us begin with a story* – one that links many aspects of the wider story we are trying to tell in this book

---

Not enough forklifts: the story of the Maoris who came to Sydney to work for the Games

Security contractors for the Games had a crisis in recruiting. To get around it there was some (it is said) unauthorised recruiting of people in New Zealand. As a result over 500 mainly Maori and Pacific Island people from small communities arrived in Australia having paid money in New Zealand for security training and a promise of work for the Games. On arrival, they found their 'licences' had not been processed, suitable accommodation had not been arranged and they had no jobs. Some were returned to New Zealand when they were found to be in breach of parole conditions.[1 16]

The Labor Council, ALHMU and the CFMEU (who had a Maori organiser) combined to assist these men and women. Some with suitable qualifications were found work in security. Most of the others, with assistance from SOCOG staff who activated the Games network of Sydney employers, organising interviews etc, were found other jobs – some in the construction industry, some in cleaning, catering and hospitality at the Games, some in jobs in the city.[1 16 34] The CFMEU assisted in the fit-out of a temporary 'Maori village' at

the old Arnott's biscuit factory.[23] Several companies involved in the 'promise of work' contributed to the cost of workers accommodation and retraining programs and the 'village' hosted a traditional Maori hangi (feast) for all those who had helped. Chris Christodoulou said of this:

"We just did our jobs – I didn't expect over 400 of the Maori community to turn up and welcome us – 30 Maori warriors with spears! It was awesome!"[1A]

The people returned to their communities with happy tales of working at the Sydney Olympics.[1 16] In itself, a wonderful human story underpinned by union, SOCOG, contractor and community collaboration in resolving a potentially difficult and damaging situation.[1]

During the rehearsals for the Opening Ceremony – all taking place at night under a cloak of strict secrecy – there was concern that some segments of the show, particularly the tap-dancing trucks and the Ned Kelly Horse segments, would chew up the running track and the grass oval (with its underground sprinkler system). The OCA insisted that plywood boards be

---

* Other parts of the 'Maori story' are told in the section on Games security later in this chapter.

A traditional Maori welcome for people who helped them get work at the Games.

laid (three layers deep on the track, entrances and truck standing points, and one layer on the grass areas) and the whole then covered with ground cloth. In the first week of September it rained and then became dry and windy and the boards buckled. During rehearsals people were tripping over the edges and corners that had lifted under the cloth. Some injuries are expected at any rehearsal but the rate was well above that anticipated and in the middle of the third night of rehearsal the decision was made to remove them. Easier said than done given the huge volume (and weight) of wood involved. There were still boards down on the running track when one young performer was badly hurt and there was a possibility that the dress rehearsal would have to be called off. [44][45]

According to Peter Himmelhoch who managed SOCOG's risk and safety program, the process was slow. There were not enough people on hand to remove the large wet heavy boards and, particularly, there were not enough forklift trucks. In the middle of a crisis meeting on the floor of the Stadium a call came through to say that a busload of Maoris were on their way! Who called them in will remain a mystery as will the name of the joker who said 'Hey, problem solved – we can use Maoris instead of forklifts!' They worked alongside the rest of the Stadium crew through the night with the rehearsal going on around them and the show went on! [45]

Getting the show on the road

After avoiding a public relations disaster by reversing the decision to exclude Australian schoolchildren who had been rehearsing for the Ceremonies in favour of American marching bands, Michael Knight made the Ceremonies operation more accountable to SOCOG and the rest of the Games planning operation.

David Atkins is widely regarded as having put the Ceremonies back on track. For the Opening Ceremony, most of the major design work was done between May 1999 and January 2000, with production between March 2000 and the Games. The show eventually had 13 segments each costing $1 million, and each involving around 1,000 performers.

Behind the spectacle were some memorable experiences in translating designs into workable props. Designer Dan Potra describes how the huge Ned Kelly Horse began as an outback windmill and came together as the shape of a horse. Just getting it in and out of the Stadium through entrances with limited height and width presented challenges, and a special frame was built for it. A six-cylinder engine (pulled out of an old cycle) and a BMW gearbox drove the seven-metre-long moving blades that made the horse's head.

Head of the 'Kelly Horse'.

"And everything had to be wind rated as well, because as you know, the way the Stadium was built, there were major cross-winds in there and it was hard to have things standing up ... We did some tests at one stage with the fish, it was flying like a kite from end to end." [8]

The Opening Ceremony also involved a spectacular collaboration between indigenous and 'white' Australian cultures. Aboriginal dancers from Grafton and Arnhem Land were involved. They met to work together at the first rehearsal. Many of the performers were moved as 'they each danced their own dances for each other'.[4] By way of acknowledgement for the indigenous segments of the Ceremony, payment was made to a committee in each community for education, sport and community development. In addition a cultural custodian deed was negotiated with the IOC. In future the contribution of indigenous people to the Olympic Ceremonies (music, dance, song, costume and props) may not be used for advertising or commercial purposes without approval of the communities involved.

The Ceremonies were live theatre, not film or TV. It was live performance and 'live to air' worldwide. It couldn't be edited or cut. The pressures on the Closing Ceremony were even more intense. The organisers did not have access to the Stadium until 2 am on the final day. The Ceremony was staged without a full dress rehearsal. There are enough stories here for a separate book. Perhaps one day it will be written.

The Ceremonies were live theatre, not film or TV. It was live performance and 'live to air' worldwide. It couldn't be edited or cut.

The creative work aside, putting on the show involved over 20,000 people. The Opening Ceremony alone involved 12,000 performers, 8–9,000 of them children. Seven thousand five hundred performers were needed for the Closing Ceremony. Behind these a small army of around 10,000: technicians, stage managers, production managers and crews of people did whatever was needed to put the show on. Professionals from the film industry built props for the events in Redfern. Two hangars, one for production and storage, the other for rehearsals, were set up at Quakers Hill.[4] Some of the thousands who worked to stage the Games Ceremonies were paid. Some were volunteers.

Performers – professionals or volunteers?

Performance is at least as much an industry today as sport. The principle negotiated early between SOCOG and the unions was that the workforce would be a carefully negotiated blend of contractor (paid) and volunteer staff. In general the tacit understanding was that volunteers would not be used to displace workers from key service jobs. But there were very different views on whether performers and the production and technical staff needed to stage the Ceremonies and other artistic events were to be volunteers or paid. The collaboration between the unions and SOCOG nearly came to grief over this issue.

The Media, Entertainment and Arts Alliance (MEAA) was part of the union team which negotiated the 'Principles of Cooperation' (1997) and the Volunteer Protocol (1999). The protocol provided that volunteers would only be used in roles where they had appropriate skills, experience or qualifications, and furthermore that the parties would consult on the exact roles to be performed by volunteers and the approximate number of volunteers required prior to the Games. In March 2000 as the Ceremonies moved into production, the MEAA raised questions about the non-payment of performers. The union argued that 'in direct breach of the protocol' SOCOG sought to engage all its Opening and Closing Ceremonies dancers and performers with specialist skills on a volunteer only basis. The union launched a campaign to achieve wages for its professional members who would be involved in the Ceremonies.

MEAA accepted that some, indeed a large number of volunteers would be needed for the Ceremonies. Lyn Gailley of MEAA says:

"We knew that dancing schools and lots of other amateurs would be involved and that hundreds of people would be needed for the Ceremonies. We were always prepared to be quite flexible. What we were not prepared for was that professional performers would be asked to work for nothing." [3]

In January 2000 when casting began it became apparent that there was a problem.

"People were contacted ... and when they or their agent asked for a contract they were told, 'Why would you need a contract?'" [3]

Jim Sloman of SOCOG argues:

"This was not originally part of the deal. The press and broadcasting side [of MEAA coverage] was. We had people asking to volunteer without pay to be part of the Games ... and once we were into [planning] the Ceremonies we had volunteers for performances. We had good people volunteering. Superstars volunteered. Some performers got upset over people taking what they saw as 'their jobs' in response to ads for volunteer stilt walkers – part of the skilled volunteer recruitment program. The situation was that we had people queuing up to do the same tasks as someone who wanted to be paid." [17]

Some of this can be seen as a consequence of the Ceremonies functions operating largely outside the rest of SOCOG so that there was little contact during the planning stages.[83] The MEAA sees the problem in part as due to the early spending and the legal costs involved in breaking the contract for the US marching bands.

"David [Atkins] had to sit on the opposite side of the table and negotiate with a budget he'd inherited. A lot of time and money and people had been committed to ideas that didn't proceed." [3]

Part of it is also the attitude towards the performance industry.

"There is this profound mindset, that people in our industry will do it for the love of it. At one point they [SOCOG] made the argument that we

should be happy to be involved for the glory, that this is what the athletes were doing, they were unpaid. Well of course they are paid and what is more we all know that once they win medals, especially gold medals, unless they are particularly stupid they're made for life." [3]

The stage was set for a major dispute, one where the union had the inside track on how to package the issues to the media.

"SOCOG knew we could get the publicity – we could produce fire-eaters, dancers, stilt-walkers, get coverage, especially the early morning shows – provide the colour and movement the media wanted and the Olympics were getting a bad run everywhere. The press were monitoring what was going on, they wanted stories, we were providing them. We would go to a meeting with SOCOG ... and take a couple of dancers or fire-eaters ... but we would have told the media that there was to be a meeting and then we'd do the media interviews outside – the dancers would be there. That's our advantage." [3]

The campaign extended over the first four months of 2000. The Labor Council provided the circuit breaker. An agreement was reached over the ratio of paid to volunteer performers and wages and conditions for performers, and technicians, particularly those involved in the 'live sites'. There was recognition of the key role of some performers as leaders of sections of volunteers. The MEAA acknowledges that there was a lot of compromise on both sides. Much of this is in the spirit of the original agreement. Some is also related to the trust established not just on the issue of payments but a sense that the whole Ceremonies program was back on track.

"We didn't assume, once David came in, that it would fail. We knew he would pull it off – create a great Opening Ceremony. In part the issue of pay for performers was our fault. We hadn't anticipated the attitude of 'perform for glory'. We know the problem areas for next time, and we will negotiate the professional stuff earlier." [3]

Much of the legacy is not passed from one Games to the next. The union was not aware until after the Games that Sydney was the first in which performers in the Ceremonies were paid as employees with defined wages and conditions.

One team; one tent?

The Ceremonies volunteers were also affected by the decision to allow this critical area to develop independently of the rest of SOCOG.[35 83] In Chapter 3 we discussed the detailed and professional planning that went into the SOCOG volunteer program.

Key elements were the attention to volunteer needs during the Games and the way their contribution to the Games success was recognised afterwards. Under Rick Birch, the Ceremonies program would handle all aspects of its own volunteer program. David Brettell who ran the SOCOG program said of this:

"The Ceremonies program was the biggest headache – we had nothing to do with this and that was a bad mistake. The Ceremonies people were creative people who wanted to do it all themselves – and this came back to bite all of us. They didn't sufficiently understand the issues of management and of recognition. The [SOCOG] volunteer program factored out the issues of training, recruitment, communications, transport, feeding and recognition of volunteers for the Ceremonies. Close to, during and after the Games the SOCOG volunteers got these but the Ceremonies people didn't. For example – volunteers got transport – free passes etc – but the Ceremonies volunteers were not included. Feeding – we made sure of the quality of food etc – the Ceremonies were not included in our planning on this. On recognition items like uniforms – Ceremonies volunteers wanted the standard official Games uniform – but they didn't need it to do the job and didn't get it – had their own uniforms for Ceremonies but that wasn't what many wanted. General volunteers were provided with a 'Swatch' watch – Ceremonies volunteers were not. The same applied to the Certificate of Appreciation etc. Ceremonies people came back and griped towards the end and the experience left a bad taste in the mouth – it was a big headache for staffing managers – but they [Ceremonies organisers] had taken themselves out of the loop."[35]

"The Ceremonies people were creative people who wanted to do it all themselves – and this came back to bite all of us. They didn't sufficiently understand the issues of ... training, recruitment, communications, transport, feeding and recognition of volunteers for the Ceremonies."

And it wasn't possible at that stage to bring them back in – the SOCOG volunteer budget had been stretched as far as it could go! Clearly Ceremonies is one area where the SOCOG mantra of 'one team; one tent' was not picked up early enough or in a comprehensive fashion.

'Live sites' – cultural change in the arts industry

The OCA coordinated the program for the 'live sites' and key venues such as the Opera House for elements of the cultural Olympics. The Opera House alone organised 175 performances of 35 different events and hosted 317,000 visitors. The Opera House was paid for the services but the revenue went to the Games. Bill Ford, a consultant to the Opera House Trust, describes a bleak situation in the workplace culture of the Opera House in 1996 –

and a dawning recognition that

"A new culture had to be in place for the Olympics. That was critical." [10]

Five years on, Kylie Bryden-Smith, Manager of Marketing and Media Relations at the Opera House, says that the Games experience prompted a lot of internal changes in the way the people in the organisation worked together, both internally and with potential partners in the arts industry.

"We are talking to the arts industry about product on-line [Internet] – to people who might otherwise be in competition with us. We recognise that while small companies can compete on-line, they recognise the advantage of working with us. The spirit is open, we want to form business partnerships and we are asking how can we do things together. There is an absolute openness and trust; we are sharing commercial information with the idea of a common goal. Also we have developed deeper relationships with Tourism NSW and the other authorities. There's a deeper commitment to reinforcing the Opera House working culture, relationships are deeper, it's not about judging people, it's about attitude, trust, understanding the need to work together for a beneficial result. No longer can you look at yourself in isolation. This is reflected in the work on the web: smaller and larger groups working in cooperation. Our goal is to be a leading learning organisation. The Olympics experience was a learning experience. Our core practices changed. We keep in mind that we must look for key things to learn: it is a learning journey." [14]

Condemned to success – protecting the Games

Security was always going to be a major concern for the Games. Fresh in the minds of people all over the world was the memory of the security breakdown in Atlanta and before that the Black September terrorist attack on Olympic athletes in 1972. In the eyes of the world, we became an Olympic City in September 1993 and **the** Olympic City from September 1996 – the target for terrorism and the press looking for any sensationalism. As well as the terrorist threat to athletes and Games spectators there was concern over the potential for public order breakdown around demonstrations by the many groups who might wish to use this world spotlight to draw attention to political and human rights issues – for example Australian Aboriginal rights groups and the growing network of groups protesting 'globalisation' of corporate control.

SOCOG and the NSW Police Service were jointly accountable to the IOC for the security of the Sydney 2000 Games with ultimate responsibility resting with the Commissioner of the NSW Police Service to establish and control the security system and advise SOCOG on operational security matters. There was no room for failure here. As Paul McKinnon who ran the security operation said: "We were condemned to success".[38]

The security command and control structure

Olympic security preparations began in May 1995 and the Olympic Security Command Centre (OSCC) was established in February 1997. This brought the Games security workforce – 5,000 police (on site), 4,500 contract security personnel and 2,000 security volunteers – under a single command structure. In addition there were specialist support personnel from Federal agencies and the Australian Defence Forces plus 'normal' duties for the NSW police force that had a special focus for the Games period. The whole was run from a single purpose-built command facility, the Olympic Precinct and Regional Operations Centre (OPRO), based at Homebush Bay. It was this Games-wide command structure that all the Games agencies subscribed to.

The command structure was negotiated through a joint committee involving all the major players including the Federal Office of the Prime Minister and Cabinet, SOCOG, OCA and the NSW Police Service. In August 1997 this committee established the fundamental principles for a security model based on NSW police control of contract and volunteer security staff. In addition, spectator services staff – around 12,000 mainly volunteers but with paid supervisors and managers – were included in the overall security command structure but reported primarily to the venue management. Thus everyone in the security portfolio reported to or came under control of the Police Commander at the Venue – who technically reported to the Venue Manager. Asked by the IOC who had the ultimate decision on a security matter like a bomb scare and a decision to evacuate, NSW Police Commissioner Peter Ryan is reported to have said that it would be the decision of the owner of the event – i.e. 'SOCOG would take that decision – but they would be mad to ignore my advice'.[51]

In the context of Australia the security threat was relatively benign compared with previous Games in Seoul, Barcelona or Atlanta. Also we should not underestimate the community spirit erupting from the single biggest peacetime event. Ultimately the capacity for control of civil disorder is in the hands of the community. As anti-globalisation protesters who planned to disrupt the torch relay through the Sydney suburb of Newtown discovered, even legitimate protest is constrained by public sentiment. The Aboriginal embassy established in Victoria Park in inner Sydney did highlight the concerns of the indigenous community but, by agreement between the Commissioner and Aboriginal leaders, consciously avoided any disruption of the Games events and transport arrangements.

That said, a sophisticated intelligence gathering and security command and control structure was put in place. Important in the planning stage was the use of the Australian and New Zealand Risk Management Standard. This was used to provide analysis of various risks and rationalise decision-making by highlighting the consequences and who needed to be responsible. As with most of the Games planning, security had to compete for its budget. The ability to indicate the nature of various security risks, their consequences and who would need to assume responsibility if the OSCC didn't have the budget, helped not only focus minds but also loosen purse strings. Even so, the Sydney 2000 budget was not bottomless as some of the private security contractors were to discover.

The overall security concept can be summarised in terms of zones of risk. Of greatest concern was welfare of athletes in the Olympic Village. Here the police provided all security as they did in the sensitive areas of each of the venues. For other areas contract security people were used and these supplemented for crowd control by spectator services volunteers. We noted above how entertainers were used to manage the movement of people as part of crowd control and security as well as maintaining the spirit of fun and enjoyment.

Contract security – recruiting a phantom workforce

We have already explored the process of recruiting and training of volunteers – a mammoth task but organised with great skill around a well-conceived strategic plan. What was to prove a major headache for the organisers was the task of recruiting the 4,500 licensed security staff to be provided by private contractors for the Games.[25]

We have noted above that in the early stages of workforce planning SOCOG saw its role as developing relationships with the private sector companies who would be most likely to tender for the major contracts. It raised questions about the task of recruiting sufficient numbers of people with the appropriate skills for the unique operation of staging the Games for a short period in September 2000. Within SOCOG a review of the capabilities of the private security industry suggested that the security industry would have major problems. Among the issues identified in the review were:

Overall the review suggested an industry recruitment capability for the Games security workforce of minus 2000 people.

- NSW Security Licensing arrangements were going through a review – the expectation was that this would reduce the number of licensed security people by half, from 34,000 to around 17,000.

- Most of those left would be part-timers – many of whom would be listed as casuals with up to five security companies. During the Games period all of these might expect to be working full time – but for just one of the companies.

- The first pick on the available pool of labour would go to companies with existing contracts who would be in demand by Games sponsors, international corporations, companies with overseas visitors, or existing companies in the city who might choose to increase security for the Games period.

- Overall the review suggested an industry recruitment capability for the Games security workforce of **minus 2000 people**.

The SOCOG/OSCC collaboration would have to develop programs to deliver the private sector workforce based on a shared understanding of the culture of the commercial security industry. It needed to manage all the security manpower requirements for the main competition venues plus warehousing and 40 test events. In this it would also be collaborating with the OCA who would manage all the Olympic Games sites up to 1 August 2000 when the police would assume command.

Given that the manpower was not out there the obvious answer was to recruit people not previously employed in the security industry. Even in this Sydney faced problems. Atlanta had a population the size of the whole of Australia's within a six-hour drive. Their call on manpower was easy. In the USA, recruiters could go to high schools and, for low-level security, if the uniform fitted you got a job. However, in NSW security was covered by legislation that required licensed staff – these were just not going to be available.

An Industry Consultation Committee added little to the depressing picture of SOCOG's own analysis. Discussions with the Australian Security Industry Association (ASIAL) revealed that

- Seventy percent of the industry was employed in just five large companies.

- The other 30 percent were employed in 300 relatively small companies.

- The majority used people like taxi drivers, schoolteachers, foremen, university students – people for whom security was a casual job – 'the kind of job you do when in between jobs or to make a quid when you need to pay the rent'.[25]

- There were few career jobs in the industry at this level even where people were licensed.

Olympic security training

In 1998 security industry representatives were invited to an 'Expo' at the NSW Police Academy in Goulburn. On everyone's mind at the time were the problems Atlanta had with security and many of the participants were interested in selling security equipment. For SOCOG, however, the priority was manpower issues – how to get the numbers for the security workforce, and who to contract for the task of managing these people for the Games. The needs analysis indicated that, as the police were in charge of the high security areas, the only people carrying weapons would be the police. The main need was for security guards who would come under this chain of command with lower level security skills requirements. This eliminated the need for weapons training and confrontation management skills – reducing the amount of training needed for Games security by a third. ASIAL agreed to this approach and with TAFE designed a course for training security people for the Games. This course was never run. What SOCOG had not realised was that the large companies, led by Chubb Security, effectively controlled the ASIAL. Paul Donato, who managed the SOCOG security program, believes the major companies in the security industry feared that the legacy of the Games might be legislation to reduce the training requirement for a security licence and this would open the door for smaller competitors to the major players.[25]

ALLSPORT/GETTY IMAGES

At this stage security was already late in the recruitment stakes. Catering companies had long been out in the field. Things got worse. There was a degree of paranoia that drove the thinking on the number of security staff required. The number was eventually cut from an initial estimate of 12,000 down to around 4,000 but getting firm numbers at this point proved difficult – prolonging the delays in actually contracting security companies to go out and recruit. For those attempting to do so the success of another part of the Games strategy worked against them. OCA and ORTA had convinced people that transport during the Games period would be a problem – prompting advance planning across the city by the private sector to reduce pressure on the road, rail, bus and ferry system at peak times. For the public and those who might be enticed to work in security this produced a reluctance to travel outside of one's own area.[25]

Low level security checks at Sydney Olympic Park.

A security resource centre?

An attempt by SOCOG to establish a security resource centre – identifying existing security workers and providing a point of entry for new recruits – was in the words of Paul Donato 'knee capped' by the larger security companies who felt that their competitors would benefit.[25] In fact all the security companies were counting the same staff on their books. Using the Olympic Labour Network was not seen as a viable option, at least for the bulk of the workforce. It is said that OLN lacked expertise in the security industry and fees of $4 per hour per worker made this uneconomic for companies paying security guards around $14–15 per hour.[12 15] * In the end both the OLN and the Labor Council helped feed people into the security workforce.

All this needs to be seen in the context of late decisions. The SOCOG budget for security was changed four times.[38] The provisional numbers required were not decided until July 99 and much modified after that.[25] And the Award negotiations designed to provide the budget certainty for labour costs were delayed by the need to negotiate with industry peak bodies as well as the key companies. By this time catering and cleaning were recruiting from the same pool of people. Both the Sydney Olympic Award and the low margins on the contracts precluded throwing money at the problem to hire the workers needed.

Olympic Security Licences

In December 1999 the NSW Parliament passed legislation for a special Olympic Security Licence (OSL). At the time the thinking was that ASIAL would administer this licensing of staff receiving special but limited training for the Games. Again SOCOG had little appreciation of the influence of the larger security companies on ASIAL and this did not work out as planned. Federal and State governments provided $11 million to the majors in the industry to train security guards but with no direct link to recruiting for the Games. People took the licence and went to

---

* In fact, security was not one of the staff categories the OLN planned to provide and Di Pass of Adecco argues that the $4.00 per hour fee was not unreasonable for recruitment, training, administration, and legal and statutory on-costs for short-term casual employment – used by a number of contractors to fill the gap in their own recruitment strategy.

wherever the work was and the Games contractors were left to recruit for themselves from the general labour pool. People were recruited from outside NSW using the provisions of the Mutual Recognition Act, which allows for recognition of comparable qualifications obtained in other Australian States and in New Zealand. People were also certified through regional training organisations where they could demonstrate the knowledge base for the Olympic Security Licence.

The original target was for 2,500 special licences. In the event only 400 were issued and 300 of these were for New Zealand recruits. These OSL workers were regarded by the police as 'warm bodies in uniforms'. Where security required 'guarding' the police insisted on fully licensed security people.[25 38] So in the end the bulk of the 4,500 security staff were certified through the normal processes. With a shortage of licensed security staff and a boom in security even without the Games security requirements, the going would be tough for the SOCOG contractors.

Contracting – power play in the security industry

In late 1999 the security contracts went to tender. There were 50 expressions of interest but only ten tenders returned. The majors had thought they were in a strong position. In the end they priced themselves out of the market.[25 38] SOCOG had a limited budget and the large security companies tender offer was more than three times the price eventually agreed for the contracts. Negotiations failed to either reduce the price or generate more money on the table from SOCOG and in the end Chubb and the other majors walked away from the process – not too unhappily as they were able to concentrate on their core business during the boom of the Games period and, as we shall see, avoid many of the pitfalls faced by those who did win contracts.

After exhaustive interviews with the remaining tenderers and assurances about their ability to fill the numbers of security staff required, SOCOG awarded contracts to a number of smaller security companies. These contractors did eventually deliver, with varying degrees of proficiency and success, but commercially it was a big call for them. All underestimated the financial commitment required up front and the scale of manpower and infrastructure required to manage this large casual workforce. Some with smaller contracts limited to a single area did better than those with contracts across several sites. Bob Morris of Sabichi had an ethnic mix of staff, drawn mainly from mid-Europeans living in Western Sydney including some ex-Bosnian police, Indians and new immigrants. These workers showed a high commitment to personal duty, though some had problems with the English language. Others like Matt Kenworthy at M.A.S. had other problems. The task involved scaling up what had been a small operation into a huge one and then back down again a few weeks later. Neither the structures nor the cash flow were in place to handle this. SOCOG staff have questioned their own due diligence in this area but feel that they 'had nowhere else to go' with the majors putting them 'over a barrel' and SOCOG/OSCC refusing to provide more funds. The SOCOG staff saw their role being 'to help these guys through'.[25]

Workforce International: a case study

In order to understand better the nature of the task, and the degree of goodwill and collaboration involved in shoring up this element of the Games security workforce, we will look in more detail at the experience of one of the contractors. Workforce International (WFI) was brought in as part of the tendering process only when the police and SOCOG had signed off on the numbers required for each area. WFI were out of their usual area, which was providing maintenance staff for industrial shutdowns, but had developed some expertise in supplying low-level security staff to sporting events such as Rugby League and horse-racing and venues such as Leichhardt Oval. This gave them project management expertise in the area of recruiting, selection and people management. However nothing in this background could compare with the Games experience where their task was to recruit 2,000 people with a security licence to fit a short two-week period. For some of these there would be work either side of the actual Games period but for all it would be work starting several months away from the tendering process. As we have shown this number was simply not available on call.

Their main problem was that the whole process was late. WFI put in an expression of interest in June of 1999. Despite discussions in October with SOCOG, WFI were not told they had the contract until early in 2000 and did not receive a signed contract until the middle of the actual Games period in late September![15] For six months the company was recruiting staff to fill the security rosters (with heavy penalties in the event that it failed to deliver the numbers) without having a signed contract. While SOCOG are critical of WFI in some areas there is also counter criticism of SOCOG's ability to manage its contractors, particularly a lack of understanding of the timetable needed to get the job done. To recruit 2,000 people who would be there on the day for a short-term job six months away WFI needed to recruit 4,000. This required putting some 10,000 people through the recruitment process. Like contractors in other areas, it was a big ask to hold the enthusiasm of people selected in March and have them hanging around until September. And many of these people were, necessarily, new to the industry of security.

To recruit 2,000 people who would be there on the day for a short-term job six months away WFI needed to recruit 4,000. This required putting some 10,000 people through the recruitment process.

From WFI there is high praise for the role played by the NSW Labor Council in negotiating the Olympic Award with pay rates that were 'fair and reasonable' and the bonus to ensure people 'completed the job'. The company says that without it the job would have been 'unmanageable'.[12] It also meant the company knew the rate of pay when bidding for the contract and knew that it would have the flexibility for rostering people across different shifts, an important consideration in '24-hour' operations. WFI initially bid for work in all five of the OSCC defined security areas but indicated to SOCOG that it could not handle all of these. Its aim was for contracts to supply a maximum of about 1,200 workers. According to WFI Managing Director Ray Roberts, SOCOG asked them to take on more and WFI ended up with the contracts for Sydney Olympic Park, the Velodrome and Rushcutters Bay.

To get a feel for what it was like we'll let Ray's words tell the story.

"It's mammoth – nothing you've done before would prepare for this – in the end it was down to a determination to do a good job, but we were still seeking to sign off on the contract as we were starting to do the job. SOCOG kept delaying … and all the while WFI was recruiting – if we hadn't we'd never have been able to deliver. WFI gambled $250,000 on getting it – and if we hadn't then the whole thing would have collapsed – there was that level of commitment to doing a good job.

"It got worse as things went on – the penalties for 'no-show' were set at $55 an hour – the police rate to cover for security people not showing up for a shift. To try to cater for the inevitable, WFI negotiated with SOCOG on the idea of a 'flying squad' located in the Sydney Olympic Park – this would be

a crew of people who could fill shortfalls for 'no-shows' – a kind of manpower insurance scheme. At the last minute SOCOG refused to agree to this. The flying squad centre was kicked out of the Olympic Park – talk about stupid – there was space, facilities for all the bigwigs but no facility for contract security. We were assembling large numbers of people on street corners and allocating them to rostered positions. Eventually SOCOG conceded we needed a location and we got part of the Old Ford Factory [at Homebush].* SOCOG were incompetent in managing us. Remember it was half-way through September and there was no signed contract – mid-way through the Games. If we hadn't been committed we could have legally walked away but we thought if we do pull out we'd be crucified so we went on in part because we wanted to make it a success but with a prayer and hoping we'd have the legal system on our side.

"Over the course of the Games we developed a knowledge of 'no-shows' that helped us with planning. Once we factored these 'no-show' rates into management we had 99 percent manning level at all venues. We were able to offer to help out police with the flying squad when there were some attempts by people to break down fences to get into venues.

"SOCOG decided to change the roster structure – decided not to send the 2,000 people through a rostering area so we had to send people straight to specific work areas. This stuffed the systems for signing on and off ... if people don't have timesheets they don't get paid – we had 700 people not paid all or part of their shifts one week. SOCOG changed the security arrangements on perimeter surveillance – had people reporting to different places, changed the deployment but didn't change the documentation. We said we wanted to be part of the discussion on this but SOCOG said nothing to us and kept us out of the meetings. We called the Labor Council and they threatened to stop work.

"WFI had 500 people who were contracted through the OLN. These were our worst experience. People [at OLN] didn't understand the logistics of signing on and off at remote venues and how we then get the timesheet to the employer to pay in a timely manner – some people were not paid for four weeks. We had no control and all the responsibility. The OLN at first refused to accept the problem – the difficulty of keeping an accurate paper trail for people working across different shifts and different pay rates – no-one had worked that out.

---

* The factory was the logistics centre for delivery of Games supplies – outside the Sydney Olympic Park security zone.

"With hindsight, rather than timesheets the venues should have used punch cards or better a swipe card – for example the security pass – the accreditation pass was already barcoded for access – but this didn't work for records. It was intended to but it was expensive therefore we ended up with a paper system. This started out as an A3 system – you can't fax A3! – we had to fight to get an A4 system. You don't realise the problems that multiply when you don't pay people – the week we had 700 people with problems – we had gridlock in the office system – and then all the other little issues pile up. Mistake rates go up and that compounds the problem – then the 'no-show' rate goes up – and that throws stress somewhere else in the system. It's OK for people out at the Games site – they see the fantastic atmosphere there – but the poor receptionist only gets complaints in her ear all day – no morale boost here!

"What stopped it all falling apart was the level of camaraderie between the public and the employees – a natural spirit of wanting to get the job done – I'm amazed at the number of people who were prepared to press on without pay for three weeks in some cases. The change in the culture of security workers – that really surprised me – never seen an attitude like it – I'd ask people on site how was it going and they'd say 'fantastic – everything going all right' then ask about pay and some would say 'haven't been paid for two weeks'. There was a fantastic level of trust." [12]

Other interviews reported Ray personally helping people with pay problems by advancing cash so they could keep working.

"The only circuit breaker in this mess was the Labor Council. This job had taught me long ago to work with the unions. We ensured union membership – encouraged people to join the ALHMU direct. Overall, though, I think the exercise was a disaster for the unions – the majority of employers didn't help sign people up for the unions. They [unions] did a lot of work behind the scenes and got little credit for it. The hard-nosed ones at the Labor Council are a bit above wanting to see benefits flowing back to the unions perhaps but they put in a lot of effort and got no reward." [12]

There is always another side to any story. Some elements of this one are still in dispute. The view of SOCOG is that WFI encountered problems that others managed to work through – with help. What seems to be beyond dispute however is that the delays in this critical area of Games planning and service delivery compounded the problems of recruiting an important section of the workforce that would, at the best of times, have presented a major headache. Late planning is usually planning on the run and rarely good planning. It is also beyond dispute that those who were carrying the major burden for this area of recruitment and management of the workforce were stretched to their limit of capability. What is perhaps even more important however is that, despite the problems, they came through and delivered an essential service required for the Games to be staged without incident. In part this can be explained as goodwill but it begs the question, what under-pinned this? What elements of the industrial and human relations architecture permitted and encouraged this expression of goodwill– beyond what anyone would have expected at the outset?

Maoris – come to Sydney to work for the Games

Let us look again at a piece of the Games story we have touched on already. The security contractors expected 20–30 percent of people recruited to drop out before the Games. About a month out from the Games the companies were shocked to find that around 50 percent of the people recruited were not available and recruiting methods 'got a bit desperate'. One recruiter with a Maori ethnic background went to New Zealand claiming that he was recruiting for several of the security firms and targeting small, mainly Maori communities with an invitation to come to Sydney to work for the Olympics. What happened next is hard to pin down but the recruiting went 'out of control' and around 500 New Zealand men arrived asking 'when do we start work?' and were not very happy when told they didn't have a job.

A few were returned immediately when it was found they were in breach of parole conditions. For the rest the story is an amazing one of inter-agency and cross-cultural collaboration. As we noted earlier, a Maori organiser from the CFMEU helped organise the construction of a 'Maori Village'. Some were found jobs in the building industry. Some were issued with Olympic Security Licences and given Games work. Personal networks built up throughout the Games planning period were used to find others jobs across the city and Games workforce. And there is the story of how a small group 'saved the day' at rehearsal for the Opening Ceremony. Many of the people involved shared in the traditional *hangi* and got to understand a bit of Maori culture. The legacy is many stories in both Australia and New Zealand of how Maoris came to Sydney to work for the Olympics.

A few lessons?

Security is a major concern at international events. What the Games achieved was a level of cooperation between agencies with very different cultures that at the end of the day resulted in an event without a security incident. We might agree with Paul McKinnon, head of the OSCC, that we were 'condemned to success' – given the international spotlight of attention on Australia and the Games we just couldn't afford to fail. We should not ignore Paul's other comment that part of the problem was the culture of SOCOG. Along with the team building and staff empowerment there was also a culture in some parts of the organisation of 'decide, delegate and dump it' where senior management failed to keep an eye on the details – this area of security obviously being one – to recognise that major problems were occurring. Later we will touch on how the OCA intervened to take over the management of some of the problematic contract areas.

None of this however should obscure the important detail of the human commitment among many ordinary people who found themselves in the middle of the mess to persevere through what, in other circumstances, would have caused them to walk away.

We should also not underestimate the achievement of having people from very different organisational cultures embrace the event command structure.[51] While security planning and operation were under police command this was seamlessly integrated with the Olympic venues management structure. It was not just about having security under police command it was also about ensuring that the public face of security was part of the broader framework of spectator services. It was about presenting a seamless security service in which people with varying levels of training in the craft of security were allocated to appropriate roles. Volunteers could check bags in some areas. A highly casualised private sector security industry workforce (whether fully licensed or trained for more limited security roles as 'warm bodies in uniform') could be recruited, trained and integrated into a fully policed security system

The IR framework outlined in the previous chapter was important in setting basic conditions for pay, and contract costs. It had rewards for commitment that overcame the 'labour churn' problems and 'no-show' rates experienced in Atlanta. The award system also gave flexibility in rostering across shifts. Paul Donato suggests this kind of flexibility could be extended.

"How about we develop a multi-skilled workforce for future events – give young people leaving school basic training in first aid, OH&S and communications – link this to a volunteer program – where venues sponsor volunteers at major events so they can get training on the job – these people then become the first option for a job of choice when a major event comes up. In security you don't need an ex-commando – in fact preferably not – better a multi-skilled person – caterer, cleaner, car park attendant, security guard, spectator services person." [25]

Clean – and Green!

Over the 16 days of the Games there were 6 million spectators, half a million in Sydney Olympic Park alone on any given day. And the athletes, officials, the volunteers and staff of the various contractors providing venue services, police and security guards, logistics and transport …

This is the story of how this huge number of people were provided with food and drink on site, the inevitable mess cleaned up and the waste food, plates, cups, containers, packaging and assorted rubbish collected and 70 percent of it either recycled or composted rather than going into landfill. It is a story of:

- strategic planning of the logistics to create an ecological 'closed loop' for all the materials involved

- unique partnerships between sections of an industry that had never before collaborated on this scale

- creative recruitment strategies for a workforce that the 'Gap Analysis' had indicated was not available in the Sydney area

- how to manage a temporary and casual 'event' workforce

- an ecological outcome that was recognised as one the 'Green Games' success stories.

Planning the logistics

Sydney's Bid committed SOCOG to a set of environmental guidelines that included waste minimisation, recycling and the use of recycled materials, and public education on ecological waste management. The target was to get at least 70 percent of the waste diverted from landfill. The aim was to showcase best practice for minimum use of material that would end up as waste as well as the maximum recycling of the material that was used.*

As well as the commitment to best practice outcomes in this field, there was also a commitment to developing cooperation between sponsors and contractors involved in providing services. It is this collaboration that we will explore here.

Like so many aspects of Sydney's Games planning, Atlanta provided the wake-up call. Atlanta had bought materials and equipment with little thought for how to dispose of them after the Games. The 'masses of junk' left at the end had been costly in terms of theft, warehousing, damage, and forced sales. SOCOG persuaded Linfox to handle logistics with Lindsay Fox reputedly overriding the arguments of some senior managers that the company would be too busy at Games time.[44]

> *The target was to get at least 70 percent of the waste diverted from landfill ... to showcase best practice for minimum use of material that would end up as waste as well as the maximum recycling of the material that was used.*

Matt Clarke had been at the Homebush party in September 1993 when Sydney was announced as the Host City for the 2000 Olympic Games. His first thoughts were 'my god we're going to have it', closely followed by memory of his parents saying of the 1956 Melbourne Games that 'there was something special about it'. Seven years later he saw 300,000 people at the Homebush site.

Moving from Lend Lease to SOCOG and then to Linfox he ended up coordinating the logistics centre at the old Ford factory just outside the Olympic Park security zone, with a staff of 1,100 (100 managers, 100 supervisors, 400 paid crew and over 500 volunteers). The first task was to change the thinking. There was an attitude that 'if you haven't done this before you don't know how to'. What was needed was some lateral thinking – not just how to buy goods **and** dispose of them but if they were needed. Best of all, the aim was not to order them at all. It involved multi-skilling

---

* For more details on the commitments and how these were achieved see (1) The Sydney 2000 Olympic Games Integrated Waste Management Solution: A waste management and resource recovery strategy for the Sydney 2000 Olympic and Paralympic Games (SOCOG, October 1998) (2) The Post Games Environment Report. (Sydney 2000, December 2000).

the people involved in purchasing, warehousing and labouring. Perhaps the biggest headache was 'how to assemble a team of committed people, turn them on to delivering 110 percent commitment for three to four months and then say goodbye after 5th October 2000'.[44]

Managing this paid and volunteer workforce was like SOCOG in miniature. Initial reactions were 'you can't have volunteers in logistics' – 'you certainly can't have them working alongside paid workers' and in any case 'they're untrained – we'll have OH&S issues'. These attitudes had to be changed. And then the volunteers needed to be recruited. Linfox did a 'homemade' video and took it on a 'roadshow' to schools, voluntary associations, logistics organisations and found the people who wanted to be part of the Olympics. Logistics is about planning the details. Sydney promised to provide transport for all the athletes **and** their equipment. Logistics made sure that both arrived before the Games started. The road race needed road cones etc. Matt Clarke remembers it as

"planning, testing, replanning and retesting. On the ground it was teamwork in groups of about 40–50: managers, supervisors, crew and volunteers – and of course the drivers to deliver everything through the security screening systems at the logistics centre and into the security zone of the Olympic Park." [44]

But that's another story ...

Closing the loop: reduce, recycle, reuse

One of the most successful partnerships of the Games involved the Integrated Waste Management Team of Visy (packaging and recycling) Cleanevent (cleaning) Pacific Waste Management (solid waste collection) and Waste Service NSW (the government waste management agency). In 1997 when the SOCOG Advisory Board on Waste Management was set up these partners were Games sponsors (contributing money and/or 'value in kind' – VIK) and/or potential contractors for providing commercial services. Their objectives were thus

- to brand the companies as Games supporters and hence good corporate citizens

- to use the Games as an opportunity for employee participation programs

- to 'leverage' their sponsorships in terms of providing goods and services (offsetting the VIK) and hence make money both from the Games and its legacy by creating a model for waste management.

The approach adopted was to control all the materials coming onto Olympic sites that could end up as waste so that the volumes could be reduced at source and as far as possible separated into three main streams:

- biodegradable for composting

- reclaimable for re-use or recycling

- trash that would need to be disposed of as landfill.

This involved tightly specifying the amount and types of packaging and utensils that could be used by other contractors, such as catering and merchandising, and ensuring that all staff at Games time were trained to use the separate waste streams. So many recycling schemes fall down because the theory doesn't get translated into practice. It only takes a small amount of trash to contaminate the other streams and make later separation for re-use and recycling so labour intensive as to be unviable.

The other feature of the team's proposal was to 'close the loop' by using the recycled material in the manufacture of further packaging and for a range of new products. Often the growth of recycling is limited by the inability of industry to utilise the material reclaimed.

Overnight kerbside collection

For Pacific Waste Management (PWM) the task was relatively straightforward. This is not to understate the scale of the task but it was limited to organising the collection of the colour-coded bins during the night hours and transporting these to the transfer station. Recruitment for the Olympics was mainly from the company's own workforce. Staff were paid a special Olympic rate negotiated with the Transport Workers Union with whom there is an established relationship. The service began on 1 July allowing lead-in and 'ramp-up' time. Max Spedding of PWM says:

"Initial nervousness, pettiness and squabbles disappeared the day the Games started and people did things way beyond their normal jobs. People, including some of the volunteers who worked with them, became convinced

Make it – take it back and remake it again. All packaging was recyclable or compostible – plus tables, chairs, bookshelves, packaging and the recycling bins were made from recycled cardboard.

they could do anything needed. We presented Olympic mementos to all employees and managers as recognition afterwards."[49]

The company reports that the Games had an impact on the corporate culture with people using more initiative and being more innovative and that the whole exercise highlighted the company's lack of logistics expertise. It is now examining how to influence customers on products used in order to increase the recycling potential rather than just collecting waste.[49]

Make it – and take it back

For Visy the Games involved providing product, developing new products and working closely with Cleanevent on the logistics for 'green' waste management. The sponsorship deal was for a total of $5 million, mainly VIK in the areas of

- paper and other materials for food packaging
- specialist recyclable food packaging, containers and utensils
- Visy board furniture
- communications, publicity, marketing, entertainment and hospitality.

For Rob Pascoe, who managed the Visy Games operation:

"*... the task was first to identify the product before it got to the consumer – some products are hard to recycle (PVC, polystyrene and even polypropylene) so all cups were either card or PET not polystyrene – then have the logistics in place to recover and recycle the materials. Our objective was to be able to take back all of the Visy manufactured products for recycling and, where possible, make these into [new] products. [For example] in the area of plastics Olympic signage was made from recycled plastic milk containers. After that it becomes a people exercise. Thousands of people and hundreds of organisations involved in creating the waste stream: the manufacturers of packaging – distributors – users – caterers and merchandisers – the public who open it – the cleaners and caterers who collect [and store] it – the waste companies responsible for pick-up and transport – to the processors who sort it to landfill, or composting or recycling – [Then] sorting the recyclables and back to manufacture again.*

"*There were 800 catering organisations in the Games. Many subcontracted their product and its packaging and most [usually] don't care what happens to it so you have to sell the opportunities and advantages of closed systems without costing the earth in terms of dollars and time etc. We had to work with all the partners – to get them to want to be involved and to indicate that we could help if they did what we told them. Selling this message involved talking to hundreds of organisations. We did presentations about product provision and how we could assist in the 'tactical partner program' – talked about the synergies. We had established [with SOCOG that] 'this is the policy for the Games' but [details of] this had to come through negotiation. It had to be commercially viable and fit for purpose. Creation of policy was part of the event management and then implementation of the program without ruffling feathers."* [41]

Visy organised an employee participation program for its 3,500 staff. The Visy Olympic Facility Leaders (VOFL) maintained a two-way flow of communication about what was going on and the development of the 'closed loop'. At Games time the VOFL supervised the recycling program ensuring the correct use of bags, bins and recycling stations, and helping the education program with caterers and merchandisers. Visy staff were also involved in the Olympic Landcare tree-planting program.* Games tickets were distributed to allow as many employees as possible to have at least one Olympic Games experience and tours were organised to see the recycling program. Across many company divisions, productivity rates were up 40 percent as a result of these Olympic participation programs.

On the production side, a lot was learned in the process of 'ramping up' production of packaging product from $100,000 per month to $6 million worth over the Games period. Though caterers were asked to order by January 2000 many of the orders came in around July and then were only indicative so the last minute ramp was even steeper than expected. Visy developed a range of cardboard furniture: bookcases, tables, desks and chairs. This was used to fit out the Uniform Distribution and Accreditation Centre (UDAC) – and recycled into other cardboard products after the Games.

As with all these stories there is more. Rob Pascoe would like to tell it.

"We should be telling the story of how we did well – the education and communication between caterers, cleaners, venues etc – understanding of the big picture – and the detail of separation – the schools program, giving

---

* We discuss some of the successes of this program in Chapter 5.

tickets for the Paralympics and the Aboriginal program — giving tickets via the Pratt Foundation — and more." [41]

Cleaning can be fun — and hard work

In Atlanta cleaning contractors had experienced haphazard planning and little emphasis on recruitment of staff. One reported recruiting 4,000 people in the lead-up period to fill 1,100 jobs at Games time with labour costs rising from $5 to $19 an hour and a fall-off rate of 15 percent during the Games. Determined to avoid a repeat of this, Cleanevent helped form the waste management team, and developed a partnership relationship with SOCOG (and OCA) as a sponsor and consultant. [40] This allowed the company to see SOCOG systems, like the pivotal role of accreditation, from the inside and to influence the development of the cleaning contracts which locked all contractors into the integrated waste management plan. The company's original target was to win about 50 percent of the contract cleaning work (six to eight of the venues). Conscious of potential conflict of interest it excluded itself from SOCOG tender processes. It was already established in several venues and advocated that all the pre-established cleaners be given preference — subject to meeting the performance criteria — for contracts at Games time. In the event many of the other cleaners decided they couldn't meet these criteria and Cleanevent ended up with around 75 percent of the cleaning work — a total of 38 venues! This required negotiations with the resident cleaning companies in the other venues over access to equipment, supplies and storage facilities for these — a collaborative partnership story in itself. In addition Cleanevent developed its own partnership network with companies supplying cleaning machinery (Karcher), biodegradable garbage bags (Biocorp), paper products (Lombards) and tractors for moving rubbish (Kubota). [40A]

Cleanevent was one of the few event cleaners specialising in short-term in-and-out operations. For the rest of the industry recruiting the huge workforce for a 60-day operation[*] placed this in the short-term contract basket. In reality the operation was at least a 180-day operation to get the management structures in the venues, key people trained and the relationships with the

---

[*] This 60-day period included the Olympic and Paralympic Games and the lead in and out 'shoulder' periods.

workforce developed. The company believes a fixed price contract for a performance-driven service with takeover in June and hand-back in November might have been better for the industry. It would have allowed more companies to be involved and greater flexibility in meeting the performance criteria. But hindsight always has 20–20 vision. SOCOG had budget problems and pressure to cut costs.

Games experiences, even hard ones like Atlanta, produce technical and cultural changes in an organisation. Cleanevent had developed event 'scoping' and rostering computer programs that allowed it to predict the cleaning and waste requirements for events and then organise the workforce needed to clean up the mess. Given data on the venue, number of spectators, catering and merchandising outlets etc, the technology assists in defining the details of the amount of waste that would be generated (by type), the numbers of cleaners and supervisors required, and the equipment, supplies, storage facilities, size of holding areas needed for wastes, number of waste bins (for each type of waste) and so on.

More important, there was a body of expertise within the organisation. Craig Lovett of Cleanevent says:

"After Atlanta the Melbourne Show was a breeze and by the time we'd finished the Sydney Show in 1997 we realised something had shifted. We had people who had confidence and who were thinking outside the box. We recruited regionally rather than in the cities. We organised accommodation and worked on making it a fun time so people we recruited stayed; and many came back to us for the Olympics." [40]

Cleanevent chose to develop its own Games recruiting strategy. It judged that many labour hire and contractor companies would be competing for the same people in the Sydney region. To build the core management for Team 2000, as it was called, the company invited many of the people it had previously employed to a work-shop in Sydney where they were offered

"a contract to work for $10,000 per month, to work their guts out, help find others, to fit into a management structure where they'd have a crew of 10 people, and they'd have fun". [40]

By June this core of people had been recruited through organisa-tions such as the Melbourne Fire Brigade, the Defence Forces (people used annual holidays to work for the Games), and community and sporting groups like the Melton Football Club and the Ballarat/Bendigo VFL. Many of this inner circle were trained on the job in the early 2000 events such as the Melbourne Grand Prix and the Sydney Easter Show. In June these managers and supervisors went through a week-long training program covering all aspects of the Games operation down to site-by-site rostering. The company believes the $100,000 this cost was well spent. On 4 September the whole of this team moved to the company's base at the Eastern Creek raceway in Western Sydney. From there they visited the sites and met with the Olympics venues management to work through the detailed script that defined the work practices for the Games. The Team 2000 people also helped build the accommodation at Eastern Creek for the workforce that became known as Camp Cleanevent.

The trick was to recruit in small groups. People who heard about it by word of mouth in small towns or through organisations could come as a group and work together for the Games.

In recruiting the cleaners, the aim was to cast the net worldwide. Through the company website 400 were recruited from the UK, 50 from the USA, and so on. Advertisements and brochures were targeted towards backpackers. An Olympic Games road tour was organised through the eastern States as far north as Townsville. Staff personal networks and the company database of people who had been employed previously were activated. In each case the message was 'come and work for the Games and spread the word to your friends'. The trick was to recruit in small groups. People who heard about it by word of mouth in small towns or through organisations could come as a group **and work together** for the Games. It could be a fun thing to do and you could make some money at the same time. By Games time 2,000 were recruited; 75 percent had not worked for Cleanevent before. The company rostering technology allowed them to make detailed choices about where they would work, when and who they would work with.

The Internet was critical to recruiting, training and retaining the workforce most of whom were recruited on the promise of a two-week job that would not start for several months. Training for management and information to and from the workforce went over the Internet. Chris Arnott of Cleanevent says of this:

"We said if you want to work for us you must have a web-based address. You can have several people via the same address but we have to be able to talk to you electronically. We assisted people with AOL 100-hour packages and Hotmail registration processes.

"Once a month, increasing to once per fortnight in the lead-up, we sent out communications about the Games; the venues; who they'd be bunking with; details on the jobs; their uniform shirt size; and questionnaires to gather details – helping to decide where to allocate them – everything from sponsor hospitality to the night shift scrubbing toilets. The aim was to have everyone turn up on the day – uniformed, knowing what to do and wanting to do it." [40]

Camp Cleanevent: one long party – lots of hard work thrown in

"The manager for recruitment was also the manager for Camp Cleanevent. Her job was to recruit and look after the people. The flow of communications and the attention to personal details meant that by the time people arrived at the Camp many felt they knew her as a friend." [40]

All the Cleanevent area and venue managers were contracted to stay on site so they could be briefed, participate in morning and evening meetings, and fine-tune the rosters and work scripts. The camp was set up as a self-contained 'village' with recreational areas, a dining hall, a bar and even chaplains and masseuses. It was there to provide accommodation for casuals who wanted it and was home for about 800 people at the peak. It was international, like the Olympic Village, with people from all over the country and the world. The company organised its own transport to and from the job rather than rely on the ORTA/Bus 2000 system (a wise move!). It also had 24-hour administration to deal with problems and sign up people for extra work as it became available. With a pool of people in reserve the company had no problems covering for the small number of 'no-shows' at contracted sites.

Needless to say all was not trouble-free. There were payroll problems – but none of the contractors completely solved this problem. There were some complaints about cost, transport, standard of the accommodation etc. The original expectation had been that there would be a shortage of backpacker accommodation in the city and this would be expensive. In fact, there were many places with prices cheaper than expected. There was an attempt to involve the unions in a dispute over the conditions. Sensibly the Labor Council refused to buy into this. The camp had been constructed from scratch. Management was addressing details, such as carpets. In any case none of the cleaning staff were obliged to stay there. [1 29 40]

In terms of waste management at the Games, the operation was an outstanding success. The system reduced the overall amount of waste generated, and only 28 percent of this went to landfill compared to the norm of around 60–70 percent for previous events in Australia. Little glitches over signage were rapidly resolved and the public response to the colour-coded bins was 'sensational'.

Behind the scenes there were some problems with compliance. The Cleanevent area managers had to liaise with caterers to ensure that the correct bags were used and placed in the right bins for composting and recycling. Coming from a military background Craig Lovett believes in the importance of communications. For the Games he set up Cleanevent 'help desks' in all the contract venues and linked these with a radio, pager and mobile phone network that allowed communication through the company control centre at Eastern Creek with any of the 150 area supervisors. All enquiries, comments and incidents were logged, responded to immediately (non-cleaning issues by referral to the SOCOG venue managers) and analysed for recurrent or systemic problems that needed attention. Summing up the Games operation Chris Arnott said:

"Most of this is classic management stuff, especially the motivators: have fun; be part of a team; hands-on stuff where management are workers – at least it is for us. What is different is that we bring to it an attitude from the events industry. The client is not the person contracting you it's the ultimate customer at the event – the public spectator. An example would be if a kid spills an ice-cream on a T-shirt then the aim is not just to clean up the mess but give the kid a new ice-cream and a clean T-shirt. We can clean it within 25 minutes and then get it back to him or her." [40]

More than loaves and fishes – feeding the 500,000 – sixteen times

'... the key area of catering which was our biggest worry'
Jim Sloman

Management of the catering program had many issues to consider. For example Games sponsorship protocols meant that some products could not be sold at Games venues. Pepsi soft drinks, for example, could not be sold as its competitor Coca-Cola had a sponsorship preference deal.[65] But these were minor compared to the overall scale of the task. Up to half a million people a day for

16 days all needing food and drink – plus the athletes, officials, media, staff and volunteers – everything from the silver service in the corporate boxes through to the sandwiches and burgers. Cooking, catering, serving customers, and then the dirty plates, food wastes, disposing of the packaging, and the rest!

Food handling, hygiene and a customer focus are important skills. Getting and retaining enough people trained in these skills was expected to be a problem.

Recruiting and training the people – one company's strategy

Catering was another of those areas where contracts were delayed until just before the start of the Games [65] and OCA was involved in sorting out some of the problems.[26 80] In 1998 Spotless Services Ltd (SSL) formed a joint partnership with ARAMARK Corporation USA as part of the SSL bid for catering contracts at the Games. ARAMARK had been involved in 11 previous summer and winter Olympics and provided international expertise to support the SSL local knowledge and experience. In a 'rival' partnership P&O Services joined partnership with Sodexho to also tender for the catering contract. In 1998 the P&O Services company, Berkeley Challenge, won the housekeeping and public cleaning services contract for the Olympic villages. In November 1999 Spotless Services acquired the non-food division of P&O Services including Berkeley Challenge. This resulted in SSL managing very different contracts for the villages, the venues catering team, and for the SOCOG joint venture management-secondment program where qualified chefs managed the venue catering. It also threw into confusion the balance SOCOG had been working towards in sharing the contracts between the major catering contractors – further compounding the delays in awarding contracts.[65]

The challenge for SSL was to recruit and train over 8,000 staff from a very shallow employment pool. There were four objectives: recruit early; develop simple cost-effective training; include awareness of the 'Green Games' recycling and waste management strategy; and retain the staff.[55] The company preferred to recruit using its own contacts and control its own payroll.[48] Staff were recruited from TAFE, hospitality colleges (in Australia, New Zealand and the USA), friends and family of staff, business schools (an opportunity for some overseas students to practise English skills), and athletes who didn't get to compete. There was also recruitment from a road show up the Australian east coast to Queensland and through high schools. Students couldn't be employed in security but could do catering, and a junior component in the award was negotiated to allow for this. The recruiting strategy involved three strategic elements:

- Borrowing competence. This involved Olympic work placements for staff and students from TAFE colleges[*] and schools with vocational education training programs. It provided learning activities that were recognised as part of existing study programs. SSL also borrowed specialist staff from across its operations in Australia, and New Zealand, and internationally through ARAMARK.

- Buying competence. Recruiting people without previous hospitality or housekeeping experience who were keen to get a start in the industry. Recruits undertook nationally accredited training at Certificate 1 or II level. All supervisors and managers completed training at Certificate IV level.

- Building competence. An extensive internal secondment program was designed to give staff the opportunity to work at the Olympics. Skills development was critical for this program in two areas:

  - training staff with the skills they would need to perform their Olympic roles
  - preparing other staff to take on additional responsibilities as they stepped up to replace staff on secondment.

The government provided $600,000 for training. This was tailored to housekeeping of the Olympic and Media Villages. It included SOCOG orientation, customer service and skills-based training. The initial stage of the training was designed to aid retention of the Games staff. It provided information and experiential learning to groups of 15–20 people at training points across Australia and New Zealand using SSL trainers and private providers. This was followed by workplace-specific training at the venues in Sydney around the themes of 'know your company, know your venue, know your team, and know your job' – closely mirroring SOCOG's key training requirements. A unique feature of the training outcome was a colour-coded 'training passport', to be worn at all

---

[*] Including from South Australia as we noted earlier.

COURTESY OF SSL

Games catering staff fed half a million people a day.

times behind the SOCOG accreditation pass. Because of the number of inexperienced staff, safety was a primary concern. OH&S staff rated all potentially dangerous equipment as either red or yellow. Red equipment was only to be used by people who had completed training and obtained a licence to operate it. Yellow meant no specific safety licence required but safe operating procedures were posted nearby. Further training was provided to about a third of the staff who went on to work at the Paralympics. This included 'Paralympic sensitivity' and orientation to the venues modified with ramps and rails etc.

One of the problems created by the recruitment and training strategies was that they were too successful. SSL planned on some loss of staff over the Games, but this didn't happen. Tim Catterall of SSL said:

"We didn't lose staff – they were there for themselves and for home country people – like the Ashfield guy who loved talking to the Yugoslav team – I'm

an Australian and also Yugoslav ... German, Philippino, Korean etc. We didn't have a language tagging program for placing staff with particular country delegations – it just sorted itself out on the job –athletes finding people who could talk their language. And the 'no-shows' turned up. The Labor Council helped ensure we had an efficient transport network – overcame problems of poor train timing, no bus services etc. The work ... on this helped us retain the early staff. Sometimes we applaud the award as helping retention – there was also pride in the culture –something uniquely Australian." [48]

We noted earlier how the catering operation ran into an overstaffing problem at Games time.

"In the venues not as much food was sold as we anticipated. People stayed longer in the venues – there was not a lot of catering in the venues, and they didn't leave to eat. Some brought their own food. The result was laying off staff which we were unable to absorb in the villages which were already fully staffed and retaining these staff. We had a lot of help from the Labor Council and SOCOG in finding employment and negotiating reduced hours. Working closely with the unions ... opens the people and both organisations to a common level of understanding." [48]

As for the 'closed loop' recycling operation:

"SOCOG were engineering a more collaborative approach – getting various industry groups to work together ... caterers, security, cleaners all part of the total delivery team. SOCOG could do this because of the size of the event and it changed attitudes – everyone involved in the customer outcome. It went beyond the product. SOCOG built the social need for a different outcome. Why do we need an event to do this?" [48]

> "SOCOG were engineering a more collaborative approach – getting various industry groups to work together ... caterers, security, cleaners all part of the total delivery team. SOCOG could do this because of the size of the event and it changed attitudes."

Selling cooperation – partnerships in merchandising

Yet another part of this partnership in service delivery can be seen in the area of Games merchandising.

Concept Sports, a small Melbourne-based company, won the contract rights to be the exclusive Retail Merchandising Concessionaire for the Sydney 2000 Olympic Games. Gary March from Concept began working inside the SOCOG office in January 1998 and spent two years planning and preparing the merchandising project. This is another example of SOCOG choosing to work closely with a company as a partner rather than just a contractor.

Bernie Smith, the Shop Distributive and Allied Workers (SDA) organiser, was involved with the other unions in negotiating the Olympic Award and went on to develop a mirror enterprise award for retail workers who would be working with Concept Sports and SOCOG specifically for the Games merchandising operation. He worked closely with Gary March from the company. Gary says he 'learnt a lot about HR and IR practices in the process'. Bernie went on to be part of the Unions 2000 team at Sydney Olympic Park and could compare the experience of the well planned and organised merchandising workforce with the chaos in many of the other service areas.

A key to success of the project was that it was fully integrated into SOCOG. Gary was involved in organising the merchandising for the torch relay and then the Games period but this meant working with all sectors of the Games organisation:

- Venue designers and architects, caterers, cleaners and waste collection to negotiate the spaces required by each group.

- Product suppliers for minimum packaging in accordance with 'Green Games' principles and waste management. It was interesting that many of the suppliers grumbled but complied because they would only get the contract if they complied.

Because of the early start the merchandising project was the first to achieve its target for recruiting, training and accrediting the workforce of 1,500 (1,600 at peak). This had been one of Atlanta's disaster areas with high staff turnover and accreditation problems, whereas Concept only needed to recruit 10 percent more than required to make up for 'no-shows' etc. Much of this recruiting was done through the SDA with some help from the MEAA. Concept advertised in SDA's journal: 1,200 forms with indication of interest, availability and experience were returned to the union and fed through to Concept Sports. In return the company gave the union open access to the workforce for membership recruiting and around 1,100 of the total of 1,600 joined either the SDA direct or Unions 2000 after it was formed in January 2000. Recruiting workers through the union was seen as an advantage in getting people with some knowledge of retailing. There was also recruiting through TAFE colleges for students. All employees were trained well before the Games. This involved the three-phase

SOCOG training approach with the work skills component being organised through the company. This skill training was short term and job specific. Retail competency-based training through a national training provider usually takes place over 12 months and this was not possible (and not seen as appropriate) for a two-week event.[54 69]

The company exceeded sales targets by 300 percent assisted by the enormous enthusiasm for Olympic merchandise, particularly by the Australian spectators at the Games. Concept Sports is now a contractor for Salt Lake City against strong competition from US companies, and in contention for Athens. The Games were a great learning experience and a much bigger task than people expected. The core staff learned the need for stronger, meticulous planning, and keeping records in minute detail. The Games drew attention to the packaging issue and waste management in merchandising, but the experience of working partnerships was probably the biggest lesson. Concept now works closely with companies like Cleanevent and Visy as part of their core business. In general it now has a policy of only working with other companies where there is this kind of close partnership, even if the cost is a little higher.

On the IR front the Games Award aided recruiting by providing real incentives for people to turn up and see the job through. The pay rates were higher than the normal award (but built into the SOCOG contract) and offered a limited junior rate structure where people 18 and over were paid as adults unlike the usual age of 21 in the Shop Employees State Award. This encouraged recruitment through colleges and universities. It also provided the flexibility necessary for temporary and casual workers. Given the cost of food at Olympic venues the inclusion of free meals and transport was a bonus – which helped retain workers for the two-week period. The nature of the event meant there were always going to be issues with pay caused by sign-on/off problems but the union assisted in identifying these and the company fixed them quickly.

For the union the major benefit was the exposure of the workforce to a positive image of the unions. As Bernie Smith puts it:

"Membership fees were never going to pay the unions for the time and work required to service people through the Games. The rewarding stuff was the interaction with young people – them seeing the role of unions and how they can help. Working with the unions resulted in issues being picked up

quickly and resolved quickly. With this size of event, management couldn't be expected to pick these up like this – they had other problems and priorities – and if they had been allowed to go on they would have had an unhappy workforce down the track." [69]

Not made in Australia – so who cares?

"The Olympic goal to contribute to building a more peaceful and better world through education, mutual cooperation, solidarity and fair play must be reflected in the activities of all those associated with the Olympics, including the manufacturers of Olympic merchandise."

Michael Knight, February 1998

• • •

"The major agreement ... was the Code of Labour Practice for the Production of Licensed Goods ... The contents of the code required SOCOG Licensees to respect ILO standards in a range of important areas plus other requirements such as fair wages and appropriate training. The serious weakness of the Code was related to the follow-up monitoring of its provisions ... The SOCOG staff responsible for arranging licences did not pay sufficient attention to the Code's requirements. SOCOG itself had a half-hearted commitment to do full implementation and we failed to put enough pressure on them to bring them into line."

Alan Matheson, ACTU, September 2000

SOCOG had set itself high standards with the Bid and generated high expectations, some of which proved hard to meet. Not only was there the idea that Sydney would be the 'Green Games' but there was also an expectation that it would showcase Australian products and Australian manufacturing. But SOCOG had a tight budget and in the area of the licensed Olympic merchandise, uniforms and sporting equipment for the Games Australia would have a hard time competing with product manufactured overseas, particularly in Asia.

Some goods, especially the soft toys of Sydney Olympic mascots Syd, Millie and Olly, were labour intensive. Uniforms made in Australia would also be more expensive than overseas product. As always there are different perspectives on this aspect of the Games story but it appears that the original intention, at least at Board level, was to source both materials and manufacturing in Australia – wherever possible. What was 'possible' obviously had big dollar constraints on it. In the end a balance between competing pressures had to be found. What follows is not the whole story, but a piece of it that illustrates the importance of negotiating meaningful agreements that build relations of trust and that address people's concerns – some of which are ethical and go to the core of the Olympic values the Games ostensibly promote.

As with other areas of the SOCOG operation production of licensed goods, including Games merchandise and the uniforms, was contracted out. Bonds (part of Pacific Dunlop) and Reebok were initially awarded two of the major contracts. Both were also Games sponsors and as such 'leveraging' their contributions in return for marketing advantage and contracted business. Reebok subsequently withdrew and Nike became the Olympic sponsor to both the Games and the Australian Olympic team. [68A]

The SOCOG uniform contracts involved production of separate uniforms for the workforce and two uniforms for the athletes. Australian manufacturers were asked to make samples and quote prices for these. SOCOG was presented with prices for goods:

- made in Australia from Australian material

- made in Fiji from Australian material

- made in China, Malaysia or Indonesia from non-Australian material.

Faced with the hard economic choice SOCOG decided on the 'lesser evil' of Australian material but manufactured overseas.[37] Some production was retained here. Bonds, who manufacture T-shirts, made most of the adult sizes in Australia and contracted children's sizes to China. Much of the decision-making and contracts for uniform manufacture occurred early and without consultation with the rest of the industry or the unions. In May 1997 a number of employers contacted the Textile Clothing and Footwear Union of Australia (TCFUA) expressing concern. They had expected that goods would be made in Australia, especially after providing samples and quotes.

Fair wear?

The labour movement has a long history of supporting local manufacture but it also accepts that we live in a global market-place. The bottom line position is to ensure that workers rights are protected wherever goods are produced. In this it has the support

COURTESY OF THE WOOLMARK COMPANY

Fair Wear?
Games
uniforms for
athletes and
volunteers.

COURTESY OF BONDS

of the International Labour Organisation (ILO), a tripartite body representing governments, employers and unions, that has a set of internationally agreed labour standards. This is an ethical issue of global significance. Recently the UN Secretary General, Kofe Annan, initiated a call for a 'Global Compact' on standards for environmental sustainability and human rights, including four of the core ILO standards. The Labor Council of NSW and the Australian Council of Trade Unions (ACTU) raised with SOCOG their concern about contracts being let (or subcontracted) offshore to countries with a poor record of labour rights violations. They were particularly concerned about use of child labour and laws that prohibit unions and collective bargaining in violation of the ILO agreements. Initially the concern was about manufacture in China where 'freedom of association' (a key ILO condition) is patently not permitted. What the unions became aware of much later – largely as a result of the continuing disagreements with SOCOG – was that there were also ethical concerns over manufacture in Fiji (see box), Taiwan, Pakistan and a number of other countries.

> In Fiji textile workers wages had traditionally been tied to those of sugar cane cutters, the lowest in the Fiji economy. A 'free trade zone' (FTZ) set up after the Rambuka coup in 1987 cut textile workers hourly wages from A$1.10 to A$0.50 – less than half the wages of sugar cane cutters. Union officials were jailed, the garment union locked out of the zone and a system of 'indenture' introduced where Asian workers imported into Fiji worked for even less than the FTZ rate – with their wages sent direct to their families at home. Even now, 13 years later, FTZ wages are only A$1.20 – still half the sugar cane cutters rate of A$2.40 per hour.

SOCOG initially denied there was a problem.[*] Rather than allaying concerns this aroused suspicion. Late in 1997 the NSW government brokered an agreement between SOCOG and the Labor Council on the Code of Practice for the Production of Licensed Goods. Michael Knight claimed this as a first in the history of the Olympic movement. It also represents a significant compromise within the spirit of collaboration between the unions and SOCOG. As one of the Minister's staffers put it:

"The unions accepted that there would be some offshore production where we couldn't produce here or couldn't meet the price in return for a respect for labour rights in overseas production." [33]

---

[*] See chronology of this dispute in Appendix 5, page 212.

Worth the paper it's printed on?

Unfortunately even the best worded agreements need commitment on both sides to make them work. SOCOG's commitment to the Code of Practice is questionable. Eighteen months after the Code was signed, TCFUA, the Labor Council and ACTU were still trying to get a list of the production facilities and a clear understanding of the processes by which SOCOG would monitor and enforce the Code. One supposedly objective investigation by SOCOG of compliance with the freedom of association clause in production facilities in Fiji, Indonesia and Malaysia reported back that there was no problem as 'no-one was forced to join a union'! Attempts to have Anna Booth (a SOCOG board member and former Secretary of TCFUA) visit Fiji were blocked. What became clear was that intentionally or otherwise SOCOG was protecting the contractors from scrutiny of the conditions under which their subcontractors were producing the uniforms and licensed goods. The problem was never with the primary contractor where the company had control over its own workforce. What was unclear were the conditions for workers where work was sub-, and often sub-subcontracted.

> Unfortunately even the best worded agreements need commitment on both sides to make them work. SOCOG's commitment to the Code of Practice is questionable.

In part SOCOG people have relied on a technicality. Uniforms are not Olympic 'Licensed Goods' but are covered by the contract with the lead sponsor (some of which is provided as VIK). Part also seems to be embarrassment at having not considered this issue important in the early letting of contracts. One thing not learned in all of this was the art of admitting there was a problem and sitting everyone down to find a workable solution.[16A]

In August 1999, over two years after first raising the issue, the TCFUA went public with its campaign for union participation in monitoring factory conditions for the production of Games uniforms. Three months later the dispute was formally resolved. SOCOG agreed to bring back the manufacture of 15,000 uniform shirts from overseas manufacture. SOCOG agreed to licensees providing names and addresses of all contractors (and known subcontractors), and agreed to ensure nominated union officials were given access to monitor compliance with the principles of the Code. The union press release acknowledges the assistance given by the Bonds company in resolving the dispute.

So the unions finally had access to inspect production facilities; but no resources went into following it up. All the letters, all the overseas trips, all the time of SOCOG and union officials ... if only a small fraction of this had been spent on actually visiting the sites, talking to the people and reporting back. But the TCFUA is a small union with limited resources and the Labor Council, as we have seen, had a mammoth task organising the Unions 2000 initiative for the Games itself. The ACTU was in the middle of some major changes. And SOCOG had no incentive to revisit this issue or provide resources for independent monitoring of some of these overseas production facilities. So, perhaps a missed opportunity – or is it one for the future?

We can hope

The unions learned much in the process of this dispute, such as how 'front' companies in Hong Kong and Taiwan are used as a cover for production in China, and what conditions are like in the FTZs in many countries. As a result, relationships were built with unions in Indonesia, Fiji, Bangladesh, Pakistan and Malaysia. The TCFUA files contain letters from Catholic priests and non-governmental organisations involved in labour rights issues all across the region. If networks and relationships are built on communication then the Pacific human rights network has been significantly strengthened. None of this would have occurred if the licensed goods contracting process had been open and transparent and SOCOG had shown a genuine commitment to monitoring and enforcing the Code of Practice. It is unfortunate these lessons had to be learned the hard way.

For the future we hope the Olympic movement worldwide has learned that questions over the human rights of people involved in producing Olympic goods (wherever they are produced) can seriously tarnish the image of the Games. Athens in 2004, Beijing in 2008 and future organising committees now have both a model agreement and a protocol for monitoring it. The model is simple. It includes basic minimum internationally agreed standards and the monitoring of these by responsible trade unionists who understand what to look for and what questions to ask. It is up to the Olympic movement to ensure that these basic standards are met and the ethical reputation of the Games upheld.

We can hope with Michael Knight, who said in March 1998 of the Licensed Goods Code of Practice:

"I look forward to the implementation of this agreement having positive impact on labour standards in the production of SOCOG/SPOC licensed products. It is also my hope that this Code of Practice will set a benchmark for future Olympic Host Cities so that labour rights continue to be considered essential to the Olympic Ideal." *

Whether this happens, or whether the principle falls at the next hurdle, remains to be seen. With Athens we may indeed hope. With Beijing we can but hope that the dialogue with the world that will take place in the lead-up to the Games in 2008 will convince the leadership in China that this aspect of human rights is an essential part of the Olympic ideal.

When the wheels nearly fell off – the transport stories

The transport of spectators to and from the Games events was one of the outstanding successes of the Games. Compared with the debacle of transport in Atlanta, Sydney's achievement was exemplary. Some of this is undoubtedly due to the early completion of the venues allowing the transport system to learn and adjust to the demands of the Games through the series of test events. The success is all the more outstanding coming as it did on the heels of a series of major problems in the months leading up to the Games (train crashes, derailments, signalling and communications disasters). What is interesting is the process of collaboration through which these lessons were learned and, as we will see, the near disaster that came to a head on the eve of the Games in the area where the shift to a culture of collaboration had not occurred.

Six million spectators, not to mention the many thousands of athletes, officials, media and Games workforce, were delivered to the events largely without incident. In addition the 'live sites' across the city entertained 1.5 million others. Most of this was achieved by the public transport system.

First let us explore the success story. Six million spectators, not to mention the many thousands of athletes, officials, media and Games workforce, were delivered to the events largely without incident. In addition the 'live sites' across the city entertained 1.5 million others. Most of this was achieved by the public transport system. Indeed the message that public transport and not the private car was the preferred way to

---

* Letter to Jenny George, President ACTU, March 1998.

go was heeded to such an extent that the anticipated road gridlock problems simply did not occur. Those who used the roads found travel, if anything, easier than usual. We have touched on some of the elements of crowd control by spectator services at the entry and exit to venues and 'live sites'. Marshalling and the more subtle process of performers providing brief attractions slowed the mass movements to more manageable flows of people through critical transport points.

The public transport system

Transport coordination was handled by the Olympic Roads and Transport Authority (ORTA). This was kept within the control of government departments and not SOCOG. In Chapter 2 we saw how this meant that transport was not included in the negotiations between SOCOG, Games contractors and the relevant service sector unions that led to the Olympic Games Award.

ORTA was more comfortable with, and better able to coordinate, the core public transport system than to manage the private bus contractors and their staff who would also be needed for the Games. The Public Transport Union (PTU)* had given thought to the potential problems over the years between the Bid and the Games. It recognised that public transport could be seen as an attractive way for people to travel. In particular the rail link to Olympic Park would be critical to moving very large numbers of people but there would need to be additional staff and training of drivers, signallers etc. Approaches to government were made as far back as 1996 and in late 1998 a high level steering group within ORTA was formed to explore potential issues in public transport. These were then passed down through the various committees of the union to focus groups of rank and file members and the suggestions from these passed back up the chain.

The major innovation supported by the union and its membership was the concept of 'sector running' – creating a dedicated shuttle system between the City and Olympic Park and isolating this from the rest of the rail network, which could then operate on normal timetables. The thinking was that most people, especially those unfamiliar with the system, would choose a route to the Games

* Technically the NSW branch of the Rail Tram and Bus Industry Union (RTBIU).

through one of two main hubs: Central Station in the City or
Blacktown in the West. By running dedicated trains between these
and Sydney Olympic Park Station (on special timetables coordinated with the main events) the rest of the system would be
relatively unaffected. A similar bus shuttle system was planned for
public transport to and from the Games. A supplementary system
using private sector buses and coaches was organised for
movement of athletes, officials, special groups of workers etc.[66]

This approach had support from senior managers in State Rail
who recognised that management-worker collaboration would be
needed for the Games. September 2000 was projected to be like
scaling up the experience of New Year celebrations and the Games
test-event movements by about a factor of four. The joint planning
helped maintain a sense of confidence through the period when
NSW Premier Carr was saying that it was transport rather than the
management of the venues, tickets and people to work for the
Games that was causing him to lose sleep.

In the lead-up to the Games, State Rail had recruited and trained
120 new drivers and guards. Three months out it recruited a
further 800 casuals to support existing staff in cleaning, crowd
control and assisting the volunteer 'rovers' in directing the public
through the transport system. Around 500 of these casuals were
subsequently employed permanently, filling a bulge in vacancies as
many regular rail staff had postponed retirement plans until after
the Olympics. From the union perspective the recruitment was
essential for the success of the Games but had the unintended
effect of reducing the overtime of regular staff and a loss of
income in some cases of around 20 percent. This was picked up in
the negotiations for an Olympic award for public transport
workers that recognised the Games pressures. The NSW Labor
Council worked to ensure that the outcome did not breach the
agreement with the government that the Games would not be
used to press special claims. The result was that rail workers
received the flat rate $2.50 per hour granted to all public sector
workers plus a $3.00 per hour all-purpose rate for the Games
period.

The collaboration had a number of other human relations
features that contributed to a highly motivated workforce.

■ In line with the practice across the public sector, senior management volunteered for secondment to Games duties. Senior

managers worked alongside blue-collar workers directing crowds on station platforms.

- Senior union delegates were rostered off normal duties for the Games period, equipped with mobile phones and worked alongside management in the rail network to sort out problems as they arose.

- Management organised lunch packs for the workers, rostering appropriate breaks for meals and providing fridges for food.

The union view is that 'simple things like this helped build morale'. For at least one visitor to the Games the result was memorable. The CEO of a Canadian company had brought his disabled father to the Games and chose to travel by public transport. Rail staff called ahead to organise reception at Sydney Olympic Park and similarly on his return through Central to Bondi. He said he'd never experienced a system like this before.

The rest is history. The timetable worked, staff were trained to the job, they felt recognised by managers and the public, and when it was all over Premier Carr congratulated everyone for their contribution to the success of the Games. For the union the lesson is about the power of involving members in the solution to a problem. State Secretary Nick Lewocki says:

"It is not about showing people that workers can be flexible and highlighting the role of the unions – this is self-evident and it really isn't a new lesson – it's about consulting with the workforce, and I mean the workforce not just the union representatives, raising the problems and asking them what to do about it, and listening. This is what builds respect and motivation and pride. The union has a 150-year history in this business; managers and the latest management tools come and go. For us it is all about how you move people and create goodwill. Whether these are long-term lessons or we drift back to the idea that managers manage and workers work – we'll have to see." [66]

The private bus industry

The contrast with the organisation of the private bus contract sector of the transport system is stark. In the days before the Games the wheels fell off the system. What is perhaps the most amazing aspect of this story is that the system was made to work. There was intervention on a number of fronts, largely coordinated through the office of the Games Minister. The collaboration was as though, 'when the wheels fell off a large number of people got under it, held the bus system up until others could put some new wheels in place and got the system moving again'. Of all the crises faced by the Games this was, above all others, the one where a major disaster was most narrowly averted. As such it can provide some valuable lessons for the future.

The Bus and Coach Association, representing most operators in the industry, realised transport would be a big issue for the Games and contributed $200,000 to the Bid. Given that Australia had a limited supply of buses, and safety standards would limit the potential for temporary imports, it foresaw a major role for the private sector in the Games. The Association's Deputy Director, Geoff Ferris, observed the problems in Atlanta and, on return, was seconded to SOCOG on the Olympic Transport Task Force for Strategic Planning and eventually, after its creation, to ORTA.

In the days before the Games the wheels fell off the system. What is perhaps the most amazing aspect of this story is that the system was made to work ... Of all the crises faced by the Games this was, above all others, the one where a major disaster was most narrowly averted.

The initial challenge was to organise a lot of buses from a large industry with many small operators. Most fleets have fewer than five buses. There are few big companies and even these are not big businesses. For the operation to work the small operator had to have some ownership of the task so the Bus and Coach Association was encouraged to set up Bus 2000. This eventually delivered 3,500 buses, from 1,200 operators, and 7,000 staff (5,200 drivers, 1,800 support staff) through the industry in NSW and sister organisations in other States. [36]

Driver recruitment

As a 24-hour a day operation the Games needed a larger pool of drivers than usual, and much larger than was available. There were always vacancies for bus drivers, lots of overtime covering spare shifts by existing drivers, and significant use of casual drivers. To illustrate the point: the Sydney Easter Show survives because it is in the school holidays and the school bus drivers are therefore available. So Bus 2000 needed to source drivers for the industry rather than just for the Olympics.

Operators were asked for lists of ex-drivers – people they could say 'yes he can drive' and 'yes I'd let him drive my bus again'. Given the extent of 'casual' driving, the existing driver pool was an unknown quantity. To reach casuals and people with a licence who might come back to work for the Olympics, the Department of Transport sent a letter introducing Bus 2000 to all registered bus drivers with an 'expression of interest' form. One of the problems was attracting people who were not Sydney based. The complexity of Sydney's road system is legendary and about half the drivers eventually recruited were from outside Sydney. These would need accommodation and, critically, would need orientation to the road system.

Driver training involved two phases. Drivers received videos and information sent to their homes. They then attended a two-day TAFE course that gave them an orientation to the Games, route maps, layout of venues etc. This was a big ask for some. All training was unpaid (though meals, accommodation and transport to Sydney were covered). Many drivers, who may have left school at 15, were uncomfortable sitting in classrooms being told how to work by an academic. Success was patchy depending on the skills of the TAFE staff.

People management – it is the little things that cause big problems

A simplified Olympic Transport Award for round the clock rostering was developed with a 'flat hourly rate for any day, any time'. This simplified payroll for management. For workers it provided ease and certainty in determining their Games period pay. It also made for equality in rostering as there was no advantage or disadvantage for day, night or weekend work. People working unsocial night-time shifts had easier work on quieter roads. All received the same rate of pay. ORTA designed the rosters and work schedules and Bus 2000 allocated the drivers to these. The rate averaged $21.70 per hour plus superannuation, accommodation, meals and transport for the drivers.

Unfortunately it is often the little things that cause major catastrophes. For driver accommodation and catering, ORTA was dependent on SOCOG who had contracts with most providers in Sydney. ORTA planning had been done independently of SOCOG and, understandably, bus drivers were low down SOCOG's priority list for these facilities. Most driver accommodation was a long way from the depots, mainly in schools – but school holidays were too late for the buses and drivers coming in early so they had to be found other, often even more scattered and less satisfactory accommodation. There was a problem with transport for drivers, getting them from accommodation to their depot for work at all hours of the day and night. ORTA planned the driver-transport schedules and Bus 2000 was to deliver it. It didn't work as planned. Food was also highly variable in standard. An individual might get a meal in a restaurant one day and from a mass caterer the next – but the drivers all knew what each other was getting.

Young workers learn early that if you want to know what is really going on in any enterprise you ask the secretaries, caretakers or the drivers. Bus drivers could see for themselves (or hear from other drivers) what was happening all over the city – and could make unfavourable comparisons.

These problems were compounded as they were across other contract areas by the steep 'ramp-up' at the start of the Games:

- The late decisions on bands and ceremonies meant SOCOG and ORTA didn't have clear numbers for people to be transported or how many would need to use the limited accommodation and catering facilities. The early stages were thus forever trying to catch up, solving today's problems but not getting ahead of those that would come tomorrow.

- Many of the buses were not even in the city until the day of the Opening Ceremony. They were still being used as school buses until the day before when the school holidays started in the other eastern States of Victoria and Queensland.[*]

- There were problems with accreditation. Drivers' passes were not available when they arrived in Sydney.

- Then drivers got lost and the government put out a call for Sydney people to volunteer as drivers assistants – 'map holders' to help drivers find their way around. These were recruited, accredited, uniformed and given instruction in what they needed to do and on the road within 24 hours, but by this time steps had been taken to take control of the situation at the highest level.

Geoff Ferris sees this as:

"the usual teething problems with a new start-up but the 'ramp-up' here was unprecedented, and fixing it overnight was not an option in transport. The result was a lot of frustrated drivers, many not knowing their way

---

[*] Many needed to travel over 1,000 kilometres to reach Sydney.

around, worried about everything: shifts, meals, accommodation etc. Some coped – gave it time to settle in. Some were vocal and made an issue out of it and we heard from these, but it was not as bad as it was made out – some went home – not many." [36]

The view from the other side of this mess is less complacent. The initial walkout involved three drivers – three who were rostered to pick up and deliver 150 other drivers from their accommodation to the depot – so they in turn could start work collecting and delivering busloads of 50 essential Games people to their venues across the city. Little things contribute to major catastrophes!

The initial walkout involved three drivers – three who were rostered to pick up and deliver 150 other drivers from their accommodation to the depot – so they in turn could start work collecting and delivering busloads of 50 essential Games people to their venues across the city. Little things contribute to major catastrophes!

Industrial collaboration?

The Transport Workers Union (TWU) covered workers on the Games construction sites at Homebush Bay and other venues. Members were involved in excavation, delivery of concrete and building materials, waste disposal, and as service providers to construction companies and subcontractors. It was a party to the agreements between the OCA and the building unions. Initially not covered by the Olympic Award, it negotiated site allowances and was part of the site agreements including induction, training, OH&S and site safety programs. For the Games it covered drivers involved in supply of goods to the Olympic site. This involved close coordination with the Linfox transport group and with the Linfox logistics team that coordinated scheduling of all supplies to Olympic Park venues. The logistics included intense security screening of all supplies and coordinating delivery between midnight and 8 am, the only hours when outside transport deliveries were permitted.

Though not involved in Unions 2000 or the original Olympic Award, the TWU worked with the Labor Council and negotiated agreements with Adecco on rates for transport workers employed through the OLN. It also negotiated with SOCOG and the Road Transport Federation and variations to the Olympic Award were made in August 2000, shortly before the Games. The late change to the award caused severe problems for some contractors who had negotiated agreements for supply of services based on previous pay rates. The new rates pushed costs for contractors well above what was expected when they negotiated the contracts.

Some organisations, particularly those from overseas, refused to accept and pay the additional costs insisting instead that the original contracted prices were binding.[15A] With an event the size and complexity of the Games it is clear that pay rates and pricing need to be resolved well in advance. This was the basis of the IR strategy developed by the Labor Council and SOCOG. The lack of involvement of the TWU in this strategy remains a sore point for many organisations.

The union makes no secret of the fact that it was concerned primarily with getting good rates for its members and using the Games as an opportunity for recruiting.[18] The negotiating tactics were described as tough but the results were broadly in line with the award conditions of other workers in the Games services and the public sector.[1 18] Rob Forsyth said of these negotiations:

"In hindsight, all parties involved would have preferred TWU involvement earlier." [16A]

Heading for breakdown

The problem was with the people-transport organised through ORTA and Bus 2000. Late in 1999 the TWU raised with Bus 2000 and ORTA the question of training of 'lead drivers'. Anticipating problems with up to 4,000 drivers from out of Sydney and some from other parts of Australia, the TWU suggested lead drivers be trained and brought in early so they could anticipate and pick up problems that could then be tackled before they became issues. Bus 2000 stalled over releasing people from companies for training. According to Wayne Forno of the TWU:

"Bus 2000 was almost equivalent to the Bus and Coach Association. We were dealing with an employer federation who was more fearful of the TWU signing members up than taking us at our word that it was a positive step. In the end we were proved right. We trained some drivers but fewer than we hoped for and fewer than were needed." [18]

The major depot was Regents Park but people were billeted at locations as remote as Picton, Hawkesbury, Blue Mountains and Windsor.* Drivers needed shuttle buses to get to work for both start and finish of shifts. Bus 2000 had problems with the logistics of this task. Buses didn't turn up and for some drivers it required

---

* Areas to the far south, north and west, and outside the Greater Sydney region.

a 4 am start to catch the only bus to get to the depot for an 11 am
to 11 pm shift and then get back to get some sleep. Some people
were 'not being fed after a 12-hour shift' – or getting 'an apple, a
sandwich and a bottle of water'. People rostered together were not
in the same accommodation. People were in bunk/dormitory
accommodation with others on different shifts – 'being woken up
by people going on and off shift and not getting a full rest'. Like
many other areas of the Games there were payroll problems.
Accreditation was one of Sydney's success stories but by far the
greatest problems occurred with the bus drivers. Late recruitment,
lack of planning and poor communication by Bus 2000 meant that
50 percent of the accreditation applications were late. The
workforce also turned up late and insufficient time was allowed for
collection of passes.[84]

Each of these problems, on its own, might have been acceptable;
together they were too much and the general dissatisfaction
flowed over into complaints about the lack of support, accommodation, passes, uniforms, food, shifts, rosters, pay – anything and
everything!

The government steps in

A week before the Opening Ceremony the State government took
effective control of the Bus 2000 operation through OCA and
ORTA and brought in its own management to run it – a decision
at the highest level.

Bus 2000 has suggested that the government overreacted, but the
union was not the only stakeholder suggesting that things were
dangerously out of control. The police commander of the OSCC
was aware of problems with transport for Games service personnel
nearly 12 months out from the Games and had built a separate
transport system for police who were stationed in the city. His view:

*"Transport underestimated how intricate and complex it would be and they
missed simple advice on planning details. It had to be simple as this was
quickly sorted out when the transport people in defence stepped in – in
support of ORTA. Command control and communications issues are
fundamental to soldiers – foreign to commercial operators and bureaucrats
... basic stuff like not having mobile phones and faxes where needed – this
was a mess."* [38]

Michael Deegan from the Minister's office had seen for himself
some of the problems.

"Ten days out from the Games Regents Park [in Sydney's inner-West] was a huge bus depot for Bus 2000. It was under-serviced, under-engineered – they had had no idea how to do it. The TWU had been saying for a long time there were problems but no-one they spoke to believed them. To be fair the buses had worked fine through the test events but these were one-off single events – no-one had done the multiple operations for transport to all events at the same time. Bus 2000 and the Bus and Coach Association would say the government panicked but it was a mess. We were dealing with a series of essentially industrial problems that no-one in the management seemed to understand. The union had photos of the accommodation, details of the hours people were working, problems with timekeeping, the logistics of scheduling, the roster, the question of food. They had the information in detail on where it was going wrong. The company wasn't listening and there was a real risk of more drivers walking off the job. This was a particular issue with the 500 drivers rostered to transport the media. Not only were these shifts arduous but out of town drivers were scared of making a mistake and getting their picture on the front page of the papers." [26]

Michael Deegan called in a heavyweight transport management team from NSW State Transit, Sport and Recreation, and Action Buses (the ACT government system). Senior departmental managers brought their senior operations staff and effectively took control, working alongside the Bus 2000 people.

"The cooperation was amazing. I rang Kate Carnell [ACT Liberal Chief Minister] and said who I wanted and she said 'he's on his way'." [26]

Bus 2000 brought in coaches to use as buses and State Transit released 500 buses that were held in reserve to meet spectator and general public transport emergencies. SOCOG accreditation sent a team out to Regents Park to get on top of pass and uniform problems. Essential communications technology was put in place and people who knew how to manage were put in to supervise key functions. It was running to catch up but the system was made to work.

Fuelling goodwill

Apart from sorting out the logistical mess the goodwill had to be re-established. The TWU negotiated a $4 per hour increase for media drivers and later an across the board payment of $2 per hour (and the $1.50 per hour Games bonus) for all the drivers. This was awarded as compensation for excess travel time, driver familiarisation time, accreditation delays, and the problems with accommodation, meals, uniforms and licensing. Workforce meetings were held over the course of the week and in the end it worked. No time was lost to industrial dispute. Some say the union 'had everyone on toast'.[17] Others, that the issues were 'not compensatable' – that the solution should have been to throw more money at the problem, not the people. If uniforms were needed then get more and quicker, and find ways of drivers getting more sleep.[36] In fact more people were brought in to make the system work and the failure to anticipate the problem was on both sides. The unions had signed off on accommodation and meal arrangements. The pressure was initially coming from the drivers rather than the union. In any case these issues were symptoms rather than the cause of the problem.

What emerges from this is a sense of amazing goodwill among the drivers and the willingness of the stakeholders to sort out major problems in the interest of keeping the show on the road. And in the end it worked. People got to where they needed to be and people, even those who were unhappy, realised it was not all bad and most of it was fun. Geoff Ferris says:

"For all the talk of unhappy drivers, I haven't met a driver or operator who has said he wouldn't do it again."

His lesson from this:

"The little things matter. Little issues were big issues, they mounted up when people were under pressure." [36]

But underneath this there is a clear example of failure to build the relations of trust and respect between the major parties and between management and the workers that was so much a feature of most of the Games. One has to ask what would have been the outcome if this kind of adversarial industrial relations had been the norm across the rest of the workforce?

And now a word from our sponsors ...

But seriously, the Olympic Games can not be conducted and Olympic teams can not participate without the contribution and financial support of the business community. For the athletes attending the Sydney 2000 Olympic Games, free travel and accommodation was provided from revenue raised by Olympic sponsorship programs. While the IOC managed the global televi-sion rights and the worldwide Olympic Partner Program, SOCOG was responsible for the domestic sponsorship program. This generated more revenue than the Atlanta domestic sponsorship program, in a marketplace a fraction of the size of the USA. The IOC marketing report states:

"The Sydney 2000 Olympic Games local sponsorship programme was the most financially successful domestic programme in Olympic history, generating US$492 million in revenue. The programme more than doubled the targeted Sydney Bid revenue and generated more revenue than the Atlanta 1996 domestic sponsorship programme in a marketplace that is nearly 15 times smaller. To provide a legacy and support to Australian sport, the Australian Olympic Committee received US$125 million in Olympic marketing funds, and the New South Wales government received US$367.5 million for the construction of sport facilities." *

Challenging for SOCOG was the high percentage of 'value in kind' sponsorships where goods and services were committed to the Games, rather than hard currency. When budget constraints began to bite, it was not possible to convert VIK into other more needy projects.

We have referred a number of times to the budgetary crises faced by the Games. Challenging for SOCOG was the high percentage of 'value in kind' sponsorships where goods and services were committed to the Games, rather than hard currency. When budget constraints began to bite, it was not possible to convert VIK into other more needy projects. Equally challenging for sponsors was the constant stream of negative publicity, forcing some to wonder if the value of their sponsorship was bleeding away with the countless gallons of ink used to print yet another negative Olympic media story.

Key to the success of the sponsor program was the two-way commitment of both SOCOG and sponsor to work in close partnership. Not only was SOCOG the 'customer' of the sponsor, each sponsor was also a valued 'customer' of SOCOG. Generally, this led to close collaboration and joint working parties to plan the operations and solve problems. Many sponsors seconded specialist staff to work with SOCOG, some for six years.

Sponsors chose to participate in the Sydney 2000 Olympic Games for many reasons but, for most, the opportunity to involve their staff, directly or indirectly in the Games, was an essential

---

* The International Olympic Committee 2000 Marketing Report, prepared by Meridian Management SA for the IOC, 2001.

ingredient. Many sponsors organised their employee participation programs in ways that aligned personal and corporate values with the values of Olympism – excellence, commitment, accomplishment, quality, experience, courage, friendship and community.

We have already touched on some of these aspects of participation and the two-way benefits in the story of the packaging, cleaning and waste management alliance. We close this section with just a few examples from among the many others. To those who have similar, or better, stories all we can say is sorry – and please do tell them within your own organisations, your networks and to the wider world because this story of collaboration has many faces. Jim Sloman was fond of saying that 'the Olympic Games is like a huge jigsaw puzzle – and nobody gets to find all the pieces'! Here are a few more of those pieces.

Calling the world

Many people saw, heard or read about the Games. For a large section of the world this was **the** news for two weeks. Telstra, a major supporter and contributor to the Sydney Bid, was the official telecommunications partner for the Games and built the 'millennium network' to carry voice, data and satellite services for all competition and non-competition venues. Given the huge dependence of the modern Olympic Games on technology, significant collaboration with other technology partners, chiefly IBM, Panasonic, Samsung, Xerox and Kodak, was critical to the success of the entire project.

The Telstra Olympic Team was formed six years out from the Games. It selected people who were particularly interested in working on the project and had some of the initial 200 working with the SOCOG headquarters team. By Games time the number had reached 2,500 with staff seconded throughout the organisation. Additional training to help the team prepare for this unique period was provided on top of the SOCOG-prescribed orientation, job and venue training.

The benefits to these staff are many. For the organisation the key lessons were about

"building accountability ... at line management; reinforcing the management principles of good listening and team involvement; proactively nullifying issues before they become difficult".[88]

For HR Manager, Mark Chilcott, one of the more significant outcomes was greater flexibility demonstrated by both managers and employees. Typically, many in the team felt the sense of loss at the end of the Games. Some needed counselling services to overcome difficulties with assimilating into their pre-Games roles.[*] Brian Pilbeam, who led the Telstra Olympic Team, shared his own experience as a Vietnam veteran to assist the team in accepting that the Games were over. It was time to move on with their lives!

More than green and gold socks

Pacific Dunlop provided a wide range of products for the Games. We have touched on several already, notably the Olex PVC-free cabling used in the construction program. Typical of Kevin Aldred who ran the company's Olympic sponsorship program, when electricians complained about working with the new material he bought them all specialist pliers. There was no problem with the material from then on. Bonds, the company manufacturing T-shirts and other Olympic garments, was also part of the Pacific Dunlop group.

The promotion saw green and gold socks worn by stars of many Australian TV shows and even the mounted police horses! Every guest at the Opening Ceremony also received a pair of the legendary green and gold socks.

One of the initiatives taken up by a number of companies and used in Games promotions was the 'green and gold socks' program. This project, recommended by a Pacific Dunlop employee, resulted in the production of 800,000 pairs of green and gold socks – each pair with one green and one gold. A percentage of the revenue from sales went directly to the AOC for the preparation of the Australian Olympic team. The promotion saw green and gold socks worn by stars of many Australian TV shows and even the mounted police horses! Every guest at the Opening Ceremony also received a pair of the legendary green and gold socks.

Other goods supplied to the Games by the Pacific Dunlop group included underwear for the women's Olympic team, gloves for doping control and food preparation, 200,000 condoms, tyres,

---

[*] This was a common feature of the post-Games experience. It was also reported by Westpac (see below). Many of the core staff of the major sponsors (and SOCOG staff) were left feeling that nothing could replace the Games as the highlight of their careers. They did not relish returning to the 'humdrum existence' of their previous work.

servicing and supply of batteries for buses and coaches and battery back-up, pillows, mattress protectors, uniforms, T-shirts, underwear, mountain bikes, helmets, tennis balls and racquets, golf bags and a few more. One suspects that if Pacific Dunlop had not sold off its food division some years before it would have been feeding the Games as well!

The company's Olympic team was kept very small, with just Kevin Aldred and two staff, but an Olympic committee brought together representatives of each brand. One of the key Olympic marketing strategies was to encourage and reward 'performance excellence'. The Personal Best Program gave winners throughout the organisation peer recognition, acknowledgement in the special personal best newsletter, and Olympic merchandise or tickets as tangible rewards. The program was the first of its kind in the organisation and has been retained post Games. The ultimate prize for the 100 staff selected as the 'best of personal best' was a complete Olympic hospitality package for themselves and their partners.

Pacific Dunlop sees the benefits of Olympic sponsorship in terms of an opportunity to develop brand identification, sales of company products, staff morale, innovative thinking and 'can do' attitudes. For Kevin Aldred it also highlighted the importance of something often forgotten:

"that passion is the most important ingredient of success — for athletes and sponsors". [56]

When it all came alight

The Games had a lot of bad press — some of it justified, some just simply because good news isn't news and so small issues got blown up. A lot of this turned around at the time of the torch relay. Negotiations with and the support of the Aboriginal community permitted this to start at Uluru,* the symbolic centre of the continent, and wend its way through many small towns as well as major cities, drawing the community into the Games spirit.

A number of Games sponsors also signed up to be sponsors of the Olympic torch relay including the 'presenting partner' AMP. Based on the experience of previous Games, sponsors were aware of the potential of the relay to capture the imagination of the

---

* Known as Ayers Rock to some.

When it all came alight.
Over land (and under water)
the torch relay linked many
Australian communities to
the Sydney Games.

population. It had already had a profound effect on people throughout the Pacific. In Australia it was to mark the turning point for the scepticism about the Games in Australia. The arrival of the torch was, for many communities, the point at which the whole event literally and metaphorically 'came alight'!

As one of these sponsors, Adecco chose to encourage and reward performance excellence with the ultimate prize, the 'once in a lifetime opportunity of being a torchbearer'. Performance excellence reward campaigns were conducted amongst Adecco internal staff across Australia and in some international countries and extended to include some 15,000 Adecco casual staff of the labour hire company in Australia. All were eligible to win the coveted prize. In the event 15 prizes were awarded. Two went to casual workers. One of these, Patrick Ganguly, said before the event:

"Being selected made me feel on top of the world, as it is an opportunity of a lifetime. I think carrying the torch will be, without a doubt, absolutely sensational. I'm excited that my friends, co-workers and family will also be part of this historic moment."[97A]

You can bank on it

Team Millennium partner, Westpac, clearly defined one of the major objectives of its Olympic sponsorship as:

"Improve employee morale and pride in working for the Westpac group and in our sponsorship activities".[96]

To achieve this objective, Westpac conducted three staff programs – Banking Site Workers, Olympic and Paralympic Volunteers and an internal staff reward program. For the team who staffed Westpac's four banking facilities at Sydney Olympic Park, a unique agreement was negotiated with the Finance Sector Union (FSU). The Olympic banking sites required operating hours of 9 am to 9 pm. The agreement included an opportunity for the Olympic workforce to forfeit overtime in return for Olympic tickets!

Westpac supported 400 employees to participate as Games volunteers at the Aquatic Centre and the Stadium (and a further 100 as volunteers at the Paralympics). The company paid wages and provided airfares and accommodation. People chosen for this Games volunteer team were selected on the basis of the volunteer work they were already doing in their own community. To assist this, Westpac worked with volunteer centres in each State to connect individuals or whole business units with non-profit organi-sations in their local area that matched their interest and the time they had for volunteer activity. A third of the staff continue this work with the community. The company assists by providing pay and flexible working arrangements for staff and financial support to the community service organisations its staff work with as volunteers. As well as providing countless hours of volunteering throughout the Australian community, the program assisted in building a positive image for Westpac, and was a highly successful recognition program for employees.

Over and above its sponsor program for Olympic tickets, Westpac invested an additional $5 million in tickets for its Olympic reward program. The Olympic sponsorship provided the necessary impetus for the executive team to define and promote the four core values of the organisation – performance, honesty, integrity and teamwork. Employees were nominated when their work performance demonstrated these core values with nominations being assessed by judging committees within each business unit. As a result one in three employees received tickets to the Games, airfares and accommodation. This program was the first of its kind that united all parts of the organisation in a consistent reward program with the result that the 'monthly morale index', an internal staff questionnaire, recorded the highest ever company morale in August and September of 2000.

Lessons beyond 2000

The extent to which these valuable lessons regarding employee involvement, staff morale, reward and recognition have continued beyond 2000 is a question which only time will answer.

Many of the lessons we have touched on in this chapter, where companies made a consistent effort to utilise the unique opportu-nity of the Games, were repeated time and time again. As we move into the final chapter of this book, we will attempt to summarise and crystallise some of the many lessons for the future. One of these is that, properly managed, there is a role for a new kind of partnership between government, industry and unions.

Another of the major lessons concerns the financing of major projects. A high profile event that attracts an international spotlight of attention provides an incentive for private sector investment alongside government funding. In particular it can be attractive to corporate sponsorship. This sponsorship (in both cash and 'value in kind') at the front end can be used to undertake projects that could not be funded by government alone. Downstream, there are significant benefits flowing to both the corporate sponsor and the community. Some of these are economic through contracts for goods or services, sales, advertising and marketing. In addition participation in the project can be the stimulus for learning and innovation – new products, new work practices – leading to significant internal cultural changes that leave the organisation better positioned in the global economy.

None of this is guaranteed. Our stories tell the tale of as many failures to seize this opportunity as they do successes – but then both success and failure provide learning opportunities – if one is open-minded enough to recognise them.

Chapter five

The legacy of 'the best Games ever'

A challenge for the future

The best stories leave you with more questions than answers. There is a big temptation to try to simply summarise the lessons of the Games here. This would be a mistake. What we have done up to this point is to give both an overview of what was achieved, some of the 'flavour' of how it was done and how it is perceived today through the eyes of people who were there. That much has been relatively easy. The stories were told to us. Our job has been merely to re-present these in a way that allows some parts of the overall picture to stand out. What we would now like to attempt is much harder. It is to suggest that the legacy is not just something we look back on with pride (which we can), but more the questions that allow us to use the experience as a springboard for a leap into the future. To do this is not easy. The Games was arguably the world's largest single peacetime event. What challenge could we set ourselves after that?

The story we have told about the Games highlights some notable successes and some – we would prefer to call them – 'opportunities'. It provides opportunities to compare and contrast different industrial relations styles and cultures, to identify some of what works and some of what doesn't and, most important, opportunities to plan for better outcomes if we are ever to tackle something like it again. The 2006 Commonwealth Games in Melbourne is an obvious candidate. This event, albeit one-fifth the size of the Sydney Olympic Games, will give us an opportunity to gather the best practices identified here and adapt these for another significant sporting event. We assume that this will be done. But to look only at this or other major events, sporting or otherwise, is to set our sights too low. Let us give ourselves a real challenge.

Major environmental restoration projects?

Let us set a target very far removed from staging a 16-day sporting event. Let us imagine that we are going to tackle what may be one of the largest human and environmental resource projects in the history of Australia – repairing the degradation of the Murray-Darling River System. Think about it. One of the world's largest river systems crossing four States on the Australian continent, extensively used for irrigation that is essential for the agricultural industries that provide a quarter of the country's export earnings, and seriously degraded to the point where long-term sustainability of the existing use of the river can no longer be guaranteed. Re-engineering both the technical irrigation systems and the human infrastructure to create a more sustainable rural economy is now essential. Yes, a huge undertaking and a challenge beyond anything ever undertaken before – and one that has to be mastered if we are to have a sustainable future! Now, looking back at the Sydney Games in 2000, what would be the legacy that we could carry into this challenging task?

Before you reject the idea as drawing too long a bow, for a moment look at what we got from the Games as if it were any other major national project:

- a level of national pride throughout the country, not seen since the Snowy River Scheme, or in wartime

- each major step of the project completed on time, and within budget

- an environmental agenda that cleaned up a site contaminated with a significant amount of toxic waste, set new standards for ecological design and construction, and piloted integrated waste management and recycling programs

- a government and industry partnership that attracted significant financial and 'in-kind' sponsorship from industry – a sharing of contracts for work on the project and a number of spin-off benefits to the sponsor companies

- collaboration between government, industry and unions that delivered financial stability and industrial harmony across all aspects of the project

- the assembling of a massive paid and volunteer workforce for a project that had the attention of over 4 billion people worldwide

- a massive training program coordinated to deliver the requisite number of people with the skills for each stage of the project and leave behind a multi-skilled workforce with valuable job experience and qualifications for the future

- significant gains in productivity – development of new products and new work systems with potential long-term benefits for the enterprises involved

- significant lessons from areas where problems arose that help to clarify the benefits of building a collaborative culture

- a recognition that national projects cannot afford to lose sight of the wider, international social justice and human rights values.

This was the Olympic Games. Could it be another major project of even greater long-term significance?

Before you say, 'But...!' We know this was the Olympic Games. Many people have said things like, 'Oh well, you would expect it to be a success. People were so worried about stuffing up, the international spotlight was on us and national pride was important. Besides, there was so much money to spend. Anyway it was sport – and a one-off project, which has little relevance to anything else.'

All true but only in part. There was a real fear of failure but at a certain stage the commitment moved beyond just getting the job done, to a determination to deliver 'the best Games ever', and succeeded. As one junior project officer with the task of training volunteers for transport work said:

"Our worst fear was that we'd be mediocre – just good enough – we wanted to be excellent – the best!"

Yes, the Games organisers did have a significant amount to spend; they also had severe budget constraints and funds had to be spent wisely and sparingly. Spending money certainly helped to solve some difficult problems, but money on its own without the strategic planning, the human relations architecture, and the incredible climate of cooperation could never have produced the outstanding results it did. We can say that goodwill made it possible to succeed – often despite what was happening behind the scenes – but this begs the question: how was this goodwill fostered? What were the elements that contributed to it and sustained it? By now you will have some idea what we think went into this equation.

Let's take another look at the Games achievements in the light of the challenge of this, or other long-term environmental restoration projects.

Gold medals for construction

We have said it many times already: this was a massive construction program delivering quality, technical and environmental innovation, on time and within budget. In terms of how this was achieved we think the following stand out:

- Close collaboration between government and private industry through 'design and construct' style contracting. This encouraged and supported the culture shift that had been taking place within the industry, from competitive and adversarial to collaborative and cooperative.

- Elements of the culture change can be seen in the relationships between contractors and subcontractors and between employers and workers.

- In the latter particularly, the collective bargaining framework – working with the unions rather than attempting to sideline them through 'contracts' with workers as individuals – established a collaborative framework for the whole construction project, which we have called the industrial relations architecture. The main elements involved:

  - An overarching Memorandum of Understanding negotiated at the highest level between the unions and the client (government and the OCA) that set common standards for all the different sites involved in the project. It also formalised the commitment of the unions to ensure on-time and within-budget completion. This ensured industrial harmony and a stable workforce. There was no incentive for workers to look elsewhere for work where conditions might be better – this was the best!

- Enterprise Agreements made with individual companies and registered as Consent Awards – based on a common pattern that defined productivity incentives for early completion of specific stages of the project. The Common Rule provisions in the NSW IR legislation bound all subcontractors into the common rules. A level playing field for everyone on the site!

- The employment of experienced union delegates to promote safety, training and constructive resolution of issues on site.

- A strategically coordinated training program that delivered the skills matrix needed by the project (not just the individual companies) on a 'just in time' basis: Overall 12,000 construction workers were trained.

  - The structure and content of the training was developed as a partnership between government agencies, construction companies, State and private registered training providers and the trade unions using both on-site and off-site training facilities.

  - A comprehensive site-induction program ensured that the overall ethos and goals of the project were communicated to all workers.

  - The health and safety component of this training delivered marked improvement in safety-conscious work practices on site. It reduced accidents and saved lives without causing delays in the progress of the work.

  - It also provided training in the new skills needed to manage the emerging collaborative culture in the industry.

We have also seen how this culture has taken root – albeit at an early and fragile stage – throughout the industry workforce, its management and its trade union structures. We also heard from several of the 'architects' of this new culture that it is the **attitudes,** not the specific elements, that sit at the core of the culture shift. The form of the agreements emerged for a specific task with its own time and place in history. They helped bring about a change in attitudes, to include trust, fairness, mutual respect, and a willingness to share responsibilities and the financial rewards; but it is the culture change that is the important outcome – the move away from competition and conflict towards cooperative, dare we say it again, collaboration.

Now take all of this out of the urban context of the Sydney metropolitan basin and spread it across half the continent, from the headwaters of our largest river system in Queensland and rural New South Wales, through the irrigated agricultural heartland to the now almost stagnant outflow to the ocean in South Australia. Go on imagine! This is a task that has to be tackled – sometime – if we are to have a sustainable future. Which elements of the Games legacy would be useful here? Which would we need to adapt? How would we bring the stakeholders in such a project together to begin the strategic planning and lay the foundations for collaboration that would carry it through to completion – step by step, stage by stage, each rural community, small town and inland city with ownership of its own piece of a comprehensive whole?

Green and gold?

The Games had its own environment program. The response, particularly from the environment movement, to the Games has not, generally, been one of wholehearted endorsement. It has been said that environmental guidelines were used to 'greenwash' the Bid for the Games in 1993, and these had been 'cherry-picked' or had the 'eyes picked out' of them. Some 'green' organisations feel they were marginalised once the Bid had been won and that many of the environment objectives were put in the 'too hard basket' as the Games approached. Some of this is fair comment. The Games certainly did not deliver on all 'green' expectations – just as it fell short in other areas. In any project there is a trade-off between the ideal, and what is technically and economically feasible at the time. Anna Booth said of this:

"We would have liked the environment program to be better but there were problems with budget constraints and technological limits. In the early days the Games had a lot of baggage. It was supposed to attract new industry, set new environment standards, set a new standard in education – so many expectations. It was Michael Knight who refocused this by saying the Games are the Games and we can't do all the rest. Take one example: I was involved in the environment program details about biodegradable plastics.

We located a supply in Newcastle but were told simply that the issue was one of dollars – they would be ten times the cost of ordinary plastic bags! People wanted SOCOG to do everything and we couldn't." [37]

Shortcomings aside, it is important to acknowledge the achievements. If nothing else, we spent $136 million cleaning up the toxic wastes contaminating the Homebush Bay site! Bill Ford recalls:

"I remember my first visit – before the Bid – to the Olympic site seeing people collecting core samples dressed in total protection suits – like spacemen. The cores revealed high levels of toxic pollution and environmental negligence. Without the Olympics we might never have had the will or the resources to clean up what is now a beautiful space." [10A]

The Post Games Environment Report suggests that the Games was a showcase to the world for a new approach to urban redevelopment. It transformed Homebush Bay 'from a land use liability into a usable public space'. It also demonstrated achievements in conservation of resources and species. As such it has set a benchmark that has already influenced planning and organisation of Olympic Games in Salt Lake City, Athens and Turin. More important from the point of view of our study it states:

> *The Games was a showcase to the world for a new approach to urban redevelopment ... As such it has set a benchmark that has already influenced planning and organisation of Olympic Games in Salt Lake City, Athens and Turin.*

"A capability now exists in the workforce to apply this knowledge and skills elsewhere in industry, government and the community, particularly in event management, construction, architecture and waste management industries. All events regardless of size can use the lessons of Sydney 2000 to enhance the environment performance of the event." *

To many people the Games **were** 'green'. The case study in Chapter 4 gives some of the details of how a comprehensive integrated waste management strategy was designed and implemented. It significantly reduced the wastes going to landfill by controlling the amount and type of packaging and utensils used in catering. Most of what was used was reusable or recyclable. Information on the system and colour-coded receptacles (themselves recyclable) were provided for public use. Behind the scenes similarly coloured waste bags and bulk bins ensured that separated wastes went to compost or recycling – diverting 70 percent of the waste from landfill. Most of us do only a half-hearted job of this at

---

* The Post Games Environment Report (Sydney 2000, December 2000).

A colony of endangered green and gold bell frogs was relocated to a protected site.

home! The Games educated 150,000 workers, 6 million Games spectators and many of the 1.5 million people at 'live sites' in the city. People understood and used the recycling system. One of the biggest fears about people bringing their own food to the Games was that this would lead to problems with the waste management program. It didn't happen. Environment consciousness around recycling went up a notch for many people. Doing it at home is one thing, doing it on an industrial scale is another. Extending this to systematic re-use and recycling in the construction program – so that this is now part of the culture of the industry – is another again.

This was not the only environmental achievement of the Games. On the opposite page is a short, selective list of the others.

Now think of this less in terms of the specific task than in terms of the process by which it was achieved. Preferred partnerships between government and industry based on commitment to the environmental objectives. Creation of partnerships and alliances between companies in what are, traditionally at least, very different fields. In Chapter 4 we explored the 'closed loop' alliance of packaging, cleaning, waste management, catering,

Selective list of the environmental achievements of the Green Games

Energy

All venues used 100 percent 'green' power for the duration of the Games. In the Olympic village 665 houses had 'grid-connected' solar panels and solar hot water systems. Passive natural ventilation saved 20 percent of energy demand in the Showgrounds.

Refrigeration and air-conditioning

Samsung provided 324 large environmentally safe 'Greenfreeze' refrigerators for use at the Olympics. Fosters Brewing banned the purchase of greenhouse-polluting HFCs and ozone-destroying equipment. Coca-Cola has agreed to stop purchasing HFC equipment by Athens 2004.

Timber

The CFMEU placed a ban on the use of imported rainforest timber. Plantation timber was used extensively in most Olympic venues. Feature grade timber that uses 80 percent of the log was used at the Athletes Village instead of select grade, which uses only 20 percent. Olympic tree planting programs planted 8 million trees at more than 500 sites across Australia. Over 4 million of these were directly attributable to the Games – 2 million in the Sydney region alone.

Water conservation

A dual water system that separates drinking water and recycled 'waste' water for landscape use and toilet flushing was used. Roof harvested water cut the Showgrounds' mains water needs by 50 percent.

Poly-vinyl chloride (PVC)

The Athletes Village reduced PVC usage by 70 percent. More than 1 million metres of PVC-free cabling were used there. At least 200,000 metres of polyethylene pipe were used as a PVC alternative.

Transport

Virtually all spectators at Olympic events used public transport. The price of tickets included transport costs. There was no public parking for private cars at Sydney Olympic Park.*

---

* For a more comprehensive treatment of the environmental benefits of the Games see the OCA website at www.oca.nsw.gov.au/oca/html/reviews.stm which has copies of reports by the Earth Council, Greenpeace Australia, and Green Games Watch. Additional information can be obtained from The Post Games Environment Report (Sydney 2000, December 2000); and Achieving the Integrated Waste Management Solution – the Sydney 2000 Waste Management Experience (Sydney 2000).

merchandising. In what other areas might collaborative partnerships be possible – or necessary – to tackle a major environmental restoration program? Strange how all too often our thinking is constrained by what we believe to be possible – rather than what we know to be necessary!

The Games project, simply because of its size, generated markets for products that could be recycled and products that could be made from recycled material ... What new technological innovation might a major environment restoration project generate – with long-term benefits for employment and exports, as we become leaders in the field?

While innovation costs money up front, it pays dividends at the back end. The Games project, simply because of its size, generated markets for products that could be recycled and products that could be made from recycled material – hence the term 'closed loop' used by Visy to describe the exercise. What new technological innovation might a major environment restoration project generate – with long-term benefits for employment and exports, as we become leaders in the field?

Still thinking of process, how would we begin to get Australia's small to medium sized industries to collaborate in partnerships with national, state and local governments to deliver the sponsorships (seed finance and 'value in kind') and recoup some of this or more by developing alliances with 'competitors', suppliers and customers to contract for the work associated with an environmental reclamation project? What are the implications for a business culture if the values of competition are balanced with those of the kind of collaboration that the Games showed to be so successful? What balance needs to be struck between competition and collaboration for major projects (particularly environmental ones) in the national interest?

Medals and flowers for people management

(And a round of applause for all who participated)

The champions got their Gold, Silver and Bronze medals. All were then handed identical bunches of native flowers!

The planning and delivery of the services that made the spectacle possible was perhaps **the** achievement of the Games. It was, as Jim Sloman put it, 'business as un-usual'. A workforce of close to 150,000 (possibly 200,000 or more if you count all those indirectly involved) assembled, trained, and Games-ready on the day and each of the next 16 days; and many coming back to do it all again two weeks later for the Paralympic Games. A 'paid and volunteer' team of people seamlessly working together, in some cases in the same uniform so that the public knew no distinction between them. In Chapters 3 and 4 we saw some of how this was achieved. The planning that went into the whole exercise and the human relations architecture that ensured industrial harmony and which, over time, built a network of collaborative relationships that weathered the storm. In some of the case studies we can see clearly how the failure to build these relationships led to near catastrophe. Near, but averted in large part because the underlying framework of agreements and relationships that had been established could be mobilised to prevent breakdown. We said there, it is as though when the wheels fell off, a lot of people got under the truck and held it up until some new wheels could be fitted and the thing put back on the road.

We need to recall that the workforce for this exercise **was not there.** The Gap Analysis indicated that, even using the best available tools for recruiting such a large casual workforce, there would be major labour shortages. Sydney learned from Atlanta. It adapted and mobilised networks of private contractors to assist in recruiting, training and managing the people needed. We have seen how these contractors were involved in helping to design the industrial relations framework which, as in the construction phase, created a level playing field and the basis for collaboration with the trade unions. How the unions responded in turn by creating Unions 2000 as a single organising focus for both recruitment of members and, uniquely, recruitment of workers for a significant number of the service jobs. We saw the strategic importance of having a pooled labour recruitment agency (the OLN) in reserve, which the contractors could use for all or some of their recruiting. There are many lessons here from the successes and the failures and the grey areas in between.

What stands out?

■ Again, the importance of the in-principle agreements[*] that set the overarching framework:

---

[*] See Appendices 4, 5 & 6 for details of these in-principle agreements.

- the Principles of Cooperation between SOCOG and the Labor Council
- the Volunteer Protocol
- the Licensed Goods Agreement.

■ The negotiation of the Olympic Games Award between the unions, SOCOG and the major contractors – before contracts were let – as a single instrument for:

- setting wage rates and the Games bonus to provide budget certainty for SOCOG and contractors
- overcoming the recruitment problems before, and drop-out rates during, the Games guaranteeing cooperation in ensuring smooth operation of the Games services.

And we note the innovative nature of this agreement with its considerable potential for a new type of collaborative project agreement that could be negotiated between parties – and how this has yet to gain acceptance as a model for the future with the main employer federations.

■ The way that, as with the construction sector, these industrial relations instruments help in creating the basis of trust from which new and more enduring relationships can be built. As we saw throughout Chapters 3 and 4, it is these relationships that are the foundations on which the culture of collaboration can be built.

■ If this point needs any justification it is surely found in such examples as the near breakdown in the private bus system. The issue is not one of right and wrong or apportioning blame. What is important is that the relationships were not established. The culture of this industry did not move from competition to collaboration in the lead-up to the Games. Yet it was the more robust framework of agreements that was used to salvage the mess. 'Goodwill' alone is not enough. When things break down something more substantial is needed.

■ A third to a half of the workforce were volunteers – some recruited because they had specialised skills that were required. Many more volunteered because they believed the project was worthwhile. There are some important lessons here that can be adopted and adapted for other projects such as how to recruit through organisations; the importance of orientation; the need to ensure that volunteers are given specific worthwhile jobs;

the costs and the heavy workload in communicating with volunteers; and the importance of recognition items – not as incentives but as rewards.

- In the middle ground between volunteers and those recruited for a project are the many who will volunteer to be seconded from existing jobs out of commitment to a worthwhile project and who gain sometimes immeasurably from the experience. There are also those who will take leave for similar reasons. And we should not forget the role of the Defence Forces in underpinning some aspects of the Games and who would both contribute to and benefit from other national projects.

- How important it was that all were given training. In the Games project this included:

  • A common orientation to the project so they could see their own job in the context of the larger picture and what would be expected of them to help make it a success.

  • Site-specific training so they were familiar with the workplace and the people they would be working with – managers, supervisors and colleagues.

  • Skills development, particularly important for young people new to the workplace who received skills training in a variety of service trades, and work experience. In the Games project much of this was short-term 'fit for purpose', but with a longer term project such as environment restoration there is scope for more training within the nationally accredited competency based training schemes and skills centres on site, as were used in the construction phase.

  • For the future we note also the suggestion for multi-skilling a new workforce with basic 'event' skills as part of school leaver training.

- We have seen how some organisations have developed the technology that can assist in planning and managing a large casual workforce, right down to being able to accommodate work rostering for small groups who want to work together, or work in a particular area of the project.

Why do people work? To live certainly, but if we tease this apart we find consistently six elements in job satisfaction:

- reward – usually income – both as a necessity and as recognition for a job well done

- purpose – a sense that the job is worth doing, meaningful, part of a wider goal

- enjoyment – not to be underestimated and closely related to

- relationships – working with people one enjoys spending time with

- education – a sense that in working we are learning something new

- competence – being able to use the skills one has.

There are other ways of framing the same story. We have given these in people's own words throughout this book. We could go on. The point is that all of this could be just as relevant to a project like the Murray-Darling Basin reclamation.

A legacy for Murray–Darling Basin restoration?

Arguably the greatest long-term problem facing Australia is water, and solving the degradation of the Murray-Darling Basin would perhaps be the biggest contribution to the water problem. On the scale of priorities this is more important than the Olympic Games. And, if the region is to have a sustainable future, it has to be done.

Some of the things in common:

- It is a long-term project. The Games was about eight years, while the Murray-Darling Basin will probably require at least a 20-year time frame.

- It will require a large budget which will have to be spent wisely. Sections will need to be completed on time and within budget.

- It is a national project that handled properly will generate national pride and commitment. It will also have the spotlight of the world on it. If successful, it will showcase Australian capabilities, set a benchmark for environmental restoration and create opportunities for exporting technology and know-how.

- It will have international ramifications – developing strategies (and technologies) for solving problems that many other countries also face. From the outset the program will need to be developed as a major learning project with international relevance.

- It will require strong leadership with a clear chain of command, but will also need to encourage innovation, participation and community ownership at the local level.

- It will be necessary to develop partnership arrangements. These will be between State and Federal governments; between governments and the private sector; between private sector businesses; between governments, unions and industry; and all in partnership with local farmers and rural communities.

- Such a huge project cannot succeed without a great deal of voluntary contribution of various kinds.

- Significant training and consciousness raising will be required. This will need to include vocational skills. It will also need to develop awareness of the big picture to ensure community support and involvement.

Arguably the greatest long-term problem facing Australia is water, and solving the degradation of the Murray-Darling Basin would perhaps be the biggest contribution to the water problem. On the scale of priorities this is more important than the Olympic Games. And, if the region is to have a sustainable future, it has to be done.

All these were achieved by the Games organisation. The difference now is that we have a legacy that might enable us to do consciously what in some cases we stumbled through during the Games.

A culture of collaboration?

We have used the term frequently. What does this mean in practice? The word 'collaboration' carries a mixed bag of images from the shaven heads of women who 'collaborated' with Germans during the wartime occupation of France to the kind of collaboration between, say, film directors and actors that produces memorable movies. Needless to say, what we are advocating is more the latter. At the same time collaboration is not all 'sweetness and light'. Just as good personal relationships require partners each to have strong yet flexible personal 'boundaries', so too does organisational collaboration between government, industry and trade unions (and equally within each of these groups as well). The ability to handle conflict is important – to be able to take a stand, argue for what we believe is right and hear the other person's point of view. It is not about always producing a 'win-win' outcome. It's nice when this happens and the flexible achieve it often. But there are times when compromise – setting aside the short term for the benefit of the long term and the whole – is essential. What makes this collaboration easier, possible even, is a cluster of attitudes that are not, and should not be adopted automatically in relations between people or organisations. These include trust, openness and respect. Respect particularly, as this is the basis from which the others can grow and without which their development is hard work if not impossible. Respect grows with the growth of relationships. It is earned, not given. The respect for the union movement's sincerity in support of the Games began before the Bid. The mutual respect between collaborating companies similarly began years ago and grew with experience. The trust and respect between company, SOCOG and union people involved in negotiating and implementing the IR agreements grew with the experience – and in this last example has continued through to the work on this study of the Collaborative Games.

Nurturing this kind of culture, especially as it so often has to emerge from one where competition and adversarial attitudes are the norm, takes real skill – something that will be essential if the kind of mega environment project we are considering is to succeed.

Nurturing this kind of culture, especially as it so often has to emerge from one where competition and adversarial attitudes are the norm, takes real skill – something that will be essential if the kind of mega environment project we are considering is to succeed. It is by no means established as the norm even among the people interviewed for this study. An acrimonious debate continues between and within several of the trade unions over whether collaboration in the Games was a 'sell-out' of the membership. Comments from some industry managers also suggested that partnership between competitors was a nice idea – but! Some also felt that unions had a privileged position in the Games because of the links between the Labor Council and the NSW government, but contributed little to the running of the Games. We hope the stories we have reported here help to dispel some myths and make a positive contribution to an ongoing debate.

Power, shame and pride?

You will recall that in the introduction we set out to ask open-ended questions. Implicit in asking people to share their strategic thinking and their perception of the major lessons of the Games we were asking 'what made the Games such a success?' The responses fell into two main groups both with a common theme that it was people's goodwill and determination that made the Games a success. For one group it was the inevitable consequence of the unique Olympic event. Listen as Tom Forrest who worked in Michael Knight's office describes it:

"All previous Olympic Games experience is that public support is highest at the time of winning the Bid. It then goes down. There are issues of cost – more than was thought, and cost blow-outs. Then realising that this a world event – tickets are going overseas and not all locally available. We had particular issues: the marching bands, Phil Coles' jewellery, the IOC scandal. Then it starts to build up again. Venues are complete – test events are held – people get to see the sites – tickets arrive in the mail – athletes arrive etc. Therefore we knew this would happen and even if we stuffed up, as long as the Games happened people would get behind it. And in our case we knew – all construction was completed one year before, on budget and this was recognised. Because we were early the transport system could be tested – it had never happened before – at all the venues. We had test events in each of the Olympic venues. Volunteers were better trained and resourced – plus we were building on the Australian volunteer mentality. There was an underlying attitude – people wanted it to be a success." [33]

People wanted it to be a success therefore it was! A different slant is given by Chris Christodoulou (quoted earlier) - that the driver for success was initially about fear of failure in the full glare of the spotlight of world attention but that somewhere in the process this turned over to become wanting to be the best. This is echoed by our ORTA volunteer driver manager – 'our worst fear was that we'd be seen as mediocre ...'. These views are not incompatible. Michael Knight summed it up this way:

"We expected that the public feeling around the time of the Bid would not be rekindled until the torch was in the Sydney area. We had the problem of seven years between these peaks. But the key figures, senior people in SOCOG, OCA, ORTA always wanted to achieve the best Games – always knew the spotlight of attention would be on the Games – knew they'd be judged by the nation favourably or critically. They knew this beforehand. Also this view was there in the unions and the workers. It was hardest to find at some

levels of SOCOG where this had morphed into an arrogance over what they were doing versus an objective assessment and a fear that it wouldn't happen. The people I liked were those who had a constructive anxiety. Some – only a few – were paralysed by fear. Some were just 'confident' they would pull it off. Both these were not much use. The third group – most of the people involved – had this constructive anxiety – an awareness of the cost of failure and the benefits of success – were a little scared the whole time – ran a little scared the whole time. These were the most useful."

There was a move away from the old adversarial culture of 'power' to one of being conscious that we were in the spotlight. Then, with genuine achievements under our belt, we saw the emergence of pride and, with it, a desire to go beyond, for many far beyond what was expected of them.

It may seem like a small point. We suggest it is a big and important one. That success in building the kind of collaboration that will be needed to sustain a large national project, particularly one that requires public support over a long period, requires something extra – call it pressure from outside or an external 'threat' – as a driver. The footy coach knows full well the importance of the 'other' team; and nations have used the external threat to unite the population in war. The challenge here is to create peacetime conditions that produce the same effect in bringing people together – to collaborate. What was it that drove large sections of the union movement and simultaneously many employers to abandon the culture of power in favour of collaboration? The answer seems to be the spotlight of attention that was focused on Sydney as a result of being the Games Host City. Everything we did was under scrutiny.

Place anyone under such a spotlight and they instinctively react with embarrassment[*] – whether they have done wrong or not. There is a 'looking over one's shoulder' and a questioning of how we are being seen in the eyes of others. The other side of this initial embarrassment is a feeling of pride which grows as we realise that we are actually doing a good job. Not inflated but genuine authentic pride in achievement. This seems to be the pattern reported by so many people we spoke with. There was a move away from the old adversarial culture of 'power' to one of being conscious that we were in the spotlight. Then, with genuine achievements under our belt, we saw the emergence of pride and, with it, a desire to go beyond, for many far beyond what was expected of them.

---

* The other and technically correct word for this is 'shame' but this tends to arouse a lot of negative reactions so we will stick with embarrassment.

All this is, of course, helped by working in an environment that encourages the taking of responsibility. Hence the importance of the workplace reform program that had taken root in the construction industry, the workforce and volunteer training programs, and the many employee participation programs that Games sponsors ran as part of their Olympic programs.

Limits to collaboration?

It would be nice to assume that what we have described as the 'collaborative culture' developed through the Games is the model for the future. This is not the view we wish to convey. This culture is still in its infancy and will struggle to survive outside the hothouse environment of the Games. It was not even a universal feature of the Games. At various points in this story we have highlighted how very different cultures came together, sometimes uneasily, to produce the Games collaboration. For example the highly centralised command and control structure of the NSW police and national security services clashed with the devolved management ethos of SOCOG. There were similar but different clashes within SOCOG over the performance culture of the Ceremonies. There were also protracted negotiations between SOCOG, OSCC and the unions over the role of volunteers in security. The major clash – and eventual, if uneasy, collaboration – occurred between SOCOG and the OCA. It is worth examining this in a little more detail. Behind it we believe there are some important lessons that are critical for the kind of mega-project of national significance we have been considering.

What we need to do here is to identify what happened and then explore why and what lessons might be learned. In particular, what are the limitations of this kind of collaboration and how might we improve on the Games model in the future?

When we began this study we were aware that a number of the key players in SOCOG had brought with them project management experience from the construction industry. In Chapter 2 we showed how a culture change towards the 'learning organisation' had evolved in the industry. It would take another book to do justice to this cultural change program. For now we note that an essential aspect of this culture is the devolution of authority down the hierarchy to the people on the front line. Providing the team framework for collective decision-making at progressively lower levels increases participation and personal commitment of the workforce to achieving the organisation's goals. The strength of this democratic organisational culture is possibly best summarised in the phrase quoted in Chapter 3 – in effect: 'when you tell someone what to do, it becomes your problem – not theirs'. There is no doubt that devolving responsibility down the hierarchy contributed significantly to the morale and commitment that was so evident in the SOCOG staff we interviewed.

Against this, however, we are faced with evidence that this organisational culture was found wanting at critical points during the Games – to the extent that significant aspects of SOCOG's work, particularly in the area of managing the contracts for Games services, were taken over by the OCA from early 2000 onwards. The whole issue of the clash between OCA and SOCOG arouses intense passions on both sides. It is easy to characterise this as a clash between the public and private sector stakeholders, or as one organisation running out of a job and looking to take over the other's. Even if true, neither offers any constructive analysis that assists us in charting a path forward. We suggest that tensions are inherent in making transitions from one culture to another. They will always exist. Both organisations had different elements of the collaborative culture we have been describing. At this distance from the event there are no mistakes – just learning opportunities. As Jim Sloman put it 'we would do it again – and we'd do it better next time'.

The basic facts of the story are that in 1999 the SOCOG Board became aware there was a major risk of failure in areas of transport, catering (excluding the villages), cleaning, waste, environment, venue management and spectator services.[33 37 38 80] An audit revealed that tenders for some of the service contracts were not being filled and that there was a major risk of the staff numbers not being delivered. It also revealed significant budget and timetable problems in each of these areas. For example the tenders for cleaning were twice the budget and this did not include provision for cleaning some areas outside the major venues. We saw in Chapter 4 how security tenders were over three times the available budget. Similar problems were identified in other areas. No-one had a crystal ball that allowed exact predictions for what scale of services would be needed at Games time but some of the initial estimates needed scaling back. More important, the contractors needed some certainty in the form of clear and precise contracts so they could plan recruitment strategies.

In conjunction with the NSW Premier, the decision was taken that a number of SOCOG's program areas would be handed to OCA to manage. OCA claim around $40 million was 'wasted through loose accounting'. The Ceremonies were identified as an area where spending 'ran rampant'. OCA claim to have saved over $1 million on the labour costs for managing the venues, and to have reduced the projected waste management contract from the tender estimate of over 18,000 tons to around 6,000 tons.[80] * Significant cuts were made to costs of many of the other contract areas. As we noted earlier, this change of control was a seamless transition. Few outside the inner workings of the contract process realised that any change in management had taken place. Despite the smooth transition there are some today who argue that it was unnecessary. Most people on the inside acknowledge that urgent action was needed and that OCA contributed significantly to this. It is also fair comment that SOCOG had done the hard yards in planning the unpredictable – which inevitably meant making mistakes.

Recriminations aside, the question we need to ask is, how did this breakdown in the orderly planning and management of the key contract services occur? What was it that distinguished this area from the other more successful programs such as the construction of the venues, the torch relay, the volunteer program (with the notable exception of the problems we identified with the Ceremonies volunteers), the management of the Athlete and Media Villages and, not least, the sports themselves?

Some of this was due to compounding problems caused by financial difficulties. In Chapter 4 we quoted the IOC reporting SOCOG's success in raising more money than any previous Games, and more than the Bid budget. This is obviously not the whole story. The AOC told us that too much of the sponsorship income was VIK rather than cash and that SOCOG's 'cash burn was too high too fast'.[71] All the way through this study people referred to budget problems. [e.g. 1 6 12 16 25 33 37 72] But to say that this was the source of the potential breakdown begs more questions than it answers. How did these budget problems arise? What strategies were adopted for dealing with them? If they didn't work, why? And what strategies might have been adopted? What were the strategies adopted by OCA in early 2000? Were these stopgap measures to

---

* The Post Games Environment Report by Sydney 2000 indicates the actual total generated for the 60-day Games period was 5,010 tons.

patch up a late emerging problem or do they offer an alternative strategy for managing a large-scale event where limited and/or uncertain finances need to be managed, some would say juggled, alongside a number of other uncertainties.

A clash of cultures?

We suggest that some answers may be found in seeing this as a clash of cultures – something that goes beyond a simple grab for power and to the heart of the story we have been exploring. Was it something in the SOCOG culture that led to the budget problems and the way these and the management of the contracts appear to have spiralled out of control? The problems certainly backed up to the point where key program areas threatened to become logistics disasters. They didn't, but as we have shown this was because there was high-level intervention that imposed a different, more disciplined, some might say more authoritarian, management structure. What characterises the cultural differences between the Games organisations that eventually came together as Sydney 2000? Are there lessons here which require us to limit or modify our perspective on the 'culture of collaboration' as the basis for future large projects?

If we conclude at the end of this study that all we have to do with the next major national project is replicate the culture of the Sydney 2000 Olympic Games then we are missing the point and heading for the same kind of potential disaster.

If we conclude at the end of this study that all we have to do with the next major national project is replicate the culture of the Sydney 2000 Olympic Games then we are missing the point and heading for the same kind of potential disaster. We could proceed on the assumption that public goodwill generated by the spectacle will carry us through but this seems both too naïve and too great a risk to run. Arguably we will get only one chance to tackle a major project such as the Murray-Darling restoration and we had better get it right – first time!

We don't have all the answers. We doubt that anyone does. We strongly suspect that anyone claiming to have them all is probably wrong. Recall Jim Sloman's comment about the Games being like a giant jigsaw puzzle – no-one gets to find all the pieces! What we have to offer are many questions (and a few tentative answers) that might help define a more mature form of the culture of collaboration – one that grows out of – literally outgrows the Games experience.

We suggest three issues that seem to us worth exploring:

- The question of **control** – how do we control functions that are contracted out to other organisations and, particularly, where within the structure of the customer organisation these are managed.

- The questions of **design and detail** – the extent to which the customer specifies what is required of the contractor. Specifically whether this includes the details of how the outcome is to be delivered, or whether these details are left to the contractor as part of a fixed price contract, which specifies performance outcomes that have to be met.

- The question of managing **conflict of interest** – specifically how to balance private and community interests. There are benefits to be had from close, collaborative partnership arrangements with the contractors (particularly where the whole venture is tackling something neither partner has undertaken before). There is also a need for open, competitive tendering that ensures that the benefits are shared by the whole community and all sections of the industries involved.

Control – the buck stops where?

In Chapter 4 we reported the comment by Paul McKinnon of the OSCC that part of the problem was the 'decide, delegate and dump it' culture within SOCOG? He was not alone in this view. Neil Fergus, Chief of Intelligence, was predicting as early as June 1999 that SOCOG management of major issues would implode and it would be necessary for the government to intervene.[38] Is this just the product of two very different cultures – one obviously rooted in a clear chain of command and control? Devolving responsibility downwards is key to the 'learning organisation' model of collaboration we have been making the case for. Does this need modification, and can this be done without reverting to the old-style management as control hierarchy? The Cleanevent story in Chapter 4 indicates that business-like control and people-oriented communication can be combined to produce a culture where hard work and 'fun' coexist. What lessons from this might apply to control between customer and contractor organisations?

Our evidence suggests that delegation of responsibility needs to be balanced with a high level of ongoing involvement of senior management. This is what we find in the areas where the SOCOG operation was successful. In the industrial relations field, SOCOG senior management were intimately involved in ongoing dialogue and negotiations with unions and contractors all the way through the Games preparation and delivery. We have seen how this built relationships based on trust and respect, particularly between key players such as Rob Forsyth in SOCOG and Chris Cristodoulou in the Labor Council. This collaboration ensured the IR agenda stayed on track (with the notable exception of the transport sector). A feature of how it was kept on track was that senior management, notably Ian Clubb, John Quayle and Jim Sloman, were brought back into the decision-making loop at critical points. Nowhere was this more important than in dealing with the 12 months delay in the ratification of the Olympic Award. Agreement on the common wage rates and Olympic bonus was essential to providing certainty over the service contract costs. Despite the delay, the message was communicated across the whole Games organisation that the essential framework was in place, that there would only be minor changes to details and that contract planning could proceed with something close to certainty that the basic IR framework would be ratified. There was also high-level involve-ment whenever it was needed in each of the potential areas of dispute: Ceremonies (paid or volunteer performers), uniforms (labour conditions in overseas manufacture) and many of the others we have identified. The result was an outstanding achieve-ment in terms of industrial collaboration that was able to 'contain' all potential industrial disputes throughout the Games.

In the area where there were difficulties – almost entirely the contracting of private sector companies to provide essential services for the Games – we do not find similar high-level manage-ment involvement (or at least no evidence of it being as effective). The contracts were managed much lower down the SOCOG structure and the problems do not seem to have been picked up early enough by senior management.

How do we get the balance right here? How would we do this in relation to the Murray-Darling project? The OCA model suggests:

- management by a much smaller organisation[*]

---

* The $3.2 billion construction project was managed by an OCA staff of about 55. The management of the $400 million Olympic 'overlay', which required much greater consultation with the contractors, required a staff of around 150.[98]

- with greater reliance on outsourcing of functions

- with very tight performance-based contracts

- with contracts managed by **senior** staff.

This 'smart client' approach is clearly 'efficient'. It also brings with it a high level of control. How do we simultaneously develop the kind of collaborative relationships with the other more subtle but important benefits we have highlighted in this study? Indeed, can we?

Design, detail and deliver?

In Chapter 2 we discussed an important feature of the collaboration between OCA and the construction contractors. This was the use of 'fixed price' and, most often, 'design and construct' contracts. In these the OCA, as the customer, specified what was required as an outcome but left much of the detail to the contractor. There was an ongoing partnership relationship with the contractor as the details were developed and, as we saw in some of the case studies, this extended into the actual construction phase. For example, on-the-ground collaboration was evident in the case of the Aquatic Centre temporary seating where the contractor encountered problems with the original design. Very important in all of this was that the senior management in the OCA came out of the industry and that the contracts were managed at a **senior** level within the organisation.

Leaving aside the obvious (and obviously significant) difference between construction and service delivery, the SOCOG management structure was larger and had, as part of its corporate ethos, the principle of devolving responsibility down to program managers at much lower levels. It also developed collaborative partnerships with a number of the companies who it anticipated would be the major contractors for the services. Some of these were Games sponsors and, as such, 'customers' of SOCOG while, at the same time, SOCOG was also their 'customer'. Some also acted as consultants to SOCOG in 'scoping' the Games tasks and setting the performance criteria for the contract tenders. The major contractors in each of the key service areas were partners in the discussions that developed the Games Award and also in the development of the contracts that they subsequently tendered for. We will return to this below.

The contract discussions continued after tender and after

selection of the major contractors. In some cases SOCOG and the chosen contractors struggled for months to define in some detail how these were to be performed. An example would be the detailed rosters in security. This appears to us to be a key 'strategic' decision – though whether this was made consciously or by default is unclear. Put simply, contracts were not finalised early because SOCOG contract managers were involved in discussing details of **how** the services were to be performed – in part as a way to contain the costs. Some of the ongoing discussion can be explained by the attempt to juggle the multiple factors, each with a large measure of uncertainty. For example the eventual number of tickets sold to spectators for each event would affect the number of people needed in service jobs (and hence the cost of the contract to supply them) – and the eventual health of the SOCOG budget. All a kind of moving feast where no-one had a clear crystal ball to show what would be the correct prediction for the actual Games. Small wonder that Jin Sloman describes this as 'business as un-usual'.

In terms of developing a more mature collaborative culture the question we might ask is how could this have been worked out differently. Obviously earlier! The contractors needed firm contracts well in advance to plan recruitment and management structures which, in many cases, involved significant scaling up from their normal operations and a massive 'ramp-up' at the start of the Games.

We have noted in Chapter 4 how some contractors suggested that 'fixed price' contracts – with SOCOG setting the performance criteria and leaving the contractor to work out the detail on how best to deliver this performance – would have been much preferred.[12 40] Is this an alternative? Does the idea of 'design and build' contracting have a parallel in the delivery of services. What would the equivalent of the 'big D' and 'little d' contracts we discussed in Chapter 2 look like in this area? Is this in fact the next step in the kind of collaborative partnerships we have been exploring – where the customer defines the outcome that is desired and specifies the performance criteria (and penalties for defaulting on these) and leaves the individual contractor much freer to design the details of how these will be met? And if so, how do we square this with the need for greater control – management of the contracts at a senior level by people who have intimate knowledge of the industry. Where for a start will we find these managers, when much of what we are describing here is innovation – by definition, never done before?

There is another aspect of the Games culture that is worth considering here. Brendan Godfrey, who managed many of the SOCOG service contracts for the OCA, suggests that part of the problem within SOCOG was that contract managers were caught up in a culture that was thinking about 'the best Games ever'. They were thinking about running the Olympic Games – to the detriment of their primary task of managing contracts. We would suggest that this problem would be compounded by the 'roll-over' of key program staff into venue management teams. If correct, this is really challenging. So much of the success that we have pointed to throughout this book relies on the fact that everyone involved shared in the big picture. This led to commitment and motivation to the extent that many people made significant personal sacrifices because they believed in the spectacular nature of the event. How do we develop an organisational culture that balances this 'spectacular' commitment – i.e. commitment to delivery of a spectacle – with the more mundane responsibilities of managing the details of business contracts? The OCA suggestion is to outsource the management of the contract details, particularly the legal aspects. This shifts some of the burden, and the risk, to outside agencies, and leaves senior management to maintain the big picture and ensure that the agreed performance milestones in contracting the services are met. While this was clearly effective in construction for the Games it has yet to be tested for the service delivery aspects of a major event like the Games.

Managing conflicts of interest

Throughout this story we have identified significant benefits from the sponsorship arrangements and close partnerships that were developed between companies and SOCOG. At the same time there is evidence that there were problems with these relationships for budget control and the orderly planning needed for such a large project.

Brendan Godfrey says starkly:

"SOCOG's exclusion of open tendering by virtue of the provider agreements was simply not proven to be beneficial." [80]

In discussing the contrast between the management of industrial relations and the service contracts he suggests:

"The unions had a direct stake in the outcome and kept pressure on SOCOG to deliver the outcomes. Many of the contractors on the other hand

had little incentive – they were writing their own cheques!" [80]

A number of sponsors were also both providers of the services and consultants who were involved in the 'scoping' and costing of the Games contracts for SOCOG. Many had effective first right of refusal for delivering contracts in at least part of their service area. Put simply they were intimately involved in defining the scope and setting the price, and then tendering for the contracts.

We are not suggesting any impropriety here. At least one contractor we interviewed was aware of the privileged position that its sponsorship and consultancy with SOCOG created. Several spoke of excluding themselves from some parts of the tendering process. Some of the contracted companies, especially in the problem areas of Games services, complained that they felt they were not managed well. Conflict of interest can rarely be eliminated completely. With the kind of collaboration we are seeking it is inevitable. What matters is how it is managed. And the evidence seems to suggest that it must be managed better, perhaps differently. The fact is that sponsor-as-partner relationships and the close collaboration with industry stakeholders who are likely to be beneficiaries of the service contracts of a major project raise important questions about how they are to be managed in the interest of the wider community. This is not just a matter of protecting the public purse. The interests of other (often smaller) companies in the affected industries need to be accommodated – especially if our aim is to spread the benefits of innovation and culture change beyond the few who are initially identified as the industry leaders.

The problem is we do not have a clear model for the kind of arrangements that are needed that will deliver:

- the kind of collaborative partnerships between sponsors, the customer/coordinating agency, and the providers of the services that will attract private sector funding at the front end – and deliver financial, technological and other non-material returns to sponsors at the back end

- and also ensure efficient, cost-effective use of public resources and safeguards for community interests and the interests of other industry players outside the initial partnership.

This presents a direct challenge to the kind of collaboration that we have been advocating. Structuring sponsorship contracts so that these do not automatically give provider status goes to the very heart of the sponsor-partner concept. Finding the balance here is not simple. There are implications for VIK arrangements and the ability of sponsors to leverage both tangible and intangible returns from their sponsorships. The budget savings achieved by the OCA might justify the assertion that the SOCOG model was, at least in some critical areas, 'not proven to be beneficial'. But it begs the question, how could it have been modified? Or, perhaps more important, how could it be modified and improved for the kind of environmental mega-project we are suggesting?

Conflict of interest is inherent in the kind of collaboration we are seeking and to some extent is to be desired and encouraged. It is not wrong to have conflicts of interest; it is a question of how we deal with them.

Few of the contractors we spoke to believe that the model was perfect. We noted above how some imposed limitations on themselves because they perceived a conflict of interest. Many, particularly the non-sponsor contractors, were not happy with the, albeit unintended, consequences of the tendering process (late contracts, uncertainty over the number of workers to be provided, and the way their contracts were managed). How can we generate the significant sponsorship and close collaboration in the planning and delivery of the services behind a major project and at the same time manage the conflict of interest in a way that is fair to all in the affected industries and the interests of the community? Note we say 'manage' not 'eliminate' conflict of interest. This is not a problem that can be eliminated. Conflict of interest is inherent in the kind of collaboration we are seeking and to some extent is to be desired and encouraged. It is not wrong to have conflicts of interest; it is a question of how we deal with them – how we manage them within principles and ethical values that recognise the dilemma. We don't have a simple answer. We raise the question. We also believe that, as we have shown, there are sufficient benefits in moving from the simple competitive model towards the kind of cooperation achieved during the Games to make it worth exploring further.

Balancing collaboration and competition?

Throughout this study we have shown that there are significant benefits to be achieved from moving away from a competitive culture towards a collaborative one. What we need is a balance between these two very different cultures. And, for all its undoubted achievements, the model adopted by SOCOG for the Sydney Games did not always find that balance. In saying this we hope that it is understood not as a criticism but as an opportunity for learning. One of the more essential aspects of the collaborative culture we are seeking is that we don't have mistakes but opportunities for learning.

Of course there are other factors involved. Some we have touched on. Many more await detailed organisational analysis to uncover the full story and make a more definitive analysis. For now, however, what we need to report is that the 'learning culture' approach that came with so many of the project managers who followed Jim Sloman from the construction industry to work in SOCOG is not, on its own, a panacea for the complex logistical problems of staging a major event or managing a large project. It may be a necessary element but the evidence is that, at least as far as the Sydney 2000 Games are concerned, on its own it was not sufficient. It may be that an intelligent mix of both devolution of responsibility and a high degree of centralisation of power and control is needed in the short term. The kind of devolved, participatory workplace culture that so obviously delivers benefits in some areas is still perhaps in its infancy and has a long way to go to maturity.

Unprecedented power and control?

A number of the people we interviewed have said that the Games would not have succeeded were it not for strong leadership from the top. A willingness to take hard decisions, to bear the consequences and to apologise for mistakes. There are many factors that contributed to the organising paralysis that occurred between the Bid and 1996; some we have touched on already. Inside the NSW government there were seven departments with Games planning units and little or no effective coordination.

"... too many bureaucracies fighting for power, not talking, no cooperation, nothing happening, this is what led to the creation of the Olympic Coordination Authority with broad planning powers to run the construction program and coordinate all government involvement in the preparation and delivery of the Games." [33]

We were told this came together at a NSW government cabinet meeting when Michael Knight, the Games President, asked for all of these to be given to him. Premier Bob Carr said you can have mine … and the rest is history.[33] If the kind of national environ-mental project we envisage is to succeed it will need similar strong leadership and a single coordinating body accountable to government but willing to cut through obstacles to progress. It will also need to balance what will be, like the Games, an unprecedented level of power and authority. We asked Michael Knight specifically what lessons from the Games might apply to other major projects like the Murray-Darling restoration. Here's his answer:

*"The short answer is, perhaps, some unpalatable things. Let me ask a question. Is anyone – apart from your study – doing any serious analysis? There's almost no analysis of the issues regarding the technology, the workforce etc. How come it worked here when it didn't work in Atlanta? It's almost eerie that there's no serious analysis. Maybe this is because some of the lessons are unpalatable. For example OCA was so successful because it was structured differently to normal. OCA massively outsourced – but it was a smart client – the outsourcing was managed by **senior** executives. SOCOG was more traditionally structured. OCA also used different core instruments in managing its contracts. For example SOCOG had its own legal department running through the organisation so legal contracts were managed quite low down from within the organisation. OCA legal work was outsourced – outside the organisation. The legal work [e.g. construction contracts and environ-ment cases] was contracted to outside firms but the client was us and was managed by senior executives.*

"There was a centralisation of authority – a level of power and authority that was unprecedented in government in NSW or in Australia. It may be that [the Games] is a one-off – that we can never replicate this."

"There was also a centralisation of authority – a level of power and authority that was unprecedented in government in NSW or in Australia. It may be that [the Games] is a one-off – that we can never replicate this. Concentrating this level of power may be needed – in that it is likely to get the job done – but there are clearly anti-democratic elements in it. So the lessons may not be appropriate to other projects – or may be unpalatable in terms of democratic principles of another government. But a strong concen-tration of power and authority, combined with high levels of political accountability, did help deliver an Olympic Games that enhanced Australia's reputation. There was a broad consensus that the Olympics was so big and so important that it couldn't be done any other way. That then begs the question: what else is important enough to our nation's future to again do whatever is necessary to make sure we deliver?"

So, as we conclude, we are not saying that the Games provides the model for another major project. We are convinced that the story behind the spectacle brings to light many lessons. Some of these lessons are clearly useful. Many point to important issues. Many more raise as many questions as they answer – and that is how it should be.

NEWSPIX

Epilogue

The Opening Ceremony reflected an awareness of the clash between – and hope for reconciliation between – the 'young' 'white' and the much older indigenous cultures of Australia. In the process of developing these segments of the Ceremony, the Sydney Olympic Games also set a new standard in cultural sensitivity and a legacy for the future of all Olympic events. A cultural custodian deed was negotiated with the IOC. In future the contributions of indigenous people (the music, dance, songs, costumes and props) may not be used for advertising or commercial purposes without approval of the communities involved.

The other, largely untold story is that of the Paralympic Games. The cultural shift in visibility and public awareness of 'disability' was a major success story. The achievement of the Paralympic athletes was an inspiration and a challenge to the wider community to review and surpass 'limits' which we traditionally impose on ourselves and others. There were also many stories of the underpinnings of the Paralympic spectacle – as with the Olympics, made possible by the seamless provision of the catering, cleaning, security and other essential services by a paid and volunteer workforce.

We hope this story will one day be told in detail and the lessons for involvement of the whole community in other major national projects identified. For now it is beyond the scope of this study.

Information on many aspects of the Olympic Games including pictures of venues, the Green Games environment program, the volunteer program and current events at Sydney Olympic Park can be obtained from the internet.
Website address: www.sydneyolympicpark.nsw.gov.au

Appendix 1

List of people interviewed for this study

Reference numbers shown as # in the text refer to data in the numbered interviews below. Supplementary information provided by an individual is shown as #A in the text.

Ref #	Person Interviewed	Organisation
1	Chris Christodoulou and Paul Howes	NSW Labor Council
2	John Robertson	NSW Labor Council
3	Lyn Gailey	MEAA
4	Julie Brooks	SOCOG (Ceremonies)
6	Michel Hryce	MEAA
7	Dave Higgon	Multiplex
8	Dan Potra	SOCOG (Ceremonies)
9	Bill Ford	Lend Lease
10	Bill Ford	Consultant, Opera House Trust
11	Michael Easson	NSW Labor Council
12	Ray Roberts and Gwillym Hughes	Workforce International
13	Ray Harty	Comet Training
14	Kylie Bryden Smith	Sydney Opera House
15	Di Pass	Adecco
16	Rob Forsyth	SOCOG (HR)
17	Jim Sloman	SOCOG
18	Wayne Forno	TWU
19	Matt Stagg	Multiplex
20	Brendan Donohue	Thiess
21	Michael Taylor	AWU
22	Kevin Brown	AWU (Construction)
23	Andrew Ferguson	CFMEU
24	Scott Gartrell	Thiess
25	Paul Donato	SOCOG (Security)
26	Michael Deegan	Games Minister's Office
27	Tim McDonald	Employers First

28	Tanya Marshall	Restaurant & Caterers Association
29	Sonia Minutello and Mark Boyd	ALHMU
30	Eric Hensley	Lend Lease
31	Mario Barrios and Eric Rolls	CFMEU/Multiplex
32	David Wilson	WorkCover NSW
33	Tom Forrest	Games Minister's Office
34	Cathy Tomkins	SOCOG (Recruitment)
35	David Brettell	SOCOG (Volunteers)
36	Geoff Ferris	ORTA
37	Anna Booth	SOCOG Board
38	Paul McKinnon	OSCC – Police
39	Barry Tubner	TCFUA
40	Craig Lovett, Darren Carter, Chris Arnott and Stephen Webber	CleanEvent
41	Rob Pascoe and Keathea Henderson	Visy
42	Mark Hartig	Adecco/SOCOG (IR)
43	Alan Matheson	ACTU
44	Matthew Clarke	Linfox
45	Peter Himmelhoch	SOCOG (Risk Management)
46	Danny Potocki	CFMEU/Lend Lease
47	Mario Barrios, Joe Brcic, and Ante (Tony) Zdrilic	CFMEU delegates
48	Tim Catterall	Spotless Services
49	Max Spedding	Pacific Waste Management
50	Brendan Lynch	SOCOG (Volunteers)
51	Jill Davies	SOCOG (Security)
52	Ian Buchan	Thiess
53	Jo Drummond	Multiplex (Ecology)
54	Gary March	Concept Sports
55	Katriona Barker	Spotless Services
56	Kelvin Aldred	Pacific Dunlop
57	Paul Houston and John Stockler	NSW DIR
58	Ian Bottrell	SOCOG (Recruitment)
59	David Richmond	OCA
60	Ian Clubb	SOCOG (HR)
61	Di Riddell	NSW DET

62	Peter Ottesen	SOCOG (Green Games)
65	Allan Whitehouse	SOCOG (Catering)
66	Nick Lewocki	PTU (Rail)
67	Chris Raper	NSW Premier's Department
68	Michael Knight	NSW Olympics Minister
69	Bernie Smith	SDA
70	Claire Houston	SOCOG (Training)
71	Craig McLachey	AOC
72	David Riordan	TAFE NSW
74	Tim Connor	University of Newcastle
75	Les Tobler	CFMEU
80	Brendan Godfrey	OCA
81	John Barraclough	OCA
83	David Atkins	SOCOG (Ceremonies)
84	Geoff Parmenter	SOCOG (Accreditation)
85	Maurice Holland	SOCOG (Villages)
86	Catriona Byrne	SOCOG (Communications)
87	Margaret Ryan	NSW DIR
88	Mark Chilcott	Telstra
89	Margaret Hird	Volunteer
91	Amanda Henrys	McDonald's
92	Raelene Harrison	Carlton United Breweries
93	Lee Price	Leightons
94	Derek Casey	Regency TAFE
95	Corin Millais	Greenpeace
96	Louise Dwyer	Westpac
97	Grant Taylor and Patrick Ganguly	Torch bearers
98	Bob Leece	OCA

Totals   **99 People**   **88 Interviews**

Appendix 2

People who contributed to the Steering Group for the Collaborative Games Study

Co-chairs	Max Ogden	Foundation for Sustainable Economic Development, University of Melbourne
	Prof. Bill Ford	
Participants	Prof. Jane Marceau	Urban Frontiers Program, University of Western Sydney
	Prof. Danny Samson	University of Melbourne
	Mile Terziovski	University of Melbourne
	Brian Tee	Dept of Industrial Relations Victoria
	David Collins	Dept of Education and Training NSW
	David Wilson	WorkCover NSW
	George Kuti	WorkCover NSW
	Greg Spierings	Dept of Sport and Recreation Victoria
	Janet Chester	TAFE NSW
	John Stockler	Dept of Industrial Relations NSW
	Justin Burney	Dept of Industrial Relations Victoria
	Paul Houston	Dept of Industrial Relations NSW
	Craig Lovett	CleanEvent
	David Higgon	Multiplex
	Katriona Barker	Spotless Services Ltd
	Ray Harty	Comet Training
	Chris Christodoulou	Labor Council of NSW
	Paul Howes	Labor Council of NSW
Research Team	Tony Webb	Project Manager
	David Williams	Director, Tier Consulting/ Oz Naturally
	Di Pass	Director, 360HR (formerly with Adecco)

Appendix 3

Memorandum of Understanding
Olympic Construction Program

Introduction

This Memorandum of Understanding between the New South Wales Government and the Labor Council of New South Wales, on behalf of its affiliated unions recognises that sound industrial relations are important for the successful completion of the Olympic program of works. It establishes an agreed framework for industrial relations during the construction of the facilities for the 2000 Olympics.

This Memorandum is the first tier of the industrial relations framework. The second tier involves the agreements reached between employers and the Labor Council of New South Wales, unions and employees.

The parties recognise the need to complete the construction of the program of works to meet defined time frames, budgets and user quality requirements, and recognise the responsibility that is associated with meeting these requirements.

This Memorandum of Understanding seeks to ensure the delivery of all 2000 Olympic and related projects on time and within budget in an industrial environment based on cooperation and stability.

Objectives

The parties have shared objectives for all the works included in the construction program, which are:

- high quality delivery of the projects within the specified time and cost parameters;

- action to improve efficiency and productivity to the benefit of all industrial parties and recognition of employee participation in achieving these benefits;

- the implementation of innovative approaches to the achievement and assessment of productivity change and in the remuneration of workers for productivity improvements;

- the creation of partnerships between unions, employers and workers characterised by cooperation, consultation and a reduction or minimisation of industrial disputation to promote creative workplace innovation;

- the highest level of occupational health, safety and rehabilitation in accordance with NSW Government policy;

- access to training opportunities for all building workers employed on the sites, recognising that they may come from the ranks of the long term and the young unemployed;

- commitment to compliance with the NSW Government's Code of Practice for the Construction Industry (July 1996 and October 1992, as appropriate), including the Code objectives; and

- prohibition of illegal employment practices including illegal cash in hand payments and illegal sham subcontract arrangements.

Application

This Memorandum of Understanding establishes the context and principles for all projects involved in the program of works. It applies to all works associated with the construction and fit-out of the facilities for the 2000 Olympics, related to the venues listed below.

• Olympic Stadium	Olympic Park - Homebush Bay
• Athletes Village	Newington
• Aquatic Centre Upgrading	Olympic Park - Homebush Bay
• Athletic Centre Upgrading	Olympic Park - Homebush Bay
• Velodrome	The Crest Bankstown
• Second Baseball Venue	Auburn
• Regatta Centre	Penrith Lakes
• Shooting Complex	Cecil Park
• Equestrian Centre	Horsley Park
• Tennis Centre	Olympic Park - Homebush Bay
• State Sports Centre - upgrading (Sports Halls,Indoor Training Centre)	Olympic Park - Homebush Bay
• New Sydney Showground	Showground Precinct Homebush Bay
• Hockey Centre - upgrading	Olympic Park - Homebush Bay
Multi-Use Arena	Olympic Park - Homebush Bay
• Media Villages	Lidcombe Hospital
• Technical Officials Village	Westbridge Centre Villawood
• Softball Centre	Aquilina Reserve Blacktown
• Various training and other venue fitouts	Various sites
• Various Infrastructure Projects	Olympic Park - Homebush Bay
• Second Water polo Venue	TBA

Project Agreements/Awards

The parties recognise the merit of Project Agreements/Awards for special projects, however, it is up to the appropriate parties under the Code of Practice to determine whether such a Project Agreement/ Award be put into place for an Olympic project.

The Olympic Co-ordination Authority, as the Principle, supports the negotiation of Project specific agreements for suitable projects.

Should a decision be taken to establish such a project specific agreement, it should be negotiated through the Labor Council of NSW. A Project Agreement or Project Award should be registered by the Industrial Relations Commission of New South Wales.

Disputes Resolution

The parties will use their best endeavours to prevent disputes arising on Olympic projects. In the event that disputes do arise, the disputes settlement procedures contained within awards, enterprise agreements and individual Project Agreements or Project Awards will be adhered to in an effort to resolve the matter.

Should these not lead to the resolution of the matter, it may be referred to the Labor Council of NSW. The role of the Labor Council will be to bring the industrial parties together and use their best endeavours to seek a resolution to any dispute. The role of the Labor Council is particularly pertinent in resolving industrial disputes involving demarcation issues between unions. Should the dispute not be resolved, the matter shall be referred to the Industrial Relations Commission of New South Wales.

While a dispute is being dealt with under the dispute settlement procedures, work shall continue in the same manner as that prior to the dispute, without prejudice to any of the parties to the dispute.

Occupational Health and Safety

The General Manager of the WorkCover Authority will nominate key Building Industry Inspectors to advise on any Occupational Health and Safety (OHS) disputes that the parties are unable to resolve at the OHS Committee level or through the normal OHS dispute resolution procedures.

The parties agree that all persons engaged on Olympic projects shall be required to have completed a WorkCover Authority accredited Occupational Health and Safety induction training course before commencing work on a site.

Redundancy and Superannuation

Given the nature of Olympic projects and the specific construction timeframe imperatives, signatories to this Memorandum of Understanding are supportive of the industrial parties negotiating redundancy payments and superannuation contributions on an enterprise or project basis in accordance with the NSW Government Code of Practice for the Construction Industry.

The signatories to this Memorandum support the payment of superannuation contributions into a agreed industry funds.

Further, the signatories see merit in isolated funds being established, for the placement of redundancy contributions, so that employees are assured some security in the event of the employer facing financial difficulties.

Insurance Coverage

The signatories to this Memorandum of Understanding are supportive of Enterprise Agreements or Project Agreements/Awards allowing for 24 hour accident insurance policies held by employers against liability for death or injury to persons employed.

The signatories to this Memorandum of Understanding are supportive of the industrial parties negotiating the inclusion of top-up workers compensation insurance where applicable, in specific Project Agreements or Project Awards.

Project Productivity Allowances

The parties are committed to innovative approaches to the achievement of improved productivity and efficiency, as well as the improved assessment of performance and the remuneration of workers for productivity improvements.

It is expected, in light of the shared objectives of the parties to this Memorandum of Understanding, that all projects with a Project Agreement or Project Award will have some form of performance payment in recognition of increased productivity in accordance with the NSW Government Code of Practice. Such payments will only be paid if agreed targets are met.

The improvement in performance is expected to flow from improved coordination, commitment and management of the various issues involved with the projects through project specific arrangements.

Training

The parties recognise the opportunity that the Olympic program of works provides for the training of workers, and both the young and the long term unemployed.

The parties are committed to the establishment of project specific on site and off site training approaches to increase training opportunities and provide training in areas in the industry where there is expected to be a shortage of skilled and competent workers.

This training will also include on site practical training in areas of work that cannot be taught in a classroom situation.

It is expected that where there are positions vacant on site, where practical, employees who have been trained using the on-site training facilities and who have the required skills and competencies, will be employed.

Hon Michael Knight
Minister for Olympics

Hon Jeff Shaw QC
Attorney General
Minister for Industrial Relations

On behalf of the New South Wales Government

Mr Peter Sams
Secretary
Labor Council of NSW
On behalf of Affiliated Unions

Mr Andrew Ferguson
Secretary
CFMEU NSW Branch

Russ Collison
Secretary
AWU NSW Branch

Bert Schmidt
Secretary
ETU NSW Branch

Phil Darby
Secretary
CEPU Plumbing Division NSW

Steve Hutchins
Secretary
TWU NSW Branch

23 December 1997

Appendix 4

Sydney 2000

PARALYMPIC GAMES
SYDNEY 2000

Principles of Cooperation

between

THE SYDNEY ORGANISING COMMITTEE FOR THE OLYMPIC GAMES

and

SYDNEY PARALYMPIC ORGANISING COMMITTEE

and

LABOR COUNCIL OF NEW SOUTH WALES

A. PRINCIPLES

The parties to this agreement recognise that the Sydney 2000 Olympic and Paralympic Games "the Games" is a unique peace time event that will provide us with an opportunity to showcase Australia. During this 60 day event the parties agree that both certainty and cooperation are necessary ingredients for the staging of a successful Games. Accordingly it will be necessary to ensure that our approach to the Games and associated activities is non political.

The parties to this agreement acknowledge that good industrial relations are a cornerstone of successful employee relations, and therefore, a harmonious and productive workplace. In particular, a harmonious industrial environment is necessary to ensure the smooth running of the Games.

Accordingly the parties commit themselves to doing all things practicable to maximise standards of service to patrons of the facilities/venues which will be operated by Sydney Organising Committee for the Olympic Games (SOCOG) and the Sydney Paralympic Organising Committee (SPOC) and to ensure that the Games will be regarded as the best run Games ever staged.

Equally, the parties are committed to ensuring that those persons who work in a paid or volunteer capacity during the Games not only benefit from the cultural experience but also assist future career opportunities by the development and broadening of their skills.

The parties agree to adopt a spirit of mutual cooperation to ensure that all issues pertaining to the utilisation of labour for the Games will be addressed.

As far as practicable, through detailed Games planning the parties will ensure that the supply and demand of labour are well balanced and that the labour market is not adversely affected by the Games.

B. THE PARTIES AGREE TO:

1. Work towards establishing conditions of employment and operational arrangements which will provide the certainty and flexibility to facilitate the smooth running of the Games

2. Where practicable, establish a consistent and complementary set of wage structures and conditions which can apply across the Games and which eliminates any potential demarcation disputes.

3. Have joint training sessions for nominated representatives to become familiar with the operational requirements of staging the Games so as to allow them to properly implement the principles inherent in this agreement and any subsequent agreement.

In addition it is agreed that the parties will support the development where possible of both internal and external accredited training for all persons associated with servicing the Games. Such training and/or induction sessions shall include the nominated representatives attending and providing written information regarding the principles inherent in this agreement and any subsequent agreement.

4. Recognise the Labor Council of NSW as the representative State Peak Council for the purposes of this agreement.

5. Provide the opportunity to employees covered by this agreement and subsequent agreements to take out and maintain financial membership of the appropriate Labor Council affiliate during the staging of the Games.

    Reasonable access will be given to representatives covered by this agreement to visit SOCOG and SPOC controlled workplaces associated with the Games, subject to prior notice being given and appropriate security arrangements being in place.

6. Assist in the development of a good industrial relations environment which is consistent with the principles inherent in this agreement with Games related venue owners/operators and contract service companies.

7. Recognise the experience skills and familiarity that existing employees of venue operators and/ or contractors can bring to the Games. Accordingly subject to probity checks, persons who normally work for venue operators and/or contractors who service the sites to be used for the Games shall be given preference of employment during the Games.

    It is agreed that such persons shall not be disadvantaged if employed by a different entity during the Games.

    Notwithstanding the above the parties recognise additional specialised staff and volunteers (including from overseas) will need to be utilised to complement existing staff.

C.   COORDINATION COMMITTEE:

In order to achieve the above, the parties have established a coordination Committee which will comprise representatives of the NSW Labor Council and SOCOG to coordinate issues associated with this agreement and any subsequent agreement. This shall include the sharing of information necessary to implement the principles inherent in this agreement and to meet as required to resolve any disputes, grievances or issues which may affect or disrupt the smooth running of the Games and associated activities. In addition the Committee shall:

*   Negotiate a further agreement which will cover the wages and conditions applicable during the Games at Olympic and Paralympic venues. In this regard it is agreed by the parties that no employees who currently work at Olympic and Paralympic venues will be disadvantaged by any such arrangement. The parties acknowledge that executive staff will be exempt from the proposed industrial agreement.

    The purpose of this agreement will be to define a framework of Games - time conditions that can be embodied in relevant agreements between employers and employees.

*   The parties agree that during the negotiations leading up to a future industrial agreement the parties will have regard to the wages and conditions which currently apply in relevant industries. In particular the parties will be mindful of the standards already adopted by the NSW Industrial Relations Commission. It is the intention of the parties to develop a modern and innovative agreement which provides benefits to all those associated with the Games and associated activities.

*   Consult to ensure that no contracts are let to companies that are based upon wages and conditions less than the relevant common rule industry awards.

*   Establish a protocol for the use of volunteers and in this regard are committed to maximising the benefits associated with volunteer work.

*   Work towards establishing the highest possible standards of health and safety, to ensure the security of employees and patrons alike during the Games.

D.   SIGNATORIES

[signature]   21 November 1997

Signature   Date

SYDNEY ORGANISING COMMITTEE FOR THE OLYMPIC GAMES (SOCOG)
PRESIDENT OF SOCOG, The Hon Michael Knight, MP

[signature]   21 November 1997

Signature   Date

LABOR COUNCIL OF NEW SOUTH WALES
PRESIDENT, John Whelan

[signature]   21 November 1997

Signature   Date

SYDNEY ORGANISING COMMITTEE FOR THE OLYMPIC GAMES (SOCOG)
CHIEF EXECUTIVE OFFICER, Sandy Hollway

[signature]   21 November 1997

Signature   Date

LABOR COUNCIL OF NEW SOUTH WALES
SECRETARY, Peter Sams

[signature]   21 November 1997

Signature   Date

SYDNEY ORGANISING COMMITTEE FOR THE OLYMPIC GAMES (SOCOG)
**DEPUTY CHIEF EXECUTIVE OFFICER /
GROUP GENERAL MANAGER, GAMES OPERATIONS, Jim Sloman**

[signature]   21 November 1997

Signature   Date

LABOR COUNCIL OF NEW SOUTH WALES
ASSISTANT SECRETARY, Michael Costa

THE SOCOG CHARTER

We have been given the honour
of staging the Games of the XXVII Olympiad
in Sydney in the Year 2000.

It is an honour which we recognise as carrying
with it great responsibilities...
to the athletes and the youth of the world,
to the international Olympic movement,
to those who are our partners and to all Australia.

We pledge to carry out our task
with a profound awareness of what is at stake
dynamically, unselfishly,
and with a level of enthusiasm
that will guarantee success.
Just as our athletes strive for excellence, so do we.
Just as they carry with them the honour of their
country, so do we.

Our vision is to stand together in September 2000
as the world celebrates the glory of the
Games of The New Millennium:
The Sydney 2000 Olympic Games.

Sandy Hollway
Chief Executive Officer

Appendix 5

Code of Labour Practice for

PRODUCTION OF GOODS LICENSED

by the

SYDNEY ORGANISING COMMITTEE FOR THE OLYMPIC GAMES

and the

SYDNEY PARALYMPIC ORGANISING COMMITTEE

Agreed between the Sydney Organising Committee for the Olympic Games (SOCOG), the Sydney Paralympic Organising Committee (SPOC), the Australian Council of Trade Unions (ACTU) and the Labor Council of New South Wales. Having concurred on the necessity for effective monitoring to ensure that the Code is respected at all levels, the above organisations are continuing discussions on practical measures to achieve these objectives.

PREAMBLE

In accordance with the goal of the Olympic Movement to contribute to building a peaceful and better world by educating youth through sport practised without discrimination of any kind and in the Olympic spirit, which requires mutual understanding with a spirit of friendship, solidarity and fair play, SOCOG/SPOC recognises its responsibilities to consumers for the quality of products produced under its licensing arrangements, and workers involved in the making of SOCOG/SPOC licensed products and the conditions under which these products are made.

Each licensee awarded the right to use the SOCOG/SPOC name or logo in the manufacture and/or supply of licensed product to SOCOG/SPOC have been audited to ensure that they have appropriate standards of operation and have, as a condition of license agreement, confirmed in writing that employee work conditions meet the relevant industrial regulations.

Licensees further agree to ensure that these conditions and standards are observed by each contractor and subcontractor in the production and distribution of SOCOG/SPOC licensed products. Licensees should, prior to placing orders with suppliers or engaging contractors and subcontractors, assess whether the provisions of this Code can be met.

Each SOCOG/SPOC licensee, and each contractor and subcontractor engaged by the Licensee, shall compulsorily implement and respect the following principles in the production and/or distribution of products bearing the SOCOG/SPOC name and /or SOCOG/SPOC authorised marks. Furthermore, each Licensee shall warrant that these principles shall be equally imposed upon all those employed or delegated by such Licensee.

EMPLOYMENT IS FREELY CHOSEN

There shall be no use of forced or bonded labour (ILO Conventions 29 and 105)

THERE IS NO DISCRIMINATION IN EMPLOYMENT

Equality of opportunity and treatment regardless of race, colour, sex, religion, political opinion, nationality, social origin or other distinguishing characteristics shall be provided (ILO Conventions 100 and 111).

CHILD LABOUR IS NOT USED

There shall be no exploitation of child labour. Workers shall only be employed in accordance with relevant State and Federal legislation, in line with appropriate ILO standards.

FREEDOM OF ASSOCIATION AND THE RIGHT TO COLLECTIVE BARGAINING ARE RESPECTED

The right of workers to form and join trade unions and to bargain collectively shall be recognised and respected (ILO Conventions 87 and 98)

FAIR WAGES ARE PAID

Wages and benefits paid shall meet at least legal or industry minimum standards and should be sufficient to meet basic needs and provide some discretionary income.

HOURS OF WORK ARE NOT EXCESSIVE

Hours of work shall comply with applicable laws and industry standards.

WORKING CONDITIONS ARE DECENT

A safe and hygienic working environment shall be provided, and best occupational health and safety practice shall be promoted, bearing in mind the knowledge of the industry and of any specific hazards held by licensees, contractors and subcontractors.

THE EMPLOYMENT RELATIONSHIP IS ESTABLISHED AND TRAINING PROVIDED

Employers should endeavour to provide regular and secure employment. Appropriate training should be available for all employees.

IMPLEMENTATION AND MONITORING

Licensees, their contractors and subcontractors shall undertake to support and cooperate in the implementation and monitoring of this Code by:

- prior to engagement, the Licensee shall provide SOCOG/SPOC with written confirmation that the Licensee, as a minimum, adheres to relevant international labour force standards;

- providing SOCOG/SPOC or its agent with relevant information concerning their operations;

- permitting inspection at any time of their workplaces and operations by approved SOCOG/ SPOC personnel;

- maintaining records of the name, age, hours worked and wages paid for each worker and making these available to approved inspectors on request;

- refraining from disciplinary action, dismissal or otherwise discriminating against any worker for providing information concerning observance of this Code.

Any licensee, contractor or subcontractor found to be in breach of one or more terms of this Code of Labour Practice shall be subject to a range of sanctions up to and including withdrawal of the right to produce or organise production of SOCOG licensed goods as per the contractual provisions. Furthermore, licensees who fail to ensure that their contractors or subcontractors abide by the Code of Labour Practice shall be subject to the same range of sanctions.

A joint Committee comprising Representatives of the ACTU; Labor Council of NSW; SOCOG staff and the SOCOG Board shall meet as required to review reported breaches of this code and make recommendations to the SOCOG Board for action as appropriate.

Chronology of the Licensed Goods Dispute

1993	Bid process acknowledges environment and human/labour rights is part of emerging Olympics ethos. Labor Council supports Bid.
1993–6	Some early sponsorship/contracts arranged re production of Licensed Goods.
1997 May	Concerns raised by unions and the ACTU that contracts are subcontracted offshore to countries with poor labour rights record or child labour use, in violation of ILO standards.
June	SOCOG writes that "manufacturing core competence [includes] a review of labour component, in particular, the focus on workers conditions and remuneration. SOCOG has made it quite clear to Olympic manufacturers that adherence to accepted recognized standards in this area is an absolute necessity and we have sought undertakings from each sponsor that this is the case." (SOCOG, 18.6.97)
July	ACTU raises issue of refusal of the contracting companies to provide details of the offshore factories used for production, particularly in China, and requests meetings to discuss this with SOCOG.
July?	Letters dated July 1997 from contractors to SOCOG contain almost identical wording: "Factories operated by us in which Sydney 2000 Olympic games merchandise is produced are operated according to such standard [Code of Practice] and, in our view, there is no evidence of what may be publicly regarded as 'sweatshop conditions'." *
November	Joint Committee of SOCOG, Labor Council, TCFUA and AWU established. Code of Practice for Production of Licensed Goods negotiated.
1998 February	Code of Practice for Production of Licensed Goods released.

* NOTE: If the code referred to here is the Code of Labour Practice for the Production of Licensed Goods, this was not signed until February 1998. In any case the language is full of loopholes, for example:

• 'operated by us' – excludes subcontractors

• 'in our view' – opinion – or fact?

• 'no evidence' – what effort was made to investigate?

Then there is 'publicly regarded as "sweatshop conditions"' – who orchestrated this identical response from all these companies?

November	Unions request briefing from SOCOG on the processes it is using to supervise the application of the Code.
1999 February	Joint Committee is told all licensees have signed manufacturing agreements but not all have been inspected. Unions seek fact-finding visit by Anna Booth to Fiji to inspect conditions in production of Games uniforms. SOCOG refuses – sends staff representative who reports 'facilities in Fiji meet the standards'.
May–July	SOCOG supplies list of licensees. ACTU contacts list drawing attention to the Code and seeking details of conditions and subcontracting – especially via front companies in Hong Kong and Taiwan to China. Responses from vague assurances to outright refusals to disclose details of factories in China lead unions to call for on-the-ground monitoring of factories, particularly where there is subcontracting.
August	TCFUA goes public with a campaign over SOCOG's refusal to allow union participation in monitoring of factory conditions for the production of Games uniforms.
October– November	Meetings between SOCOG, Labor Council, unions and ACTU reach agreement to settle uniforms dispute. SOCOG agrees to source 15,000 uniform shirts in Australia; SOCOG removes objections to providing names and addresses of all contractors (and known subcontractors); SOCOG will ensure nominated union officials are given access to contractors to monitor compliance with the Code.
2000	Resources for monitoring are not available. On-site monitoring deferred.
September	During the Games, political unrest in Fiji holds up delivery of 166,000 uniforms produced under licence.
	ACTU writes to Italian unions: *"The major agreement involving the ACTU was the Code of Labour Practice for the Production of Licensed Goods ... the contents of the Code require SOCOG Licensees to respect ILO standards in a range of important areas plus other requirements such as fair wages and appropriate training. The serious weakness of the Code was related to the follow-up monitoring of its provisions. For example, despite requiring the Freedom of Association convention to be respected there were still numerous contracts let to China. The SOCOG staff responsible for arranging licences did not pay sufficient attention to the Code's requirements. SOCOG itself had a half-hearted commitment to do full implementation and we failed to put enough pressure on them to bring them into line."*

Appendix 6

SYDNEY OLYMPICS AND PARALYMPICS
VOLUNTEER PROTOCOL

1. Title

This agreement shall be known as the Sydney Olympics and Paralympics 2000 Volunteer Protocol.

2. Intention

The Sydney Organising Committee for the Olympic Games (SOCOG) and the Sydney Paralympic Organising Committee (SPOC) and the Labor Council of NSW have signed a Principles of Cooperation in which both parties agree to:

"Establish a protocol for the use of volunteers and in this regard are committed to maximising the benefits associated with volunteer work"

This agreement shall facilitate the implementation of the "Principles of Cooperation" and assist in the efficient running of the Sydney 2000 Olympic Games.

3. Area and Incidence

This agreement shall apply to all volunteers who come under the control of SOCOG with respect to those volunteers who are used within SOCOG controlled areas.

4. Arrangement

Subject	Clause Number
Title	1
Intention	2
Area and Incidence	3
Arrangement	4
Parties	5
Period of Operation	6
Definitions	7
Determination of Roles to be Assigned to Volunteers	8
Volunteer Recruitment	9
Volunteer Training	10
Benefits	11
Health & Safety	12
Income Protection Plan	13
Public Liability	14

5.   Parties

The parties to this agreement shall be:

a.   the Sydney Organising Committee for the Olympic Games

b.   the Sydney Paralympic Organising Committee and

c.   The Labor Council of New South Wales.

6.   Period of Operation

This Protocol shall operate prior to, during and after the Olympics and Paralympics in accordance with Clause 3 of this Protocol.

7.   Definitions

A "Volunteer" shall mean any person who is an unpaid person who has agreed to assist with the running of the Games and registered as a volunteer with SOCOG.

"The Games" shall be the activities associated with all aspects of the setting up, administration and facilitation of the Sydney Olympic and Paralympic Games within the designated SOCOG controlled areas.

"SOCOG Controlled Areas" shall be the venues and other areas including but not limited to roads, beaches, and waterways promulgated by SOCOG as locations of competition and non-competition activities.

8.   Determination of roles to be assigned to volunteers.

SOCOG has identified the types of functions that may be filled by volunteers with these functions being outlined in the Volunteer Information Booklet. Volunteers will only be used in roles where they have the appropriate skills, experience or qualifications.

Notwithstanding the above, the Parties agree to consult on the exact roles to be performed by volunteers and approximate numbers of volunteers required prior to the Games.

9.   Volunteer Recruitment

Recruitment for the specialist volunteers was launched in September 1997. This phase has targeted those organisations that will commit to providing a specific number of specialists including sporting federations, tertiary institutions, language schools, St John Ambulance, Australian Medical Association, Surf Life Saving clubs, and the Rural Fire Service.

For other volunteer roles, a publicity campaign consisting of press advertising, promotion in shopping centres and other public areas will commence in August 1998.

10. Volunteer Training

All volunteers will be provided with training which will equip them to perform their tasks with confidence. Such training will encompass three components, Olympic orientation training, followed by job specific training and finally venue specific training. Volunteer training will be facilitated by Volunteer Services through TAFE NSW. Where accredited training is conducted, volunteers will be provided with records of that training.

11. Benefits

Volunteers will be entitled to the following during the period of operation of this Agreement:

a.   Catering - Volunteers will be provided with meals whilst at work during the Games

b.   Uniforms - Volunteers will receive a distinctive volunteer uniform that will be in keeping with the look and image of the Games. On satisfactory completion of their assignments, ownership of the uniform will transfer to the volunteer as a valuable memento of their participation.

c.   Transport - Public transport will be utilised to provide transport to and from venues at no cost to volunteers. It is anticipated that in remote locations a limited number of volunteers will be able to access special "park and ride" services.

d.   Accommodation - If necessary, SOCOG will seek to meet the accommodation needs of volunteers as practicable.

e.   General - The most valuable reward for volunteers will be the opportunity to participate in the world's greatest sporting and cultural event. Volunteers should also gain from the training provided, the broadening of skills and the Olympic experience.

f.   Each volunteer will be acknowledged in the following manner.

   •   A certificate to commemorate participation in the Games..

   •   Certificates covering all training.

   •   Post Games Functions.

   •   Acknowledgement of their contribution in the media.

   •   Acknowledgement of volunteer names in the Program of the Opening Ceremony (to be confirmed).

   •   Acknowledgement of volunteers as a group, at the Closing Ceremonies.

Opportunities for volunteers to see some events, rather than work continuously in the background, will be examined in terms of practicality and cost.

12. Health and Safety

All volunteers should be encouraged to take rest breaks at a time convenient to both SOCOG and the volunteer.

Volunteers should not be normally required to perform their duties for more than 12 hours per day.

13. Income Protection Plan

Volunteers shall be covered by an income protection plan as selected by SOCOG in consultation with the Labour Council. The income protection plan shall be taken out and funded by SOCOG.

14. Public Liability

SOCOG shall be responsible for providing liability insurance to cover the volunteer workforce.

Glossary

The 'alphabet soup' of the Sydney 2000 Olympic Games

There is a tendency to speak in the 'specialist' language of acronyms – known to people on the inside of a story, but alienating to people on the outside. We have tried to avoid this in the story of the Collaborative Games but sometimes repeating 'the Sydney Organising Committee for the Olympic Games', the 'Olympic Coordination Authority', or some of the specialist names of the trade unions gets too long winded. Each of these is given in full at least once in the text with the acronym shorthand (SOCOG), (OCA) etc. We also use the shorthand of 'the Games' to refer to the Sydney 2000 Olympic Games throughout the book. For easy reference the acronyms and shorthand words we use are listed below.

ACTU	Australian Council of Trade Unions
ALHMU	Australian Liquor Hospitality and Miscellaneous Workers Union
AOC	Australian Olympic Committee
ASIAL	Australian Security Industry Association
AWU	Australian Workers Union
CELTA	Centre for Entry Level Training
CFMEU	Construction, Forestry, Mining and Energy Union
DET	Department of Education and Training
DIR	Department of Industrial Relations
FSED	Foundation for Sustainable Economic Development (at the University of Melbourne)
HR	Human Relations (management)
IOC	International Olympic Committee
IPC	International Press Centre
IR	Industrial Relations
Labor Council	Labor Council of New South Wales
MEAA	Media Entertainment and Arts Alliance
OCA	Olympic Coordination Authority

OLN	Olympic Labour Network
ORTA	Olympic Roads and Transport Authority
OSCC	Olympic Security and Command Centre
RTBIU or PTU	Rail Tram and Bus Industry Union, commonly known as the Public Transport Union
SDA	Shop Distributive and Allied Workers Union
SOBO	Sydney Olympic Broadcast Organisation
SOCOG	Sydney Organising Committee for the Olympic Games
SPOC	Sydney Paralympic Organising Committee
SSL	Spotless Services Ltd – Catering Company
TCFUA	Textile, Clothing and Footwear Union of Australia
TWU	Transport Workers Union
The Bid	The Sydney Bid for the 2000 Olympic Games considered by the IOC in 1993
The Games	The Sydney 2000 Olympic Games
UFP	Urban Frontiers Program at University of Western Sydney
VIK	Value in kind – the value of goods and/or services contributed by Games sponsors in addition to (or instead of) cash to the Games Organising Committee
WFI	Workforce International Ltd – Security Company

Index

Tony Webb, the author and manager of the research project for the Collaborative Games Study, holds a Master of Science degree in Energy Resources Management and is currently doing doctoral research at the University of Western Sydney. He has spent 30 years working at the interface between the trade union, consumer, environment, public health and workplace change movements in Europe, North America and Australasia.

In this time he has worked as researcher, campaigner and consultant to many of the major environment, consumer and trade union organisations in the UK, USA, Canada and Australia. For seven years in the 1980s he was Associate Researcher with the London Food Commission, producing several books on food irradiation with Dr Tim Lang and contributing to the award-winning food safety campaign.

In the 1990s he coordinated the Food Policy Alliance of Australian farmer, consumer and trade union organisations. It was through the work on this alliance that he developed the relationship with Max Ogden, then an Industrial Officer at the ACTU with responsibility for the food and pharmaceutical industries and now the Manager of the Foundation for Sustainable Economic Development at the University of Melbourne which commissioned and raised the funds for this study.

The research team for the study included David Williams and Di Pass. David has developed and managed construction projects incorporating advanced ecological design and is currently Director of Oz Naturally, an ecotourism and ecological restoration foundation. Di was National Director for the Adecco Olympic program and is now Director of 360HR, a recruitment and human resources management consultancy.

Tony lives in the Blue Mountains where he is also active in the men's health and well-being movement. Max lives in Melbourne. Di and David live in Sydney. All are committed to the next stage of the project – translating the lessons of the Games to major environmental restoration projects in Australia.